PLATO'S DIALOGUES
PATH TO INITIATION

PLATO'S DIALOGUES
PATH TO INITIATION

CAROL DUNN

PORTAL BOOKS
2012

PORTAL BOOKS | 2012

An imprint of SteinerBooks / Anthroposophic Press, Inc.
610 Main St., Great Barrington, MA 01230
www.steinerbooks.org

Copyright © 2012 by Carol Dunn. All rights reserved.
No part of this publication may be reproduced, stored in a retrieval system, or transmitted, in any form or by any means, electronic, mechanical, photocopying, recording, or otherwise, without the prior written permission of the publisher.

Book/cover by William Jens Jensen
Cover image: *Scuola di Atene* by Raphael;
fresco, 1510; Apostolic Palace, Vatican City

LIBRARY OF CONGRESS CATALOGING-IN-PUBLICATION DATA
Dunn, Carol.
　Plato's dialogues : path to initiation / Carol Dunn.
　　p. cm.
　Includes bibliographical references.
　ISBN 978-0-9831984-6-8 (pbk.) — ISBN 978-0-9831984-9-9 (ebook)
　1. Plato. Dialogues. I. Title.
　B395.D86 2012
　184—dc23
　　　　　　　　　　　　　　　　　　　　　　2012036663

Contents

Introduction	vii
PART ONE	
The First Stage: Definition of the Virtues	3
The Second Stage: Higher Spiritual Teachings	23
The Third Stage: Mystic Teachings	41
The Republic	49
Transcendence and Immanence	84
PART TWO	
Plato and Pythagoras	107
Commentary: Two-Principle Theory	147
Was Number Immanent for Pythagoras?	191
Comparison of Plato and Pythagoras	206
PART THREE	
Tracing the Source of those "Foreign" Doctrines	225
Conclusions	282
Bibliography	301

INTRODUCTION

My purpose in writing this book is to offer a re-evaluation of Plato that will radically alter and expand our view of his purpose in writing *The Collected Dialogues*. Some of the great exponents of Plato's philosophy are W. K. C. Guthrie in his six-volume set, *A History of Greek Philosophy;* W. D. Ross, *Plato's Theory of Ideas;* and A. E. Taylor, whose several books on Plato—especially *Plato: The Man and His Work*—have elevated the discourse to a high level by providing a probing analysis of the dialogues. Francis Cornford's books, *Plato's Cosmology* and *Plato and Parmenides,* are seminal, and Aristotle's interpretations are crucial to an understanding of the historical development of Plato's thought up to the present time. There are also many scholars both ancient and modern whose names will emerge as we embark on our re-evaluation of Plato's dialogues.

My position is that in the main modern scholars interpret Plato with an overwhelming focus on understanding the rational content of the dialogues, but omit or neglect the project of their *purpose*. Once they have mined the individual dialogues for their meaning, they neglect to share with the reader what they are *to do* with the knowledge gained from their investigations. I will argue that Plato is engaged not only in *thinking* but also, and more important, in *doing*. What we *do* with the knowledge is crucial because it can determine the meaning and purpose of our own life.

It became clear to me, as I read Plato, that he was not merely engaging in rational philosophical discussion—important as that is—but that in effect The *Collected Dialogues of Plato*[1] especially up to the *Republic,* embody the Socratic exhortation for each individual to "take care for the soul." This entails actively reaching for the highest aspirations to guide one's journey through life, and attempting to understand its deeper mystery and meaning. What I will argue, therefore, is that Plato's dialogues

---

1 Edith Hamilton and Huntington Cairns, *The Collected Dialogues of Plato.*

embody a rational philosophy and, at the same time, a system of spiritual/religious principles and doctrines whose purpose is to lay out—in a public forum—the path a true disciple needs to take in order to have a personal and direct experience of spiritual illumination, or enlightenment. Thus this book's title, *Plato's Dialogues: Path to Initiation*.

That journey starts out from humble beginnings, with the definition and instantiation of the virtues, and it proceeds at the next stage into higher knowledge—that of immortality of the soul, recollection, transmigration of the soul (reincarnation), and the law of cause and effect (karma). If the second stage is successfully navigated, the aspirant gains access, at the third stage, to higher esoteric truths embodied in the sciences of mathematics, geometry, astronomy and music. Finally, the worthy disciple would have been adequately prepared to engage in the ultimate science of dialectic, beyond which, as Socrates points out, there is nothing but the Good. The *Symposium* and *Republic* reveal that the goal of all seeking is a sudden and direct experience of the Good that would engulf the soul in what is termed a state of illumination or enlightenment.

All of these stages are found in *The Collected Dialogues of Plato*, and upon examination, the manner of their exposition is found to be not accidental, but deliberate, and in my view constitutes a complete course of spiritual/religious study. Such a course of study requires more than mere philosophical discussion. It requires continuous effort and active engagement on the part of the student. In effect, the journey perfects the soul and radically changes each life. What I am suggesting, then, is that Plato is a spiritual/religious teacher laying out a set of spiritual doctrines in a similar fashion as Jesus of Nazareth laid out for Christianity or Gautama Buddha set out for Buddhism. Where Jesus taught the masses by way of parables, Socrates engaged citizens in the search for definitions of the virtues, and where Jesus taught the apostles higher truths in secret, Plato reserved knowledge of the higher, esoteric truths for the inner circle of students and for the guardians, those who would eventually rule their cities with justice and truth.

The Collected Dialogues of Plato embody, in effect, a grand design, and the exposition of the spiritual/religious principles and doctrines actually constitute a major part of Plato's philosophical endeavor. The first section of the book lays out just what this grand design entails and how Plato

Introduction

develops it according to his higher purpose. Specific references to salient dialogues provide evidentiary proof of Plato's intentions, and the grand design itself confirms throughout that Plato is involved in active *doing* and not mere passive philosophical *thinking*.

In Part I of the book I also focus on two major topics that I feel have not been adequately investigated, or have not been allotted their proper context within Plato's dialogues. The first of these major topics concerns the doctrines of the immortality of the soul; transmigration (reincarnation); and the law of cause and effect (karma) that are the focus of the *Meno, Phaedo, Phaedrus, Symposium,* and *Republic*. What I am suggesting is that these doctrines were quite "foreign" in fifth-century-BCE Greece, and it is important to trace them back to their original source.

The second major topic has to do with the meaning of the Good. Plato's form of pedagogy throughout the dialogues is not to provide an answer to a student's question, but to discuss the topic in such a way that students can come to the answer for *themselves*. This is the reason, in my view, why so many of the dialogues have no specific conclusion. They were not meant to! It was for the student—and us—to arrive at our own conclusion. Thus, I would not expect Plato to give a direct answer to the question of the Good. But in the context of his spiritual/religious endeavor, leading ever higher into transcendental realms, and considering his many *statements* about the Good, it is hard to escape the conclusion that when Plato speaks of the Good it is the concept of God to which he refers, however we may interpret that term. I have documented his statements on this matter with particular care, since I am well aware that many philosophers are unwilling to make that inference from the Good to God.

These main topics, then, constitute the first section of the book.

Part II, "Plato and Pythagoras," investigates the possible sources of those doctrines, with an analysis of the influence upon Plato of the teachings of Pythagoras. These investigations include crucial philosophical topics such as whether there are two principles governing the cosmos, or only one; whether number is immanent or transcendent; and whether there is a conflict between the Pythagorean Monad and the concepts of the Unlimited-Limit. Important sources for these arguments are Philolaus of Croton, Plato himself, Aristotle, and others. This examination of Pythagoras is important because in addition to being renowned as providing the foundation of Greek mathematics and music, he is known to have had a school and to have taught mystery tradition doctrines to his inner circle of disciples. Thus, it is important to understand whether a case can be made that Plato is also to be viewed as operating within the Pythagorean tradition as well as the mystery tradition.

Part III, "Tracing the Source of those 'Foreign' Doctrines," focuses on the doctrines of immortality of the soul, transmigration (reincarnation) and the law of cause and effect (karma). I take the conclusions of the Plato-Pythagoras analysis and trace the findings backward in time to the legendary musician, Orpheus, who was claimed to be the founder of the mystery schools; and through the Persian Empire, upon which the religious teacher, Zoroaster, had such a major influence. I continue tracing the sources even further back, to the most ancient history of the Persian Empire, which had its beginnings on the steppes of central Asia—in Iran—and eventually to India. The results of these investigations were not only quite surprising, but may change our view of Plato. In short, I claim we need to understand him as a teacher of the mystery religion, but, using the new garb of his own age—that of reason.

Having completed a brief overview of our project, let us go back to the beginning and establish some ground rules and procedures. First, I have used *The Collected Dialogues of Plato*,[2] edited by Edith Hamilton and Huntington Cairns as my standard translation of Plato's dialogues. All footnotes are from this work, unless otherwise stated. I have also abbreviated the titles of footnoted books after the first mention of them. For example, A. E. Taylor's book, *Plato: The Man and His Work* (abbreviated Taylor, *PMW*).

Second, the question of the themes and chronology of the dialogues is complicated and inconclusive. I have, therefore, used the basic chronology from W. D. Ross's book, *Plato's Theory of Ideas*[3] as it provides a useful framework for this investigation, ably augmented by the Hamilton/Cairns compilation of the dialogues published by Princeton University. Scholars still differ on assigning accurate chronology to the dialogues, but it is sufficient for my purpose to assign them to the early, middle and late periods, understanding that the early dialogues mainly deal with the definitions

---

2   Edith Hamilton and Huntington Cairns, *The Collected Dialogues of Plato*.

3   W. D. Ross, *Plato's Theory of Ideas*.

Introduction

of the various virtues, Courage (*Laches*), Piety (*Euthyphro*), etc.; the middle period deals with the themes of immortality of the soul, recollection, transmigration, the law of cause and effect (karma) that inform *Meno, Phaedo, Phaedrus, Symposium,* and *Republic* in particular; and that the *Symposium* and *Republic* also deal with the themes of illumination and enlightenment, and the Good. The later dialogues, such as *Laws, Statesman,* and *Sophist* (excluding Plato's cosmology, the *Timaeus*), deal—in my view—with the *application* of the principles derived up through the *Republic to* those later themes. What I mean here is that Plato's collected wisdom through the *Republic* is applied on a specific and rational basis to the institutions and principles that embody the very structure of Greek life in the fourth century BCE. Having broad categories of early, middle, and later gives the flexibility to read any dialogue within a specific category in any order, and not lose anything of substance when discussing those dialogues as a group, or placing them within the total structure of Plato's philosophical intention.

Third, as I have already hinted, Plato's philosophy is *doing, not just thinking.* While most scholars define Plato as a rational thinker, one whose philosophy they can compare with those of other philosophers, it isn't usual to take the principles of Plato and actually understand them as a system by which to *live.* I have come across only one other scholar (besides Guthrie) who has made this point—namely John Gould, who states in his book *The Development of Plato's Ethics:*

> There is an almost universal tendency to assimilate cases of knowing *how* to cases of knowing *that...* what is required is a form of moral *ability* comparable in some respects to the creative or artistic ability of potters, shoemakers and the like (and that what) Socrates envisaged was a form of knowing *how,* knowing that is, *how to be moral.* (Gould 6–7)

Fourth, since Plato's dialogues depend upon his metaphysical principles, central among which is his concept of the *Forms,* or *Ideas,* some clarification of this term is required.

Socrates became famous in fifth-century-BCE Athens, because he was arguably one of the first to seek the definitions of things, definitions that sought *essences* and not just their temporal or mundane particulars. W.

D. Ross, in his book *Plato's Theory of Ideas,* tells us that the search for piety, courage, and the other virtues "led Plato to recognize the existence of universals as a distinct class of entity, and that he took over as names for them the words *eidos* and *idea,* words that in ordinary Greek had already begun to be used in the sense of *quality* or *characteristic*" (Ross 14). He continues that both *idea* and *eidos* are derived from the word "to see," which originally meant *"visible form."* Ross also uses a quotation in which Socrates uses the word *form to* define universals:

> You said there was one *Form* which made impious acts impious acts, and pious acts pious?... Tell me then, what is the nature of this *Form,* so that by looking at it and using it as a *pattern* I may say that any act done by you or another that has such a character is pious, and any act that has it not is impious. (Ross 13)

Ross mentions that there are a number of interpretations of the term *universals* put forward by other scholars, and that A. E. Taylor (*Varia Socratica*), in studying the use of Greek words before Plato's time, believed Plato's definition had its basis in Pythagorean ideas of geometry, where Form meant a *geometrical pattern or figure.* Ross also footnotes the work of C.M. Gillespie, who held that *idea,* or *eidos,* had first a physical definition meaning the *form* or *shape* of a physical object; that it was sometimes seen as *the outer, visible shape* and at other times, *the structure, the inner form, the nature* (Ross 13). As noted above and throughout the dialogues, Socrates most often is translated as using the words *Form* or *pattern* to describe the *Ideas.*

Therefore, it is important to state that scholars have different interpretations of the very words that supply us with the definition of the word *Ideas.* Of all these possible choices, Ross prefers the term *Ideas.* My own choice is *Form,* or *pattern.* Today, I would call it an archetype. Regardless of what name we use, however, Plato makes clear that unless we could "account for"—i.e. *define* the *essence* of any word, including the word *universal*—it could not be applied correctly, and that this would prevent true discourse from taking place. This is, of course, exactly what happens in the early dialogues. Each participant has his own provisional view of the virtue under examination, or different views of the same virtue as the dialogue moves along. But, in each case, Socrates seeks from them a

Introduction

universal, a Form, a definition of its essence that would cover all possible instantiations.

Fifth, it is important to understand the *context* of the Forms or Ideas. And here I want to comment on Ross's book, *Plato's Theory of Ideas*, mainly because he is representative of so many other modern investigators. The title gives me pause for two reasons: First, it describes Plato's work as a *theory;* also, it denotes the Forms as *Ideas*. Given the statements in the *Republic* about the long and arduous studies undertaken by the guardians in order to take their place in ruling the city (whether of the soul or the external city) and Socrates's constant efforts to show us how to live rightly, I do not see the Ideas as mere *theory*, but see them instead from the perspective of *practice*. I reiterate John Gould's statement that what Socrates envisaged was not a form of *knowing that* but "was a form of *knowing how*, knowing how, that is, how to be moral" (Gould 6–7). Second, I find the term *Ideas* to be an unfortunate choice of word to describe the Forms because our habits of thinking in the twenty-first century lead us to the mistaken belief that the Forms are ideas in our *minds*, and not, as Plato describes, eternal patterns that guide our behavior. I am supported in this view by A. E. Taylor who states: "But, it is misleading to call them, as they have so long been called, *Ideas*. That suggests to us that they are some one's thoughts, 'ideas in some one's head' precisely what the theory does not mean."[4] This view is also confirmed by W. K. C. Guthrie, who declared that the translation of the Greek word *idea* meant *form or pattern* and that "the English word *idea* is about as unsuitable a rendering as could be found, for to us it suggests what has no existence outside our minds, whereas to Plato the *idea* alone had full, complete and independent existence."[5] For these reasons I will use the term Form, or pattern, and occasionally the term archetype to describe the eternal principles to which they refer, only resorting to the term Ideas for the sake of the understanding of those who still prefer the use of that term.

Sixth, it is inconceivable to attempt to evaluate the essential meaning and importance of Plato's dialogues without emphasizing the enormous weight of Aristotelian interpretation. He is still the pre-eminent authority for so many modern philosophers. However, I think it is essential to

---

4   A. E. Taylor, *Socrates*, footnote 1, 165.

5   W. K. C. Guthrie, *The Greek Philosophers—From Thales to Aristotle*, 89.

disentangle *facts* reported by Aristotle with *judgments and interpretations* he made about philosophical doctrines found in Plato and Pythagoras. I will go into this topic more deeply later on, but let us remember that Aristotle was by nature a scientist, and his scientific skills of observation and classification that were to prove so influential, for example, in the realm of biology, were not the same skills needed to penetrate the transcendent nature of the *metaphysical forms* revealed by Plato or the mathematics of Pythagoras. Despite the decision by so many twentieth-century philosophers and scholars to defer, ultimately, to Aristotle's judgments about Plato because he was a contemporary, and historically so influential, I find Aristotle to be a far less reliable, objective, and fair judge of Plato's metaphysics than should be expected.

Seventh, and last, Aristotle was one among many who dismiss as fanciful or meaningless the myths found in Plato's dialogues—*Phaedo, Gorgias, Republic,* and *Timaeus*. In my view, given the rigorous exercise of reason needed to understand the thrust of each of the other dialogues, Plato didn't suddenly fall into a fanciful heap when it came to the myths. Just as each dialogue has an intrinsically purposeful *theatrical* setting, so the myths are to be seen as expressions of Plato's thought when dialectic—having reached its limit—could no longer reveal the truth Plato sought to communicate. Just as Socrates in the *Republic* was unable to give Glaucon the *experience* of the Good, even though he might have wished to do so, Plato is similarly unable to reveal the loftiest realms of the Good except by symbol or analogy. In other words, he is, perhaps, unable to reveal his own or Socrates's *direct* experience of the Good, illustrating once again that Plato's students were required to use *all of their own faculties* in order to attain the direct experience of the Good *for themselves*. And where students had not yet reached those heights—as with Glaucon—the symbol and the allegory would have for the time being to suffice. I allow then that the myths have an intrinsic place in Plato's philosophy and, like the consummate playwright that he is, he introduces them when and where appropriate.

PART ONE

The First Stage: Definition of the Virtues

Having established the ground rules, let us turn to the dialogues and examine them, keeping in the keen lens of our perspective the view that Plato is engaging in a philosophy of *doing* and not merely *thinking*. And, since we have established that Plato's endeavor will start with the cultivation of the virtues, it is there that we must start. I will take two of the virtues and, from an examination of them, attempt to find a pattern or principle that we can apply to the rest of the virtues found in the early dialogues. And, it is always useful to remember that the theatrical setting of any dialogue provides a key to its inner meaning.

In the first case, Socrates is discussing the virtue of courage, not with just anyone, but with two distinguished generals—Laches and Nicias—fighting men in the army whom common knowledge would esteem for their understanding and experience of this virtue of courage. After having established that any virtue is a good, and that Socrates himself is ignorant of the matter in question, he presses the generals for the definition of courage. Socrates asks: "What is that common quality which is called courage and which includes all the various uses of the term?" (*Laches* 192-b). Laches replies that a man of courage is he "who does not run away, but remains at his post and fights against the enemy" (*Laches* 190-e). Socrates points out that Laches is speaking of a specific application of courage to infantry men, but he wants to know how courage may apply to every other kind of soldier. He wants to know the common quality that would define courage in all cases. After reflection Laches answers that courage "is a sort of endurance of the soul, if I am to speak of the universal nature which pervades them all" (*Laches* 192-b). Socrates points out to Laches that there can be a *foolish* endurance of the soul, and that therefore every kind of endurance of the soul will not fall under their sought-after universal definition. Socrates guides Laches to admit that only *wise* endurance is courage, and yet Laches immediately contradicts that definition by stating he believes that the soldier who endures, having knowledge, i.e. the skills needed for use of the sling or the bow, is not as courageous as one who has not similar knowledge of these things. (*Laches* 193-b). Socrates replies that in his opinion those who do not have skills of their trade are foolish compared to those who fight with such skills. He finishes this little skirmish by showing that Laches holds foolish endurance above wise endurance, and that as a result his words are at variance with his deeds.

Laches admits his error. He says, "I fancy that I do know the nature of courage, but somehow or other, she has slipped away from me, and I cannot get hold of her and tell her nature" (*Laches* 194-b). At this point the general, Nicias, enters into the discussion. Nicias comes up with a statement that he has already heard, and attributed to Socrates—"that every man is good in that which he is wise, and bad in that in which he is unwise" (*Laches* 194-d). He adds that a brave man is also wise. Socrates takes him to mean that courage is a kind of wisdom. But when pressed Nicias holds that "courage is the knowledge of that which inspires fear or confidence, in war or anything" (*Laches* 195). Laches intervenes at this point, claiming that courage is one thing and wisdom another. Socrates points out that this is just what Nicias has denied. Laches claims that Nicias is talking nonsense. After further discussion as to whether courage is knowledge on the grounds of hope and fear, and questions of whether wild animals or children have courage, Nicias says to Laches that there is a difference between rashness and courage and that Laches favors rashness whereas he, Nicias, defines *courage* as wise actions.

At this point it is clear that the two generals completely disagree about the definition of courage. In fact, Laches becomes upset believing that Nicias's definition of courage would "deprive of the honor of courage those whom all the world acknowledges to be courageous" (*Laches* 197-c). Now the argument has taken a serious turn. Nicias is challenging the common understanding of courage, and Laches hotly wants to deny Nicias such a victory. The question arises as to whether or not Nicias might be a Sophist, one who, in Plato's estimation, is an expert is spinning untruths and deception. To one seeking understanding, that could be a great insult. Socrates persuades Nicias to begin again with the definition.

In recapping the argument so far, Socrates points out that they have accepted that courage was one part of virtue, and that justice and

The First Stage: Definition of the Virtues

temperance are likewise *parts* of virtue (*Laches* 198). Socrates circles back to an earlier definition that the terrible and the hopeful are the things that may or may not create fear and that fear is expectation of future evil. But Socrates goes further, stating that it is his notion that *there is only one knowledge*—and it applies to the past, the present and the future. As a result, courage cannot be concerned only with good and evil of the future but of all times. Nicias's argument is flawed since he only includes a part of courage but not its whole, and courage must apply without reference to time. Extrapolating from that, Socrates goes on to show that if a man knew *all* good and evil he would be perfect, would not be wanting in any virtue, whether it be justice or temperance or holiness, that he alone would be competent to judge between what is to be feared, or not. In fact, Socrates slyly wonders whether justice and temperance are *parts* of virtue, but this statement falls on deaf ears. The denouement comes when Socrates points out that if that were not true, courage would be the whole of virtue and not merely a part. And clearly it is not. The discussion has ended in contradiction. Socrates concludes that they have not discovered what courage is. Nicias points out to Laches that they are both ignorant of things that they as generals ought to know. And he gracefully admits that if he were choosing someone to educate his children, he would not choose either himself or Laches to do so, but would request Socrates to undertake this important task. Socrates replies that he is no better equipped than either of the generals to do so. Nicias wonders if Socrates will listen to Lysimachus, the father of one of the youths needing education. Socrates maintains that *all* of those present should seek out the best teacher that they can find. They should concern themselves with their *own* education as well as that of their children. Lysimachus agrees that he will be educated along with his children. The dialogue ends with Lysimachus requesting Socrates to come to his house at dawn to advise him further about the situation.

This dialogue—the *Laches*—represents the pattern undertaken by Socrates in his investigations. First, he seeks to define the essence of the virtue under consideration, stating that unless the definition was understood, it could not be applied correctly, as this lack of understanding and consensus would prevent true discourse from taking place. This, of course, is what happens in the early dialogues. Each participant has his own provisional view of the virtue under examination, or different views of the same virtue as the dialogue progresses. But in each case Socrates seeks from them a *universal*, a Form or pattern, or as Ross would describe it, an Idea, namely a definition of its essence that would cover all instantiations.

The participants in the early dialogues are never able to arrive at an all-encompassing definition of a Form that will satisfy all cases. Therefore, this same lack of a definition can be found in the *Euthyphro* dialogue that focuses on the virtue of piety; the *Charmides*, of which temperance is the subject of discussion; and *Hippias Major*, which investigates the nature of the *beautiful*. In all these and similar dialogues, any conclusions arrived at are merely provisional. If participants want to arrive at a universal Form or pattern they must start their investigations all over again. This is not because a Form or pattern does not exist, but because those particular participants in the discussion were unable to arrive at it. This does leave open the possibility that a truly wise student *would* have been able to penetrate to the ultimate definition of each virtue, but such a student did not present himself. And, since Socrates's pedagogical style is to encourage the participants to reason for themselves and not to merely allow someone else's ideas to fill them—even if they are those of Socrates—Socrates must conclude the discussion at the point where the participants can proceed no further.

The fact that there are so many definitions of courage shown in the dialogue reveals something interesting about Greek life and Greek thinking at the time of Socrates and Plato. Each of the participants in a dialogue is applying the virtue in question in a merely relative situation, and fails to reveal the universal definition sought by Socrates. In fact, the probing clarity of Socrates's questioning is in stark contrast to the confused and error-prone level of thinking exhibited by his fellow Athenians. In the case of the *Laches* the participants are generals, men whom one would surmise *ought* to know what courage is since the soldiers under their care have more need of courage than, say, merchants or Sophists. Socrates reveals this unclear thinking on the part of the populace as it pervades the entire spectrum of Greek life.

In the next dialogue we shall examine the consequences of ignorance, revealing a darker side. A man's father may be put to death due to the beliefs of his son. The theatrical setting for the *Euthyphro* is outside the law courts where Socrates himself is headed to answer a charge of corrupting

The First Stage: Definition of the Virtues

the youth of Athens. He encounters Euthyphro at the entrance to the law court, and upon asking him why he is there, is somewhat shocked when Euthyphro says he is there to prosecute his own father on a charge of murder of a servant. Euthyphro self-righteously states that he knows he is acting in the spirit of true piety. When asked by Socrates to give a definition of piety, Euthyphro's first answer (*Euthyphro* 5-d) is "what I am now doing, prosecuting the wrongdoer." We note that Euthyphro is not a general, a man of action like Nicias. Euthyphro is a theologian, a man who interprets religion and claims to know what piety is. He thinks that one must prosecute the impious man, no matter who it might be. But when challenged by Socrates he defended his actions by responding that Zeus, the father of the gods, swallowed his own children, and that Athenians who do not think Euthyphro should follow in the footsteps of Zeus contradict themselves. Socrates wonders whether Euthyphro really *believes* all those stories about warring gods, and Euthyphro responds that he does believe them.

Socrates resorts to his usual method of questioning and asks Euthyphro for a universal definition of piety, or holiness, one that would be instantiated in all cases. Euthyphro's second definition (*Euthyrphro* 7) is that "what is pleasing to the gods is holy, and what is not pleasing to them is unholy." Socrates parries that Euthyphro has just admitted that the gods war among one another, so how could there be common agreement among them about what is holy. Socrates points out (*Euthyphro* 7-e) that in that case "what each of them thinks noble, good and just, is just what he loves, and the opposite is what he hates." Socrates points out to Euthyphro that perhaps his prosecution of his own father would be pleasing to Zeus but hateful to Cronus or Uranus, but Euthyphro is unmoved. He thinks one who murders ought to pay the price. When pressed further, Euthyphro admits that in fact there are all kinds of disputes about what constitutes whether a person killed someone wrongfully. And, having made that admission, Socrates is free to challenge Euthyphro's position on the grounds that Euthyphro has no proof that the gods would think the father murdered his servant unjustly.

Socrates asks Euthyphro whether they could both agree on a definition. They might agree (*Euthyphro* 9-c) that "what the gods all hate is unholy, and what they love is holy, whereas what some of them love and others hate, is either both or neither." Euthyphro is willing to go that far. Next, Socrates wonders (*Euthyphro* 10-a) whether "what is holy (is) holy because the gods approve it, or do they approve it because it is holy?" After discussion (*Euthyphro* 10-d), Socrates shows Euthyphro that "it is because it is *holy* that it is loved: it is not holy *because* it is *loved*." The conclusion from this is that what is pleasing to the gods is not the same as what is holy, and thus Euthyphro's initial definition is found to be in contradiction. The dialogue continues on, but our examination is sufficient to show, once again, that Euthyphro, a theologian, an interpreter of religion—the very person one would suppose to have a sound definition of what is holy—is sadly wide of the mark. To discover the true and universal meaning of piety they would once again have to start over in their deliberations, something from which Euthyphro conveniently excuses himself.

In fact, the early dialogues show participants who have relative, confused, or contradictory beliefs or opinions. Socrates has as his purpose a form of questioning that will reveal to the participants a deeper and more universal definition of each of the virtues. It is important to underscore the fact that for Socrates, without a correct understanding of the *definition* of each virtue, the individual would not be able to apply it fully or correctly in his life. In addition, it cannot be over-emphasized that for Socrates and Plato philosophy is *doing*: it is first understanding, and then applying a set of spiritual or religious principles that will contribute to the whole meaning of life. It therefore *matters* to Socrates how the participants fare in their investigations of virtue. It is important to Socrates that students go beyond relative interpretations of the virtues and discover their universal nature. It is essential that students penetrate to the level of universals in order to discover the deeper truth of life.

At this juncture, we need to probe deeper into the nature and expression of the virtues. In the early dialogues, the starting point is the discussion of particular instances in which a person has engaged in an act of virtue—for example, an act of piety or an act of courage. The person who engages in a virtuous act is described as having *shared in* or *participated in* the Form of courage. These virtuous acts are considered to be *immanent* due to the fact that they are evidenced *in* the person's actions. However, in the case of the virtues, there are no sensible *objects* in which the virtues are exhibited. Instead, there are only sensible *subjects* engaging in personal acts of virtue that can be *observed* in the everyday, sensible world. In the *Phaedo* and *Republic,* Socrates will deal with questions as to whether everyday objects such as couches or tables, or relative terms such as tallness and shortness can be assigned Forms. For the present, however, when we speak of the Forms as being *immanent* in particular instances, Ross says we mean the Idea, or Form, is "present" in them; it is placed "in them" by the craftsman; it comes to be "in them"; it is "common" to them; the particulars, in turn, "possess" or "share in it."[1] Parenthetically, only once, in the *Phaedo,* did I actually find the term *Form* translated as the word *universal.* Plato, using Socrates as his mouthpiece more often than not, uses words like *pattern* or *Form.* Whenever Plato is discussing universals he uses the **concept** of *Forms* to designate universals, **in his sense of the word**, without actually using the **term universals** to convey his point. Let me reiterate that for Plato, in the early dialogues, the term universal means the definition of the word's *essence* and that it carries a metaphysical status and meaning.

Universals

Before proceeding with the debate about universals, let us focus momentarily on the *status* of universals. The *Philosophical Dictionary* states that, "universals are features (redness, tallness) shared by many individuals; each instantiates the universal. The metaphysical issue is whether these features exist independently of particular things that have them." Notice that this modern, well-publicized definition does not include "features" such as courage or justice, those very features that Plato assigned a metaphysical status (meaning that at this stage they are described as non-sensible, intelligible objects). This points to the very nature of the problem with universals. Plato's interpretation has been entirely omitted. Our modern *Philosophical Dictionary,* and many commentators, ascribe to a universal a strictly *scientific* definition as a *quality,* whereas for Plato it was most certainly a non-sensible, *metaphysical* object. In fact it is here, on the question of universals, that Aristotle was to break with Plato in his complete rejection of the metaphysical definition of the Forms, or universals. For

---

1 W. D. Ross, *Plato's Theory of Ideas,* 21.

him, as for countless scientists down through the ages, the term *universals* has come to be understood in its entirely scientific meaning of *quality*, or *characteristic* belonging to a person or object.

The big question is: *Do* universals exist independently of particular subjects (or objects) that have them? Realists say they do; Nominalists say they do not, and Conceptualists say that they do so only mentally. (Here again, the problem surfaces—no mention is made of "features" such as courage or wisdom, which Plato would claim, at the very least, are non-sensible and should not be treated in the same way as sensible objects.) On this reading then, Plato is a Realist, for he claims the Forms exist independently of us. Aristotle, on the other hand, is a Conceptualist, because the gathering of different species (*sensible* particulars) such as dalmation and poodle under the genus "dog" is a mental abstraction of classification; it structures more order into our *thinking* about dogs, but it does not posit an independent *existence* for the universal.

For the above reasons, and because it is key to an interpretation of universals, I will state my understanding of the Socratic and Aristotelian methods of arriving at universals, and then compare them. In the case of Socrates, this method involves looking at, for example, particular instances of courage, and trying to define the term by *stripping away all the accidentals* of time, place, and event in order to arrive at the definition of courage *itself*. The Socratic universal has a moral and ontological purpose—to help people live rightly, and seeks to establish truth in the unchanging Forms. The Platonic Form of courage is the *essence of courage*.

Aristotle's method of dealing with universals is quite different from that of Plato. For him, all known species of dogs—dalmation, retriever, standard poodle, etc., fall under the genus "dog." In this process, however, there is no stripping away of accidentals to arrive at a definition *in itself*: instead there is a *gathering together* of all appropriate identifiable *sensible* characteristics in order to arrive at the definition of the genus. In the Aristotelian case, external or unchanging Forms simply do not exist, and "potentiality" in the sensible object replaces the ontological purpose of the Platonic Forms. Here, then, we are talking of a scientific process of *classification,* which has little in common with Socrates's search for higher truth—in fact, quite the opposite.

The First Stage: Definition of the Virtues

On its face, the debate boils down to whether intangibles such as "courage" and "tallness" are instantiations of universal and unchanging Forms, or whether they are scientific classifications/logical propositions that specify courage and tallness as qualities that an individual person or object possesses. But the crucial battle is between diametrically opposing metaphysical and scientific/logical views of interpreting the world.

Logic is another issue that impinges greatly on the question of the status of universals. Many commentators, notably Richard Robinson in his book *Plato's Earlier Dialectic*,[2] Ross himself, and many others, it seems to me, have interpreted Plato's work in either scientific or logical terms. And perhaps they have assumed more technical or Aristotelian logic to be evident in the early dialogues than is actually the case. If so, it would seem to make a significant difference as to our conclusions about the Forms. How we interpret the meaning of Forms is crucial not only for the all-important definitions, but also in respect to the equally important task of how we will tackle the issue of participation later on. Ross himself declares that some of Plato's answers to questions show that "in principle he was assuming, as Aristotle proceeded to do explicitly, that definition is analysis *per genus et differentiam* (Ross 13). However, as Ross himself admits, Plato did not explicitly use *genus et differentiam* until the *Sophist*, a dialogue that according to his own chronology is a late one that dates after the *Parmenides* and the *Theatetus*.

I also find it unfortunate that Ross's first translation of the words *idea* and *eidos* is "quality" or "characteristic" because if we proceed using *only* these *scientific* translations of the definitions, we have already prejudged the entire argument about universals on the side of logic and science, for these terms "quality" or "characteristic" are precisely the ones that will be fought over in the major battle between the metaphysical and scientific/logical views of the world. These terms most certainly do not convey what *Plato* meant by Ideas or Forms, namely that they were independent of our mind, eternal, unchanging, and were *patterns (or archetypes) that could guide people to live rightly.*

Regarding this issue of logic, Guthrie states the nub of this problem quite clearly: "One must always remember that his (Plato's) *concern with language, logic or method was only ancillary to a larger purpose.*

---

2   Richard Robinson, *Plato's Earlier Dialectic*.

The end was right living."³ And F. M. Cornford confronts the issue even more bluntly:

> Dialectic is not what is now known as "Formal Logic".... Formal Logic may be described as the study of 1) propositional forms—not actual significant statements, but the patterns or types under which statements can be classified; 2) the constituents of these propositional forms (subjects, predicates, relations between terms, etc.); and 3) formal relations of inference between propositional forms. The beginning of Formal Logic is marked precisely by the introduction of symbols.... The introduction of symbols means that the attention is now fixed on the form of statements apart from their content.... The science of Dialectic...does not study formal symbolic patterns to which our statements conform, nor yet to these statements themselves.... What it does study is the structure of the real world of Forms.... There is nothing to show that he (Plato) had ever conceived of such a science as Formal Logic.⁴

Last, let me frame this argument about universals with respect to Plato's philosophical purpose in writing the dialogues. According to Guthrie, it was to "rescue" knowledge from the Heraclitean flux of the sensible world. Heraclitus, it may be recalled, held that knowledge was not possible in an ever-changing world. Socrates's search for definitions—for *essences*—was conducted in order to oppose this view vigorously, because he (Socrates) believed that skepticism could result from Heraclitus's extreme philosophical position. Socrates had "the belief that...*an (ideal) standard did exist*; it was not something we arbitrarily fixed for ourselves but something that was there for us to discover, and in his belief it was single."⁵ Arguing then, as Plato does, for a Realist interpretation of the Form stabilizes definitions in unchanging values, and doing this guarantees their truth, because truth comes from the eternal Forms, and the Forms are part of the divine world. *Not* to argue in this way, for Plato, would be to risk allowing his definitions to fall right back into the Heraclitean flux. The result would be to pull the eternal truth enshrined in the definition—i.e., the Form of

---

3   W. K. C. Guthrie, *A History of Greek Philosophy*, vol. 4, 244.
4   F. M. Cornford, *Plato's Theory of Knowledge*, 264–265.
5   Guthrie, *HOP*, vol. 4, 243.

The First Stage: Definition of the Virtues

Courage *itself*, back to the sensible world where it would indeed become merely a "quality" someone possesses that could be scientifically classified. The scientist might say that Plato has turned his back on the sensible world, but Plato can reply that the scientists have turned their backs on the metaphysical world and the ideal standard of truth.

And that is exactly what happens with Plato's student, Aristotle. He rejects Plato's metaphysical Forms in favor of scientific classification and/or formal logical propositions. These logical propositions about tallness or redness may give us sensible classifications of universals but they make no ontological claims about the essences of things in the way Platonic Forms do. The fact that tallness and redness *can* be interpreted solely on an empirical basis is precisely where the scientists find Plato most vulnerable to attack. It is also the place where the epistemological claims, both for and against, are most murky. For Plato the Form of Courage is a non-sensible object, immanently instantiated. However, logicians and scientists end up discussing Plato's metaphysical questions from the level of logic or science, or even from the level of sense impressions. They reject Plato's metaphysical truth and substitute a truth that is scientific or logical. This is the major flaw in their position from a metaphysical point of view.

We must also bear in mind that the *Philosophical Dictionary* tells us that "it is *often difficult in practice to establish the truth of universal propositions*." On this view, the scientists have no more claim to truth than Plato does, because first it is difficult *in practice* to establish truth, and also, as often happens, later research may show their original propositions were provisional, or even wrong. From this perspective scientific truth is relative.

As for logical proof, the x's and y's may "work" in regards to formal logical propositions, but they are incapable of defining the *actual content* of the virtues because, first, the virtues are eternal, not temporal, and second, scientists don't recognize them as such. They restrict the virtues to mere "qualities" on a par with redness and tallness. The x's and y's of the proposition are really empty forms, signifying little but a formal pattern. The very formal nature of the argument precludes a definition of the very real virtue of courage. Personally, I find this to be a static form of logic, perhaps a clumsy and mechanical imitation of Plato's dialectic, but lacking in Plato's eloquent grace and vital intellectual movement. One can already sense the danger in a logical conception of truth—it would squeeze the life out of dialectic, mechanize the dialectical procedure, and dismantle metaphysical truth. And this, I sense, was its aim.

Clearly scientific and logical truth have their place in the scheme of things, but if they are going to oppose metaphysical truth without first, in good faith, *examining* the selfsame metaphysical truths, then their attempt to discredit Plato's Forms fails because they have failed to engage him in his own metaphysical territory. In fact, logic and the scientific method *cannot* reach into the eternal, because it is elusive and incommunicable. This is the nub of the problem.

One probable reason for misunderstanding of the issue can be found in Plato's discussion of the Divided Line in the *Republic*. I take Plato at face value when he presents this analogy. He means us to understand that he categorizes four different groups of people according to their ascending levels of mental capabilities. He extols the virtues of the man of reason, operating at the fourth and highest level because *he alone* can engage in dialectic and contemplate the pure Forms without reference to sensible particulars. In Plato's scheme, the logicians and scientists fall into the third level, which corresponds to the faculty of understanding, with its mathematical and geometric objects. To this I think we can add logic and science, which also deal with theories. Therefore, for scientists and logicians to truly understand the issues related to Forms, they would, for Plato, have to be operating with the faculty of reason. Instead, they are operating at the level of understanding because they are still tying their investigations to diagrams illustrating assumptions that ultimately refer back to the sensible world. They have not learnt to "do away" with hypotheses in the search for the unhypothesized first principle. To put it bluntly, they do not have the tools for the job. And to be fair to them, neither do most of us. According to Plato, unless *we* are operating at the level of reason we simply will not understand the Forms as they are intended to be understood. I think it fair to say that Plato would have felt that someone criticizing him from the third level was like the man at the fairground who tries to shoot at the swiftly moving line of ducks that constantly move across his field of vision. He usually misses the mark.

The enduring, age-old question remains: *Is* there an ideal standard of knowledge? As Socrates says, at the end of the *Cratylus* (440), "Whether there is this eternal nature in things, or whether the truth is what Heraclitus and his followers say, is a question hard to determine." We may add that eternal truth cannot be captured by science and logic. A crucial passage in the *Symposium* later reveals that *personal and direct experience* of the transcendental unity of things would provide the answer to that question, but the experience is not only rare, but almost *incommunicable*. This is the age-old problem for metaphysicians. That Plato managed to communicate *so much* about universals is a tribute to his genius. Meanwhile, investigators here in the twenty-first century must continue to examine their own assumptions in order to answer the question as to whether the virtues, such as courage, piety, and justice are merely scientific classifications, logical propositions, or metaphysical essences.

I would like to indulge in my own Platonic argument for universals, or as Socrates calls them, Forms. Since Plato will, in the next section, argue that the soul is immortal, and stores within itself a record of its good and bad deeds (deeds that will be judged by the impartial law of cause and effect, or karma), the inference is that the soul, a non-sensible "subject" that outlasts the body, is the part of the human being best equipped to apprehend and understand the virtues (non-sensible objects). The virtues exist on higher, intelligible planes of consciousness, and this is why Plato exhorts students to *detach* from the senses in order that their judgment of universals and higher truths are not obscured by bodily concerns and a sensible world orientation. This could also apply to scientists. Despite their abilities to theorize from their experience of the world, most are still *oriented* to the sensible, material world.

Be that as it may. Three observations may be made about these early dialogues. First, Plato is introducing the notion that each virtue is in fact a *"good."* For example in the *Charmides* (15-d), translated by Jowett, Socrates asks: "Then, in reference to the body, not quietness, but quickness will be the more temperate, if temperance is a *good*?" Second, Socrates is already hinting that courage, temperance and the other virtues are a *part* of virtue. This pattern can be observed throughout the dialogues. And third, at the conclusion of each dialogue, Socrates and the participants have to accept that they *were not able to discover an adequate definition of the virtue under review*. To proceed further, they must, in each case, start all over again.

Now, to return to the main theme of this book, namely that Socrates and Plato were committed to *doing*, not merely *thinking*, we can recall the statement in John Gould's book, *The Development of Plato's Ethics*, that *doing* had the connotation of learning *how to act rightly, to be moral*. I have argued that this occurs when a person tries to apply themselves in a serious manner to the cultivation of the virtues—courage, piety, justice, and the like—for when they do so on a consistent basis, the embodiment of these very virtues will also correspondingly diminish the lower appetites and ambitions. Those seeking the higher road of life are shown that the very *meaning* of life is wrapped up in the search for higher ideals by which to live.

Before we move on, let us review the collective significance of the early dialogues that refer to the virtues. The virtue of piety, correctly understood and applied (*Euthyphro*), would help an individual have the right understanding of their own actions in relation to the higher meaning commanded by the gods; the virtue of beauty (*Greater Hippias*) would help a person be open to beauty in the arts, thus influencing their cultural life; the virtue of courage (*Laches*) would help anyone, not just soldiers, to respond appropriately when the safety of their person, another person, or their city was in danger or during times of war; the virtue of justice (*Republic*) reveals itself to be indispensable to human civilization but is, at the same time, a mere shadow of a higher, divine law. *Gorgias* discusses the pitfalls of wrongly understanding power; *Crito* discusses whether laws should be set aside in extenuating circumstances; *Ion* shows that art is not just of balance but it represents the realm of higher knowledge; *Phaedrus* and the *Symposium* discuss the many faces of love, but place divine love far above its mundane human expression.

As we have seen, personal reflection by individual students on each of the virtues was the form of pedagogy utilized by Socrates and by Plato. However, close examination of this group of early dialogues confirms that even though they are presented individually, for the sake of clarity and understanding, they are, in fact, *parts* of a whole. Put together—as pearls on a single string—these dialogues constitute nothing short of a clear *system* of moral and ethical behavior, and provide a firm foundation as a necessary prerequisite of seeking higher truth and then esoteric knowledge. The individual having the mindfulness to understand the definitions of

The First Stage: Definition of the Virtues

these virtues, and to make the persistent effort to live by them on a daily basis would, in Socrates's opinion, already be demonstrating the values of the higher individual, who could contribute those values to the greater community, in this case the city-state of Athens.

Is Plato, in Greece, alone in his search for the higher meaning and values? Assuredly not! In fact, if we are to include Plato as a spiritual-religious teacher, we would expect to find examples of similar religious systems of teachings all over the world. Before we do so, let us remember, first, that at least two of these systems were derived hundreds of years after Plato's time and may reflect a general evolution in human consciousness; second, that Socrates and Plato were among the first to emerge from mythological thinking and to utilize the faculty of reason in their spiritual/philosophical researches, and that makes it understandable that their first task was the search for definitions, and especially definitions of the essences, the virtues. Our first task, then, is to show how they may be understood in terms of the later systems. A list makes this more clear.

DIALOGUE	VIRTUE	PURPOSE
EUTHYPHRO	Piety, holiness	To act in accordance with commandments of the gods.
LACHES	Courage	To act with courage—whenever needed, not just in war.
CHARMIDES	Sophrosyne	"Know Thyself"; act from laws of inner harmony/proportion.
REPUBLIC	Justice	To act justly at all times, as individuals and as a city-state.
GORGIAS	Power	The pitfalls of wrongly understanding power.
CRITO	Law	Should a state set aside laws in extenuating circumstances?
APOLOGY	Sacrifice	This is the noblest act of a good man—such as Socrates.
LYSIS	Friendship	What is true, higher friendship?
ION	Art	Is it balance of emotions/mind or does it belong to divine realms?

These are the virtues discussed in the early dialogues. There are other important virtues revealed in Plato's later dialogues, but let us leave them aside for the moment. We merely want to know whether Plato's early dialogues provide a parallel to religious/spiritual systems in other places and times. I have taken the clearest and simplest of descriptions in order to highlight the basic correspondences.

In Christianity a good place to start is the teaching by Christ of the Beatitudes at the Sermon on the Mount, which is found in the fifth, sixth and seventh books of Matthew. They are as follows:

> Blessed are the poor in spirit, for theirs is the kingdom of heaven.
> Blessed are those that mourn, for they shall be comforted.
> Blessed are the gentle, for they shall inherit the earth.
> Blessed are those who hunger and thirst for righteousness, for they shall be satisfied.
> Blessed are the merciful, for they shall receive mercy.
> Blessed are the pure in heart, for they shall see God.
> Blessed are the peacemakers, for they shall be called sons of God.
> Blessed are those who have been persecuted for the sake of righteousness, for theirs is the kingdom of heaven.
> Blessed are you when people insult you and persecute you and falsely say all kinds of evil against you because of Me.
> Rejoice and be glad, for your reward in heaven is great; for in the same way they persecuted the prophets who were before you.

In addition Jesus gave new, Christian, teachings about murder, adultery, divorce, falsehood, and revenge. He then exhorted everyone to love their enemies, turn the other cheek, and pray for those who persecuted them.

I think Socrates would have felt vindicated by Christ when, in the *Crito,* his friends tried—unsuccessfully—to persuade him to flee Athens in order to save his life when he knew it was his duty to sacrifice it.

Let us turn now to Judaism, and The Ten Commandments:

1. I am the Lord your God and you should have no other gods before me.
2. You shall not take the name of the Lord your God in vain.
3. Observe the Sabbath and keep it holy. Six days—labor, but the seventh is God's and you will not work.
4. Honor your father and mother.

5. You shall not kill.
6. You shall not commit adultery.
7. You shall not steal.
8. You shall not bear false witness against your neighbor.
9. You shall not covet your neighbor's house.
10. You shall not covet your neighbor's wife.

A cursory comparison between Judaism, Christianity and Plato already reveals a core of similar beliefs and practices. Let us, however, move to the East and review the basic tenets of Buddhism. The Noble Eightfold Path constitutes the practical steps needed to be taken by one who wishes to live according to higher truth. The Noble Eightfold Path includes:

1. Right view. This means to understand things as they really are, to possess wisdom.
2. Right intention—describes commitment to ethical and mental self-improvement.
3. Right Speech—the first principle of ethical conduct, for our words can affect others in good or bad ways.
4. Right Action—the second ethical principle—means one abstains from wrong actions. It means to act compassionately to others, to be honest, to respect the belongings of others, and to avoid harmful sexual relationships.
5. Right Livelihood. One should earn one's living in a righteous way, and wealth should be gained legally and peacefully.
6. Right Effort. Our mental state can fuel unwholesome states of desire, envy, aggression and violence, or wholesome states of self-discipline, honesty, benevolence, and kindness.
7. Right Mindfulness refers to a higher faculty of cognition whereby we can begin to perceive and control our mundane thoughts.
8. Right Concentration. This is where all the mental faculties are unified, and due to this one pointed focus, the mind can concentrate on higher realities by way of meditation.

As explained, the Noble Eightfold Path describes principles that will engender wisdom, ethical conduct and mental development in the serious student, and these practical steps are then harnessed in the service of higher spiritual doctrines described as the Four Noble Truths. To clarify, it needs to be stated that Buddhists believe in the concept of reincarnation, or as Plato would call it, transmigration, whereby one lives a succession of lives in the pursuit of higher perfection of the soul. With that understanding, these Four Noble Truths are:

1. Life means Suffering—because of disease, old age, death, and because our mundane world is imperfect and impermanent. We must seek for what is changeless, for that will relieve our suffering.
2. The origin of Suffering is Attachment. Because we attach ourselves to transient things due to our desires—for wealth, for power, for fame—we are unable to see the suffering we are creating now and for the future.
3. The Cessation of Suffering is Attainable. We can learn to undo our attachments by understanding their negative fruits, and thus avoiding them. We detach from the passions in order to reflect and meditate upon what is changeless and brings true happiness.
4. The Path to the Cessation of Suffering is a gradual path of self-improvement (shown in the Eightfold Path) that eventually leads to the end of the cycle of births and deaths in a human body. When that occurs, the one who has reached Buddha-hood enters *Nirvana,* a state of cosmic consciousness that is identified with the *Void,* the sum total of existence. It is said that Nirvana is incomprehensible for those who have not attained it.

Lest we think that we have gone too far afield in including Buddhism in our review, let us first remind ourselves that the system of self-improvement, including the virtues, is very clearly set out, and the parallels to Plato's virtues are unmistakable. Second, it is absolutely clear from Plato's dialogues (*Phaedo, Phaedrus, Meno*) that he, too, accepted the idea of reincarnation or, as he calls it, the transmigration of souls. He shares with Buddha the notion that the eternal and changeless world is something people on earth forget when they don their earthly bodies. Plato also shares with Buddha the understanding that the passions, ambitions and lower desires lead us astray from our higher nature. As with Buddha, it is the *effects* of the passions and desires that cause the soul to be born again in order to resolve those issues.

It is precisely the concept of reincarnation (as well as the immortality of the soul, and the law of cause and effect, karma) that connects Plato to the East, which has held fast to those doctrines for untold thousands

The First Stage: Definition of the Virtues

of years. As we observe today, except for those engaged in the study of Eastern philosophies and yoga, the concept of reincarnation is, in the main, still somewhat alien to the western mind. Parenthetically, we might add that recent Biblical scholarship, and some of Jesus' own statements, attest to the fact that he too touched upon the doctrine of reincarnation. Jesus said of John the Baptist that he was the prophet Elijah come again. Christ's own words about John the Baptist indicate that for him the issue of reincarnation was a familiar one, and we may speculate that perhaps the Christian teachings were originally intended to include reincarnation and the more expanded sweep of time than one mere life, which that doctrine offers.

But to return to our point, whereas Christ taught by example and by his parables, Socrates (Plato) achieved his purpose in having people think for themselves and understand the definitions of things, starting with the virtues. Buddhism taught not only all the forms of moral/ethical thinking and action, but in addition the practice of *meditation* on the higher realms. Even here we can find parallels to Plato, for detachment from the senses taught by him achieved much the same goal of the Buddhist centering his mind in meditation. Both were attempting to rise above the sea of passions, ignorance, and imperfection of the temporal world in order to gain a solid foothold in the higher realities of the inner world. And both shared the ultimate goal of merging their soul with the eternal while they were living in a human body.

In this respect, Plato and Buddha are, unexpectedly, in accord. And when we examine the more esoteric aspects of Christ's teachings, we will see that he confirms the same view. The higher teachings were reserved for the disciples and were not meant for the masses. For the ordinary people, the higher knowledge was clothed in parables, much as in Plato higher knowledge was veiled in myth or subsumed in the arts.

Let us leave this section on the early dialogues by reminding ourselves that they are to be taken as a whole, and that Plato's purpose in writing them—in addition to the cognitive aspect of understanding the sought-after definition—was that they provided a basis for moral thought and action in *all* aspects of life—spiritual, religious, political, the arts, law, and the cultivation of the virtues—central among which was the virtue of justice. The virtues, however, were merely the lower slopes of the mountain.

As such they prepared the disciple to be worthy to gain higher knowledge, some of which was esoteric, or hidden.

The Second Stage:
Higher Spiritual Teachings

These dialogues constitute the next level of the spiritual/religious teachings, and the specific focus is an examination of the immortal human soul. Perhaps Socrates himself reflects the inspiring nature of these particular dialogues (*Meno Phaedo, Phaedrus*) because in places he seems almost to be transported into the higher realms about which he is speaking.

A few observations need to be made here to place Plato's investigations of the soul in the context of fifth-century-BCE Athens. For example, at that time the focus of life in Greece was very much on the activities of the here and now. The Greek people loved life and appreciated its physical gifts. They attempted to live life to the fullest today—here in this body—and they had little concept of what happened when they died. In fact, one might say, they were not particularly interested in knowing. Their concept of the soul was derived from Homer, who had described it as a mist or a wraith that dissolved or dispersed at death. Therefore, the Greeks approached the question of death more or less as a negation of the physical vitality of their earthly life, not something about which to be actively interested.

However, in fifth-century BCE Athens, many of Homer's views were beginning to come under attack. Some of the Pre-Socratics were quite critical of the mythological Homeric account of the universe, and Socrates took exception to Homer's view that the gods disagreed with one another and created wars among themselves. The search for *definitions* by Socrates was itself an attempt to move beyond Homeric mythological thinking toward the emergence of Greek reason, and at the same time encouraged students to think for themselves, a doctrine that would find itself decidedly unpopular with the political authorities of the time.

Given these conditions, and with the benefit of historical hindsight, Plato's investigations of the soul appear to constitute an important (r)evolutionary development. They certainly would not, at that time, have taken root among the ordinary people—the tailors, merchants, and soldiers—least of all the slaves and women. But they did take root in the civilized upper classes, the Athenians with money and leisure, and time to apply themselves to philosophical subjects.

Those who took part in these dialogues dealing with the more transcendent aspects of existence were fortunate indeed to have Socrates himself as their mentor and guide. For, according to our theory, they had been so successful at living a life of virtue that they had attained the right of moving on to the next phase of the inner search. It would be to this relatively small group of students that Socrates would impart his teachings on the immortality of the soul, recollection, transmigration (reincarnation), and the law of cause and effect (karma)—beliefs that were completely foreign to the average dweller of Athens of the fifth/fourth centuries BCE.

The Apollonian and Dionysian mystery schools were definitely in existence at the time, but it is known that Socrates refused to belong to either one of them because their teachings required an oath of secrecy. Socrates wanted the freedom to be able to discourse with other citizens, in public, about many topics, but one surmises that the knowledge of the immortality of the soul and its related doctrines could have been seen by those in power as part of that secret knowledge that belonged to the mystery schools. However, as Socrates points out in the *Symposium*, he had received his philosophical education from a wise woman of Athens called Diotima, and it does not say in the dialogues that she extracted from Socrates an oath of silence. Quite the opposite! For, from that time onward, Socrates had encouraged his fellow citizens "in obedience to the divine command" to take care of their soul (*Apology* 23-b).

Meno: Doctrine of Recollection

As stated, in the second stage of inquiry the topic is the immortality of the soul and its ramifications. As usual, Socrates takes us into the topic in a step-by-step fashion, one that will deepen and expand with each successive dialogue. But he begins the investigation in the *Meno,* where the stated topic is whether virtue can be taught. However, the dialogue is significant because it provides an exposition on Plato's central doctrine of recollection.

Every philosopher knows the scenario of the *Meno*. A discussion is taking place between Socrates and Meno about whether virtue can be taught, and after eliciting from Meno that virtue is the desire of the *Good*, Socrates replies that they need to find out what virtue *is in its essential nature*. While he agrees that courage, temperance, and wisdom are individual virtues, he emphasizes: "I asked you to give me an account of *virtue as a whole*" (*Meno* 7-c). What is good? What is virtue? "Does anyone know what a *part* of virtue is without knowing the *whole*?" (*Meno* 79-c).

In this regard Socrates exhorts Meno to recall that inspired people like poets and priests believe that "we are not born in entire forgetfulness nor yet in entire nakedness but that "the soul of man is immortal. At one time it comes to an end and at another time is born again, but it is never finally exterminated" (*Meno* 79-c). So this is Socrates's first point—that the soul is immortal. In this dialogue Socrates does not explore the reason or purpose of future lives. He is content to introduce the topic in such a way that it can connect up humankind's immortal soul with its divine source. Socrates further posits that if we tried hard enough we could *recollect* what our souls knew in other lives and in the divine world in the period between lives. Here is Socrates's second point: that because man *can* recollect knowledge he had gained in prior lives, or even in the period between lives, knowledge is *recollection* and not learning as we understand it. Socrates gives a proof of learning as recollection when he summons Meno's slave boy to participate in an experiment. The slave boy has had no education, but, by following Socrates's directions and using his own native intelligence, the slave boy is able to correctly reason to the principles of geometry that underlie squares and triangles. The slave boy's success in reasoning to principles he had never been taught in this life causes Socrates to ask whether those present agree "that his soul has been forever in a state of knowledge?" (*Meno* 86-a). For Socrates, this is sufficient proof that the boy is revealing knowledge that he once possessed but did not recollect until provided the appropriate opportunity.

He then turns back to the issue whether virtue can be taught, and wonders whether it is some form of knowledge, or a form of good. After discussion, Socrates famously states, "If there exists any good thing different from and not associated with knowledge, virtue will not necessarily be a form of knowledge. If on the other hand knowledge embraces everything that is good, we shall be right to suspect that virtue is knowledge" (*Meno* 86-d). Socrates argues that even the virtues—courage, temperance, justice—could be used for harm unless they were guided by the goodness of a person's nature, and goodness was dependent upon wisdom. Socrates muses that if virtue is learning it could be taught, but he points out that famous Athenians known for their virtue, such as Themistocles or Lysimachus, were unable to pass on their virtue to their sons. Socrates concludes that virtue is a part of wisdom, and if there was ever a person who *could* teach virtue he would be as a true reality among flitting shades.

Plato achieves several purposes in the *Meno*, apart from introducing the topics of the soul's immortality and its innate ability for recollection. Socrates's very method of pedagogy—that of encouraging young people to ponder things for *themselves*, reinforces the notion that learning is not blindly accepting facts and theories put forth by teachers and other authority figures. The mind here is no "tabula rasa" such as we find in Enlightenment figures such as John Locke and David Hume. Plato would have fought vigorously against the idea that knowledge was "outside" of oneself, and that the helpless individual merely absorbed it like a sponge. For him, the soul of man was always in dialogue—so to speak—not only with the external world but also with its own immortal source. It is for this reason that Plato accomplishes another of his goals in the *Meno*. He would argue that because man has an immortal soul, he has the ability to be linked to all aspects of life, even to those areas whose principles might seem on first view mysterious or obscure.

Because of this link—its faculty of recollection, and its immortality—the soul could not be swept away or drowned in the temporal flux of phenomena—as was argued by Heraclitus in fifth-century-BCE Athens. His position was that because everything in the world was in constant flux, there was nothing stable in human beings by which to arrive at certain knowledge. Knowledge of immortality of the soul advocated by Socrates confirmed that human beings are *not* left adrift in an alien universe by an uncaring or distant god. Quite the reverse! Because human beings have an immortal soul, they could be certain of their transcendental source, and, owing to the of faculty of recollection, they could remember knowledge they had learned from other lifetimes or in the divine realms before birth. Thus, human beings could be saved from the skepticism, even nihilism, of the darker social effects of the Heraclitean position.

One recalls here Socrates musing in the *Phaedo* on his past where he shares with his friends that once upon a time he occupied himself with scientific theories dealing with the origin of our planet as found in the works of the Pre-Socratics, but he found their explanations to be too materially-minded and in the end rejected them. In fact, he refers to them as absurdities. For Socrates, *God* is the artificer of the universe and that firm conviction pervades Plato's writings on the matter. The fact that human beings *have* an immortal soul gave them the certain point of stability that allowed them fearlessly to contemplate their place in the world, knowing that they were connected to the fluctuating world of change and, at the same time, to the unchanging divine realms presided over by God. Equally important, it opened people to the possibility that they, too, could become poets, priests, or *disciples* who could have *personal experience* of the mysteries of their own soul.

Phaedo: Immortality of the Soul

This dialogue contains Socrates's arguments for the immortality of the soul, a poignant topic since it takes place on the day of his execution. Ironically, the day before Socrates's trial began, a boat crowned with garlands was sent on an annual sacred mission from Athens to Delos, and a law was in effect that no executions could take place until the mission returned. Because of this, an unusually long interval occurred between the time of Socrates's trial and execution. The mission had been greatly delayed by stormy weather—possibly a subtle hint that the gods themselves were displeased by the order to execute a man the Delphic Oracle had once pronounced the wisest man in Greece.

Socrates is in his jail cell, together with a few other disciples, including the Pythagoreans Cebes and Simmias, and the subject naturally turns to Socrates's views on the future life. Socrates states that "the gods are our keepers" (*Phaedo* 62-e) and that in the next world he expects to enter the company not only of wise gods, good men and those who are dead, but also "divine masters who are supremely good" (*Phaedo* 63-c).

Socrates then wonders whether there *is* such a thing as death—and if it is not simply the release of the soul from the body. He adds that a philosopher is one who has lived his life preparing for death because rather than directing his attention to mundane things such as food and drink, sexual pleasure, or smart clothes and shoes, he has spent his time directing his attention toward the soul. It is Socrates's contention that the body is a hindrance to knowledge because the senses do not reflect things accurately, and that the soul can only get a clear view of things in the course of reflection and contemplation, free of the pull of the senses. Socrates points out that the soul recognizes things in the invisible world—namely absolute uprightness, beauty, goodness and the like, all of which are apprehended by "applying his pure and unadulterated thought to the pure and unadulterated object" (*Phaedo* 65-e). This entails separating the soul as much as possible from the body and by cultivating the virtues such as courage and self-restraint, but Socrates emphasizes it is *wisdom or goodness* that makes possible courage, integrity, and self-control.

Socrates points out that most people see death as an evil because they are afraid of losing their earthly pleasures, but the wise man has no such fear because he has spent his time in living the philosophical life, detached as much as possible from the senses. That is why Socrates expects to be welcomed in the other world by good rulers and good friends.

Cebes declares that the average person has grave misgivings that when the soul is released from the body it may cease to exist, or be dispersed like breath or smoke and simply vanish. Thus, Cebes characterizes the Homeric version of the soul. Socrates answers his concern with a question. Do the souls of the departed exist in another world or not? He reminds them of an old legend that says that souls do exist in another world after death, "and that they return again to this world and come into being from the dead" (*Phaedo* 70-d). He supports this by saying that souls could not come into being again if they did not exist. In fact, by the law of opposites, life comes from death and eventually death comes from life.

Socrates's first argument for the immortality of the soul is that just as sleeping is opposite to waking, so death is opposite to life, and that both are generated out of their opposites. If death is the opposite to life, and if the living come from the dead, then our souls do exist in the next world.

Socrates's second argument depends upon the doctrine that he introduced in the *Meno*, namely that learning is recollection. Here, in the *Phaedo*, he expands and extends that inquiry, declaring that if recollection is valid, then our souls must have originally learned the knowledge they now recollect at some other time before they entered the human body. In other words, the knowledge was gained in the divine world, which is a proof for the immortality of the soul, since it is the soul's faculty of recollection that allows such knowledge to be remembered. Socrates gives an example: when a lover sees a musical instrument or a piece of clothing that belongs to the person they love, their mind conjures up the picture of its owner. Similarly, a portrait of Simmias would remind those present of Simmias. From these examples Socrates extrapolates that recollection may be caused by similar or dis-similar objects, and that one must also be conscious whether similarity is perfect or only partial. To press his point, he takes as a further example that of two sticks or two stones: by looking at two sticks or two stones one understands that there is a principle by which they are measured—not equality, but *absolute* equality. "So long as the sight of one thing suggests another to you, it must be a cause of recollection, whether the two things are alike or not" (*Phaedo* 74-d).

Then Socrates touches upon a major issue of the *Phaedo*—that of *imitation*, or *participation* of the soul in the virtues. He explains that sometimes when you see one thing that has a tendency to be like something else the comparison falls short and it is only a poor imitation. Nevertheless "anyone who receives that impression must in fact have previous knowledge of that thing which he says that the other resembles, but inadequately" (*Phaedo* 74).

In the same way, we must have had some previous knowledge of absolute equality before we saw equal sticks or stones and realized they were striving after absolute equality but fell short of it. Socrates concludes that we must have had knowledge of absolute equality before our birth, and of all other absolute standards as well—absolute beauty, goodness, uprightness, and holiness. "We must have obtained knowledge of all these characteristics before our birth" (*Phaedo* 75-d). Therefore the recovery of that knowledge is not learning, but recollection, and the objects in this world that *remind* us of these absolute values are as copies of the original pattern.

Simmias is convinced of Socrates's arguments for the existence of the soul prior to its human birth, but Cebes's concern still has to be addressed as to whether or not the common fear is justified that, at death, the human soul disintegrates like smoke or the wind. Socrates replies that he has already given a proof of this, but will approach it from another direction. He asks to which class of things do souls belong—composite, natural, inconstant things, or is it one thing that is not affected by change. Is absolute reality constant and invariable? Does absolute equality or beauty "or any other independent entity that really exists ever admit change of any kind? Or does each one of these uniform and independent entities remain always constant and invariable," he asks. Cebes agrees that these things must be constant and invariable, as well as invisible. Socrates reminds Cebes that they had agreed that the soul uses the body, but when engaged in philosophy it detached itself from the senses. Now he argues, "When the soul investigates by itself (detached from the senses), it passes into the realm of the pure and everlasting and immortal and changeless, and being of a kindred nature, when it is once independent and free from interference, consorts with it always and strays no longer, but remains in that realm of the absolute, constant and invariable, through contact with beings of a similar nature. And this condition of the soul we call wisdom" (*Phaedo* 79-d).

Socrates reinforces that the soul is most like what is divine, and therefore it will not disintegrate at death. The soul that is good goes into the presence of the good and wise God, whereas the soul that is contaminated by its earthly pleasures and desires will be dragged back down into the visible world and may even turn into an apparition that haunts graveyards. Socrates also hints that those who have cultivated gluttony, drunkenness, and selfishness may be born as dull animals such as donkeys. But true philosophers restrain themselves from bodily desires in order to cultivate purity of soul, so that upon their death they will be admitted to the divine realms.

Simmias and Cebes are not yet won over. They still have concerns about the soul's survival of death. Simmias tells Socrates that he is a Pythagorean and their definition of soul is that it is held together in a tension between extremes—of hot and cold, dry and wet and so on. He says if the soul is an invisible attunement as of the strings of a musical instrument, what happens if the musical instrument is broken. Does the soul's attunement still exist or is it destroyed. Socrates answers Simmias by using the analogy that a human (soul) can change many coats (bodies, as in transmigration, reincarnation), but that the soul exists ever constant throughout. Cebes's concern is that even though the soul takes on many bodies, he thinks that the soul could itself eventually become exhausted and perish at the end of one of its lifetimes. Cebes still needs to be convinced that the soul is absolutely immortal and indestructible. After establishing that Cebes does find the doctrine of recollection convincing, Socrates asks him whether he prefers the doctrine of learning as recollection (which supposes preexistence of the soul) over the Pythagorean view that the soul is an attunement (in which the instrument is a composite thing and therefore subject to change and destruction). He chooses the former, and Socrates shows him that if the soul's attunement is a composite thing, it should therefore follow the lead of its elements but not control them. Socrates argues that if the soul was an attunement, then whether a soul is good or bad, it would have the same amount of attunement, but if the attunement was an absolute attunement it would not contain a share of discord and thus all souls would be equally good—a view that Simmias has to agree is false (*Phaedo* 94-b).

Cebes still requires Socrates to prove that the soul is indestructible, and Socrates replies that that is no light undertaking, for it requires a full treatment of the causes of generation and destruction. Socrates begins by stating that in his youth he was much taken with natural science and sought the causes for things. But when he learned that there was no causality and no order in the pronouncements of Anaxagoras, and that he had hypothesized the four elements as causes, Socrates dismissed all such studies as absurdities. Socrates now puts forth his own view of causation that, he says, assumes the existence of absolute goodness and absolute beauty. He wants Cebes to consider whether an object such as a beautiful rose is beautiful because it is participating in *absolute beauty,* one of the Forms. For Socrates, this amounts to a form of causation. He uses examples of largeness and tallness, claiming that "there is no other way in which any given object can come into being except by participation in the reality peculiar to its appropriate universal" (*Phaedo* 101). Socrates doubles back to his earlier argument about the two sticks or stones that cause the mind to recollect the Form of equality, and he applies the same argument to tallness and shortness.

He is careful to make a distinction that, while "opposite *things* come from opposite things,... the opposite *in itself* can never become opposite to itself because it is eternal and changeless.

He gives a further, mathematical example. Although three and five are numbers, they also both share in the Form of being odd, and odd is a Form that must be applied to all odd numbers. A similar situation obtains between the Form of even and all even numbers. The Forms of odd and even *in themselves* cannot change because if they did their whole character or essence would be destroyed. Just as the Form of odd must accompany an odd number such as five, what enlivens the body is the soul, and the soul, being a Form, does not admit its opposite, death. Therefore the soul is immortal. Socrates is thus able to convince Cebes that our souls, after death, will exist in the next world, and if such is the case, Socrates said it "demands our care not only for that part of time which we call life, but for all time." Since the soul is immortal, there is no escape after death for those who do evil; they will be taken by their guardian spirit to a place of judgment and undergo corrective experiences for a required time, and then their guardian spirit will bring them back to another human life. Socrates concludes that, to guard itself against evil, the soul should become as good and wise as it can.

The Question of Participation

The major theme of Ross's book *Plato's Theory of Ideas* is that the Forms (or Ideas) go through an evolution from immanence to transcendence. As Ross states, the "whole group of early dialogues treats the Ideas as being immanent in particular things. It is "present" in them; it is placed "in them by the craftsman; it comes to be "in them"; it is "common" to them; the particulars, in turn, "possess" it (the Idea) or "share in it'" (Ross 21).

There is not much explicit exposition of participation in the early dialogues because they are mainly taken up with the search for definitions. However, the person engaging in a courageous act was said to *participate* or *share* in the Form of courage. From the side of the individual, Laches is seen as participating or sharing in the Form of courage. From the side of the Form itself, it is present in the particular person (i.e., Laches). It is placed in the person or comes to be in one.

By the time of the *Phaedo*, however, Socrates had made the remarkable statement (*Phaedo* 79-d) that "when the soul investigates by itself, it passes into the realm of the pure and everlasting and immortal and changeless, and being of a kindred nature, when it is once independent and free from interference, consorts with it always and strays no longer, but remains in that realm of the absolute constant and invariable, through contact with beings of a similar nature. And this condition of the soul we call wisdom."

This passage contains a number of remarkable ideas, which we will only mention in passing. The first is that the immortal soul is of a *kindred nature* with the divine realms. The second is that when the soul contemplates or is *absorbed* in those divine realms it is in a state of wisdom, and the third is that the realm of the divine, the absolute, is constant and invariable, pure, immortal and changeless. In the context of our current topic, the above statements reveal that the Forms are not known by use of the senses, but only by pure thought, which means that the soul contemplates things directly and clearly *only* when it is detached from all bodily concerns or sensible conditions. Socrates also makes the point (*Phaedo* 75) when talking of absolute equality that the sensible particulars are only a "poor imitation" of the Form against which they are measured. Socrates declares that if the Forms of beauty and goodness (described as absolute realities) really exist, "it is to them, as we rediscover our own former knowledge of them, that we refer, as copies to their patterns, all the objects of our physical perception" (*Phaedo* 76-e).

As Ross comments, "The Ideas are not now seen as a relation of universal to particular, but as Ideals, Standards, Limits to which individual things only approximate" (Ross 34). We notice that the definition of the Forms has shifted significantly—from immanence toward transcendence. Let me make two points here. Ross claims that the Ideas are no longer seen as a relation of particular to universal. This reveals that Ross has a completely different interpretation of *universal* from Socrates, in fact a scientific interpretation. But as Socrates makes clear, the universal is a *Form*, and thus the relation between a particular instantiation of it and the absolute reality of the Form is unchanged whether or not he *expressly designated* it as such in terms of participation in the early dialogues. What is added is the understanding that because Forms are divine, *any* instantiation of them in the sensible world is bound to be considered a poor imitation. The reason for this is that the soul is encased in the three-dimensional world of the flesh, and the lower aspects of the mind are prone to error-filled judgments—about sensible objects as well as eternal realities.

The second point concerns the issue of imitation, and Ross's interpretation of the term. As he says: In the *Phaedo*, another element comes into the theory; the particulars are spoken of as falling short of the Ideas, not only by being particulars and not universals, but by not being genuine examples of the Ideas but only approximate examples of them; the language of imitation begins to creep in without, however, either displacing the other or being reconciled with it (Ross 35–36). Both Ross, and R. K. Gaye in his book *The Platonic Conception of Immortality and its Connection with the Theory of Ideas,* insinuate that because instantiations of the Forms were imitations, they were not in fact genuine, and that Plato himself had become aware of the flaws in his Theory of Ideas.

This is an understandable objection if you are a scientist, but I think Plato would have defended himself by saying that the source of a Form (Idea) was the divine, intelligible world, and that the very nature of the sensible world of time and space was composite, and this meant that no instantiation of a divine virtue or higher truth would ever be perfect or complete. Perfection was the province of God alone. But the aspiring student or disciple could make genuine efforts to embody the virtues, and *when* a person engaged in a virtuous act, he was indeed *participating in* or *imitating* the divine nature of things. As Socrates declares in the *Phaedo*, the Forms were divine patterns that human beings imitated as they endeavored to embody divine truth. Thus, I think we can dismiss as unsubstantiated Ross's objections about imitation not being *genuine* and also his claim that Plato, by using the term imitation, had come to find flaws in his theory of Ideas. Plato was only too well aware of the frailties of human nature, but that did not prevent him from encouraging humankind's higher angels toward the divine realms. In fact, it was the impetus behind his entire philosophical enterprise, especially up to the *Republic*.

In the discussion of universals, the scientists, beginning with Aristotle, sought to disprove Plato's claims for the divine (and metaphysical) status of virtues such as courage, holiness, beauty and justice. For them the Forms simply did not exist. Universals were sensible-world descriptions and amounted to *qualities* that a person or an object *possessed*. If that scientific project had been entirely successful the result would have been to obliterate the metaphysical realms as a sphere of investigation, and to have tied all truth to the mundane, sensible world that was beginning to be described, especially by the Pre-Socratics, in more scientific and material terms. One might say that Plato's entire philosophical enterprise, especially in evidence in the *Phaedo* and *Symposium*, is to *resist* the scientific interpretation of the world and to restore the divine world as the central focus of the human search for meaning in life.

Lest we should think the evolution of the Forms stops with the description in the *Phaedo* of Forms as ideals, standards, or limits, Ross tells us that by the time of the *Symposium*, Plato has moved to the designation of the Form of beauty as *a being apart from its embodiment in any beautiful thing*. And, the last phase of the evolution of the Forms from immanence to transcendence is revealed in the *Republic*, the dialogue on justice, where Plato uses the example of the macrocosm of a city (a visible, sensible object) to serve as analogy for the city of the soul (an intelligible, non-sensible object). In this dialogue Socrates uses the deceptively simple image of the *mirror* to suggest that the true relation between the divine and natural world is one of *resemblance*. This is where Socrates gives his famous teachings on the *transcendent* nature of the Good. (These issues will be examined more closely in the corresponding dialogues, but the above gives a hint of our direction.)

The term *participation* is also used to explain other relationships in the dialogues. In *Hippias Major* the question is raised as to whether one is participating in a Form in whole or in part. In the *Republic*, Socrates tells us that we may designate specific names for the various Forms, but that is *just a way of speaking*, and in the end they are all parts of the Good, and as such, "have communion" with one another and also *participate* in the Good (*Republic* 79-b). And finally we must not forget the participation of the soul in the transcendental *experience* of illumination, expressed so eloquently in the *Symposium*.

Whether we use the term *participation, imitation, or resemblance,* the question then, as now, is how to deal with the issue of the Forms (universals). *Are* virtues non-sensible, intelligible, metaphysical objects, or are they qualities that a person possesses? In my view there is no resolution to this question, because the scientists/logicians and the metaphysicians stand in direct opposition to one another like armies on a battlefield. In the end it is not a question of what *evidence* will prove the case for or against their reality and existence. When all is said and done, the *evidence* will be interpreted by using one's *assumptions* or *beliefs* as a guide. If you are a scientist by nature, no doubt you will reject the Forms as fanciful creations imagined by dreamers detached from sensible reality. The virtue of courage will be seen to be a *quality* that one possesses. If you are a metaphysician by nature, you are more likely to accept the truth of the Forms because your assumptions have already allowed you to believe in the reality of the divine world. Thus, the issues of universals and participation will never be solved scientifically. Metaphysical objects, by their very nature and description, are beyond the province of science's boundaries to make a determination for or against them. That is why, as Socrates says, individuals must make their own decision as to truth and then live by it.

My view is that if virtues are metaphysical objects, then participation is possible because the intelligible, immortal soul, being akin to the Good, has as its corresponding objects the intelligible virtues and the other Forms.

PHAEDRUS: THE LAW OF CAUSE AND EFFECT (KARMA) AND THE LAW OF TRANSMIGRATION (REINCARNATION)

The stated topic of this dialogue is whether a youth should favor a lover or a non-lover, but the underlying theme is the relationship between the divine and earthly realms and the part played by love in reconciling them. In fact, Plato uses this dialogue to reveal the place the human soul holds in the grand design of the cosmos.

The dialogue starts innocently enough, with Phaedrus reading a speech by Lysias, a famous writer, on the reasons why a youth should favor a non-lover over a lover. Socrates is not impressed and reluctantly agrees to give his own speech on the subject. However, he covers his head with a handkerchief before he launches into his discussion. After defining love as pleasure and holding it in opposition to what is best, he offers several cynical arguments as to the many damaging effects a lover could have upon a favored youth and is glad to be finished with his speech. Alas, his divine sign comes to Socrates and tells him he has to atone for an offense against heaven. Socrates *knows* that his speech against love was foolish, even blasphemous, because Love is a god, a divine being, and thus could not be evil. In fact Love is a form of divine madness, which is a gift of the gods.

Socrates begins his defense of Love by building on the arguments established in the *Phaedo* for the immortality of the soul, adding here in the Phaedrus that the soul is "ever in motion," a characteristic of first principles, which are by their nature unchanging and eternal. As to the soul's nature, it is likened to a pair of winged steeds controlled by a charioteer. The steeds of the gods are good, but in the case of humankind, they have one steed that is noble and good and the other that is the opposite—i.e., unruly and prone to evil and, as a result, the charioteer has a difficult task controlling them.

The centerpiece of this dialogue is the soaring vision of the soul before its birth when it experienced the nature of things in the heavens: "And behold, there in the heaven Zeus, mighty leader, drives his winged team. First of the host of gods and daemons he proceeds, ordering all things and caring therefore, and the hosts follow after him, marshaled in eleven companies "with each god leading his own company...and Hestia abiding alone in the god's resting place" (*Phaedrus* 247).

As Socrates explains, there are many spectacles of bliss on the roads where the gods travel, and those souls that have the capacity travel with them to the summit of the world, where "the revolving heaven carries them round, and they look upon the regions without" (*Phaedrus* 247-c). However, the ultimate place is *beyond* the heavens where "true being dwells without color or shape, that cannot be touched; reason alone the soul's pilot can behold it, and all true knowledge is knowledge thereof" (*Phaedrus* 247, c-d). Those souls of the gods (and those who can follow them) because they are well-balanced and readily guided, behold true being and are nourished with the soul's proper food, for she contemplates truth and justice and temperance in themselves and knowledge of all that is (*Phaedrus* 247-b-c).

As to the other souls, those who are unable to become most like the god they follow, they are carried around in the revolutions, and because their steeds are "confounded" have a difficult time understanding the things that are. The unruly nature of the bad steeds obscure the truth and, in their haste and violence, they trample one another, are lamed, their wings are broken, and failing to receive the vision of being, they depart and feed upon the food of semblance.

This vision of the truth of things is what sets in motion the journey of the human soul, and in the three-dimensional world it is embodied in the *law of necessity, cause and effect,* or *karma*—which is the vehicle of cosmic justice. As stated, the pure soul who has followed in the train of one of the gods and who has beheld the truth is "kept from sorrow and free of hurt" until another revolution begins. But the soul that is unable to see the truth falls into forgetfulness and wrongdoing "and because of that burden sheds her wings and falls to earth." Such is Socrates's explanation of why souls are here on earth.

It is the law of necessity, or cause and effect, that determines human fate, which is to incarnate into a human body under the law of transmigration, or reincarnation. The soul who has seen the most of true being will have better circumstances, and those who have seen the least of true being will have more difficult circumstances. Socrates explains the order of those births: first will be into a seeker after wisdom or beauty, a follower of the Muses and a lover; second, in a king who abides by the law, or a warrior and ruler; third, in a statesman, a person of business or a trader; fourth, in an athlete, physical trainer, or physician; fifth, in a prophet or mystery priest; sixth, in a poet or artist; seventh, in an artisan or farmer; eighth, in a Sophist or demagogue; and ninth, in a tyrant (*Phaedrus* 248-c-d).

Socrates explains that in each of these incarnations, the soul who lives righteously has "a better lot for his portion, and he who lives unrighteously, a worse portion. Once upon the earth, it is extremely difficult for the soul to regain her wings, because it takes ten thousand years for the soul to "return to the place from whence she came" (*Phaedrus 249*). There are two exceptions—one who has pursued the philosophic life of wisdom; the other, one who, having passion for one's beloved, conjoins that passion with the search for truth—can be freed after only three thousand years.

But as to the rest of the souls, after they have lived their first life they will be brought to judgment. Those who have lived righteously are taken to a place in the heavens to receive the rewards of their past life, while those who lived unrighteously are "punished in places of chastisement beneath the earth" (*Phaedrus* 249-a-b). After a thousand years these souls are brought to the choice of their second life, "each choosing according to her will" (*Phaedrus* 249-c).

These lifetimes are under the strict control of the law of necessity and the law of transmigration, and the soul will continue to incarnate into human bodies until, at long last, it comes to understand the language of Forms. This is because the Forms provide the springboard for the recollection of what the soul saw when it was aloft with their god looking down upon things "which we now suppose to be, and gazing up to that which truly is" (*Phaedrus* 249-c).

Socrates has told us that those souls that are pure have beheld the truth of being, while those souls with unruly, unmanageable steeds have fallen to earth and feed on the food of semblance. This means that their judgment of things is impaired, and that they cannot appreciate the Forms—of justice, temperance and the like. But human beings have a saving grace, in that while they journeyed with Zeus and the gods human souls beheld the form of Beauty and were "initiated into its most blessed of mysteries pure and whole and unblemished."

The form of Beauty inspires people through the faculty of sight, and when one who is close to remembering the truth of the divine world sets eyes on a beautiful bodily form, one can experience "a shuddering and a measure of awe...and reverence as at the sight of the god." For such a soul, the bodily form leads to the recollection of the divine forms and to the truth of being it once knew. But, for those souls who are goaded by selfish desire and wantonness, their evil steed dashes their chariot, brings them to their knees and causes anguish (*Phaedrus* 254-e). Socrates tells us this happens time and again until the evil steed is cured of is wantonness, and at long last follows after the beloved with reverence and awe. Such, says Socrates, are the great and glorious blessings of Love and is the reason why, all other things being equal, a youth should favor a lover over a non-lover.

Summary

These three dialogues—the *Meno, Phaedo,* and *Phaedrus*—contain the doctrines that separate Plato from all other Greek philosophers, with the possible exception of Pythagoras. The *Phaedo* focuses on immortality of the soul, the *Meno* deals with the faculty of recollection that connects the human soul to the divine world, and the *Phaedrus* reveals the grand purpose of the soul's journey in its earthly incarnations. Where the *Phaedo* outlines the *arguments* for the soul's immortality, the *Meno* and especially the *Phaedrus* reveal the *mechanism* by which the soul finds its progress while in a human body. As we saw, it was purity of the human response to the original vision of the divine world that determined which of the nine possible lives would be selected for incarnation.

This serves as an introduction to the law of the transmigration of souls, the doctrine that the merits or demerits of one's past life will determine the circumstances of one's future births. In the East, this cycle of transmigrations is described as the *wheel of rebirth* and has been accepted since time immemorial. In the west we know it as law of reincarnation. As stated, the series of births lasts until the soul is purified, whereupon it finally comes to contemplate the reality of the transcendent Forms that embody the Good.

The law of necessity, or the law of cause and effect, is that cosmic law that impartially judges one's actions in each life as right or wrong. In the East this is referred to as the law of karma. One receives good karma, or beneficial circumstances, in one's next earthly incarnation for a life righteously lived, or difficult circumstances in the next life if one has fallen into ignorance and wrongdoing. The law of cause and effect has no favorites. All are equally responsible under the impartial rule of divine justice. It is for this reason that Socrates says that in order to avoid evil, the human soul should ever strive to live righteously. Some have objected that the knowledge of reincarnation would make us defer to the next life what should be accomplished here and now. That objection would be refuted by Socrates and Plato because for them the care of the soul did not apply just to this current life but for all time.

The Third Stage: Mystic Teachings

These are the highest teachings and are restricted to those of the inner circle, including Phaedrus, Agathon, and in the *Republic*, Glaucon. Such students must have safely passed the earlier two stages and been found worthy. They had to have demonstrated exceptional virtue, morality, understanding, and persistence in the pursuit of the highest truth and a noble life. In addition, as will be shown in the *Republic,* the guardians, those groomed to rule their cities with justice and wisdom, were required to offer their lives unselfishly in the service of humanity.

Symposium: Mystical Illumination of the Soul

The *Symposium* is Plato's dialogue devoted to Love, but—let us pause. What on earth is a dialogue on *Love* doing in the work of a *philosopher, Plato,* perhaps the most influential philosopher in history! In the introduction to the dialogue in the Edith Hamilton/Huntington Cairns edition of *The Collected Dialogues of Plato*, a comparison is made between the *Symposium* and Christianity, especially the paean of praise afforded human love by the apostle Paul—but as is admitted, Socrates takes that message an octave higher into a *eulogy* for divine love. We would have to turn back many historical pages to find a time when *Love* was considered an acceptable topic of philosophy!

Most philosophers in the western world today would groan, throw up their hands in despair, or blush for sheer embarrassment if questioned as to why Love, that most "subjective" of topics, should be included in Plato's discourses on philosophy. And that, of course, is the nub of our argument. Judged by western philosophical standards, Love is an orphan who has been banished from the kingdom. But not for Socrates! For him, Love was not only an integral part of the mystery and wonder of existence, but its highest pinnacle! That is why the *Symposium* is considered one of Plato's greatest dialogues.

The setting for the *Symposium* is a dinner party, and entails several of the participants giving their interpretations of love. Phaedrus begins by lamenting that, for all the hymns and anthems that have been addressed to the other deities, not one single poet has ever sung a song in praise of so ancient and so powerful a god as Love (*Symposium* 177). Those present are in agreement that each should praise the god of Love in their own way, with Socrates adding, "I couldn't very well dissent when I claim that love is the one thing in the world I understand" (*Symposium* 177-d). This is an extraordinary statement. A philosopher is claiming that *love* is the *only* thing he understands! This is not what we would expect, and when it is his turn to speak Socrates will be required to explain himself! In the meantime, several other praises of the god of Love are offered.

Phaedrus opens the discussion by stating that Love is the oldest god because he is so ancient and primeval as to be unbegotten. He claims Love is the source of the highest good and caused the ancient heroes as well as the lover to make great sacrifices for the beloved.

Pausanius adds that there is not one kind of love, but several. Of these the main divide is between human love, governed by the earthly Aphrodite, called Pandemus, and the heavenly Aphrodite who governs divine love. Pausanius points out that the laws of love are different in other city-states and that some things that are considered acceptable in one country are held to be disgraceful in another.

Erixymachus, a medical man, expands the previous hypotheses by claiming that love governs not only human existence, but also the animal and vegetable kingdoms. In fact, he argues, Love is so powerful and all–embracing that it governs *every* activity whether sacred or profane. He applies this standard to the body and states that Love tends toward the *good*.

Aristophanes steps forward with an explanation of the "real" nature of human beings that hearkens back to an ancient belief that in the *beginning* the human race was divided into three sexes—male, female, and a third, the androgynous, which partook equally of male and female characteristics. As he tells it, originally human beings were globular in shape, and he gives a description of them, stating that males came from the Sun,

The Third Stage: Mystic Teachings

females from the Earth, and the hermaphrodites from the Moon. Then he explains that they tried to combat the gods to wrest power from them, and in punishment Zeus split each globular being in two parts, and that these two parts, being separated, would forever be yearning for the other half. Aristophanes says this argument explains the love humans have for one another, and that what they are seeking is nothing less than to be merged with the beloved.

Agathon is looking for a definition of love. He says Love is the youngest of the gods, and has imperishable youth, dwelling in the softest part of human nature, the heart. He has moral virtue and the ability to control his desires; he can inspire creativity in the souls of others and is the inspiration for the Apollonian arts of archery, healing, and divination. Agathon closes by holding that Love, besides being the loveliest and the best, is the cause of those same virtues in all around him.

Inevitably, attention turns to Socrates, he who had been standing in a trance in a nearby doorway while the speeches were being given. What will *he* say about Love, he who shared with his companions that Love is the *only* thing he knows anything about! He begins by stating that Agathon has merely *flattered* the god of love, and not praised him. Socrates says he won't have anything to do with Agathon's eulogy of love, but he, Socrates, doesn't mind telling those present the *truth* about Love.

Although he doesn't explicitly verbalize it, Socrates knows from the various speeches that each of the speakers has only spoken of a *part* of love and not the *whole* of love. (Does this sound familiar?) They have given descriptions of love as an individual god with rulership over certain aspects of existence. But, as with the definitions of the virtues, Socrates is seeking the interpretation of Love that will cover *all* the instantiations of it given by his banquet companions. He wants the *ultimate* definition of Love.

But Socrates didn't *say* that. Instead he mentions some teachings he received when he was a young man. They came from a wise woman called Diotima, she whom Socrates describes as having postponed for ten years a great plague of Athens owing to a certain sacrifice she had made. It was Diotima, a *woman* in a totally male-dominated society, who taught Socrates the philosophy of Love, and we may notice that Socrates is capitalizing the word. In addition, it was Diotima who taught him the question and answer format that was, ever afterward, to be the hallmark of the Socratic method of inquiry.

She explains that Love stands halfway between the mortal and immortal worlds, and that while the divine does not mingle directly with humans, it is through the mediation of the spirit world that man can have connection and exchange with the gods. She declares that people who are wise do not long for wisdom because they already have it, and by the same token none of the gods are seekers of the truth because they are already wise and know the truth. Socrates wants to know: who *are* the seekers of truth? She replies that between wisdom and ignorance is placed Love. Wisdom is concerned with the loveliest of things, and Love is the love of what is lovely. And so it follows that Love is, ultimately, a lover of wisdom (*Symposium* 204-c). Socrates is not satisfied. He asks: What is it that the lover of the beautiful is longing *for*? She asks Socrates to consider substituting the word *good* for the word *love*. What is it that the seeker is searching for? To make the good his own, replies Socrates. Diotima asks him whether it is not true that *everyone* seeks to make the good his own, and whether it follows that everyone is *in* love. For her, being in love is only a single aspect of love. Their definition, so far, falls far short of the mark. And so she expands it. "For Love, that renowned and all-beguiling power, includes *every* kind of longing for happiness and for the good" (*Symposium* 205-d), but she explains that we would not characterize athletes, businessmen or philosophers as lovers. She has heard that lovers are always looking for their other halves, but for her, Love is never longing for anything other than the *Good*. At this point, Socrates asks Diotima to enlighten him as to the cause of all the various aspects of Love.

To encapsulate her teachings, she says, "To love is to bring forth the beautiful, both in body and soul. (Furthermore)...there's a divinity in human propagation, an immortal something in the midst of man's mortality which is incompatible with any kind of discord. And ugliness is at odds with the divine, while beauty is in perfect harmony" (*Symposium* 206-c–d). Diotima explains to Socrates that Love is in fact the longing in man for immortality. Those who seek procreation by way of the body turn to a woman and create physical children, while those who turn toward the spirit conceive things of the spirit—and those things are wisdom and all the virtues. She explains that the most important wisdom is what governs the ordering of society, when that includes justice and moderation, and that if a young man had those qualities as a youth, and was drawn to higher things, when the time for procreation came, he would not turn to woman to beget children, but would seek a beautiful youth and undertake his education. She mentions Homer and Hesiod, Lycurgus and Solon as examples of the attainments possible to one who follows in their footsteps.

She tells Socrates, she has no doubts that he might be initiated into the more elementary mysteries of Love but she doesn't know if he could apprehend the final revelation, because their discussion is taking place at the "bottom of the true scale of perfection" (*Symposium* 210). Nonetheless, Diotima agrees that she will do all she can to help him understand, and here begins the famous discourse often described as the "Ladder of Love."

First a seeker will fall in love with the beauty of one individual body; next he must reflect upon the beauty to be found in *all* human bodies; and then he must become the lover of every lovely body. After that the seeker must understand so thoroughly that the beauties of the body are nothing compared to the beauties of the soul, that he must be able to discern spiritual beauty even in a deformed physical body. This, says Diotima, will help the seeker for initiation to build a noble nature. The next step on the journey upward is to contemplate beauty in all institutions, and after that to divert his attention to *all* the sciences and to find beauty there. This is done so that the seeker may know the beauty of *every* kind of knowledge.

From this rarified vantage point, the youth, "turning his eyes toward the open sea of beauty, he will find in such contemplation the seed of the most fruitful discourse and the loftiest thought and strengthened, he will come upon *one single form of knowledge*, the knowledge of the beauty I am about to speak of" (*Symposium* 210). She tells Socrates that whoever has viewed the various stages in due succession is drawing near to the final revelation. This revelation is nothing less than the description of a mystical experience of the soul as it merges with the divine in a transcendent moment of illumination or enlightenment.

Diotima continues:

> And now, Socrates, there bursts upon him that wondrous vision which is the very soul of the beauty he has toiled so long for. It is an everlasting loveliness which neither comes nor goes, which neither flowers nor fades, for such beauty is the same on every hand, the

same then as now, here as there, this way as that way, the same to every worshiper as it is to every other. Nor will his vision of the beautiful take the form of a face, or of hands, or of anything that is of the flesh. It will be neither words, nor knowledge, nor a something that exists in something else, such as a living creature, or the earth, or the heavens, or anything that is—but *subsisting of itself and by itself in an eternal oneness*, while every lovely thing partakes of it in such sort that, however much the parts may wax and wane, it will be neither more nor less, but still the same inviolable whole. (*Symposium* 210-d–22-b)

Diotima tells Socrates that apprehending universal beauty is the only way that the seeker must approach—or be led—to the sanctuary of Love. For such a seeker, who has once gained the vision of the very soul of beauty—a transcendent experience that will stay with him forever—will nevermore be distracted by the seductions and charms of the beauty of physical bodies and visible things because upon him has been bestowed the ultimate, transcendent experience of Love.

This is an awe-inspiring statement, difficult to apprehend if you, as that seeker, had not fulfilled all the requirements outlined in the ladder of Love. A. E. Taylor appears to have a remarkable understanding of it. As he states,

> In the end the study of the separate sciences leads up to the supreme science of "dialectic" or metaphysics, in which we are confronted with principles on which all other knowing depends, so here Socrates describes the man who is coming in sight of his goal as descrying "one single science" of Beauty. And in both cases, in the final moment of attainment, the soul is described as having got beyond "science" itself. Science here passes in the end into direct "contact" or, as the schoolmen say, "vision," an apprehension of an object that is no longer "knowing about" it, knowing propositions that can be predicated of it, but an actual possession of it and being possessed by it.[6]

What this possession amounts to is rightly the subject of *transcendence*.

At this *sublime* moment of the proceedings, Alcibiades barges into the high-minded dinner party quite drunk and wishing to lower the tone by

---

6 Taylor, *Plato, the Man and His Work*, 230–231.

tempting everyone present to involve themselves in drinking when they had agreed before the dinner party that they would abstain from wine. Despite this, it falls to Alcibiades to render a tribute, even a *eulogy*, to Socrates. This tribute is one of the most valuable statements of praise because it comes from Alcibiades, arguably Socrates's greatest disappointment as a student because later on he betrayed his highest principles by going over to the side of Sparta and fighting in the war against his own countrymen, the Athenians. Alcibiades is described as a deceitful youth, an adventurer, a politician, an intriguer, and a charmer. When Pericles, the greatest of Greek statesmen, died, the people chose Alcibiades to succeed him despite his betrayal of Greece during the war with Sparta. Under his rulership he led his country to ruin.

Thus Alcibiades could represent the evil steed who was unruly and drawn to wrongdoing, but whose good steed, while in the actual company of Socrates, could be inspired toward a noble life. Alcibiades, a favorite of Socrates, is in a position to document the virtues that make Socrates an exceptional being. Alcibiades says Socrates reminds him of Marysas the satyr, or a *seleni* (*Symposium* 215-b), a statue that opens up down the middle to reveal a figure of a *god* inside. He thinks Socrates is as impudent as a satyr, and has a greater ability to bewitch everyone than the magic found in Marysas' flute, music that showed who was a fit subject for divine *initiation*.

Alcibiades, who is involved in politics and is in with the mob, says he has heard the oratory of the great Pericles, but even that great leader of Athens pales beside Socrates, whose speech turns his whole soul upside down and makes him feel ashamed of the impurity of his lower nature. He realizes his attention spent on politics is making him neglect the care of his soul. Alcibiades charges that Socrates attracts good-looking people but is not attracted by them, that he is impervious to sexual relationships, and that no matter how much wine Socrates might drink, he could never be made drunk. He tries to appear ignorant and uninformed on the outside, while all the time the *inner god* exists within him. Alcibiades says he had once seen the images inside Socrates's seleni—and that they were godlike, golden, beautiful, and utterly amazing. Alcibiades recounts their military service together in Potidaea where Socrates withstood the hardships of the campaign better than anyone else. Socrates continued to go barefoot even in a shockingly cold and icy winter, and wore only his usual coat. And then there were his trances! Alcibiades recounts that Socrates would go into such trances when wrestling with a problem and would not emerge again until he had found an answer, something that had, on occasion, taken over twenty-four hours to accomplish. Then again, Socrates was the bravest man because he'd saved the life of Alcibiades in the campaign, and he was humble because when it came time for military decorations Socrates was passed over in favor of Alcibiades himself, who had powerful family connections. In addition, when fighting at Delium, Socrates had shown he was fearless in the face of death, and his very glance had probably intimidated the enemy.

Alcibiades knows that Socrates makes his arguments using images and ideas that even common people could understand, and that his arguments were elusive in that they appeared to be reiterating common truths that sometimes appeared nonsensical while, if you probed further, you would open him up like the seleni and there would be revealed the only arguments that made sense. These arguments are precisely those that had the power to bewitch the inner soul into a noble and righteous life. Alcibiades concludes that Socrates is absolutely unique and that no comparison among men will suffice, only the comparison with those godlike seleni and satyrs.

When we review the elements of this tribute, Alcibiades clearly likens Socrates to a god—in fact, a god of *love*. Does he mean us to understand Socrates as an embodiment of a god of love, such as the other participants have praised? Or does he mean to insinuate that by his superior virtues and extraordinary, unique nature, Socrates embodies the godlike nature that alone attains the mystic experience of the soul, merged in divine Love, of which Diotima had spoken? Once again, Plato leaves that judgment to us, the readers.

The Republic

The *Republic* is considered to be Plato's greatest achievement, dealing as it does with the role justice plays in the life of the individual and the state. Socrates begins by saying that it is difficult to pinpoint justice in the individual man (the microcosm) and so he proposes to his companions that they enlarge their scope to encompass a city (the macrocosm) where it will be easier to define the subject of their investigation. We will not go into detail, except where the subject matter has a bearing on our theme of transcendence, but in order to set the stage for the dialogue, it is useful to know that Book I sets out a description of the city and its needs and underscores that the city is best served when each man performs his own one function of work and no other. Book II contains Socrates's criticism of the old mythic stories of the Homeric gods, and Book III launches into Plato's rules for the conduct of the guardians, that elite group who will eventually rule their cities. In fact, it is important to take into consideration that the entire dialogue is devoted, in one way or another, to this overarching theme.

Let us also note that the *Republic* begins with Socrates declaring that the just man is the happy man. His companions Glaucon and Adimantus challenge Socrates to show that the just man—and not the unjust man—is the *superior* man. Several definitions of justice are put forward in Book I. For Cephalus it is "truth-telling and paying back what one has received from anyone" (*Republic* 331-c). Simonides claims that it is "to do good to friends and evil to enemies" (*Republic* 332-d). And boorish Thrasymachus holds "that the just is nothing else than the advantage of the stronger" (*Republic* 338-c). As we know, Socrates will not rest until he has arrived at a universal definition.

It is no accident that those who offer these early definitions of justice fade from the scene in the later developments of the dialogue, a veiled hint that their definitions do not qualify them for the higher truths that justice renders solely to the worthy and tested student. Thus, of those present, Glaucon is the only one who has the capacity to question Socrates on the higher aspects of justice.

This brings up the question: Who *will* teach these worthy students and exemplary guardians? It cannot be lesser persons, as they would not have been found worthy. It could only mean that teachers would have to be those who had passed through a similar course of study. And if we were to fathom a guess at the singular and extraordinary nature of such a teacher, would not the first name that came to mind be none other than Socrates?

Remembering the eulogy of Socrates by Alcibiades in the *Symposium* might help us decide whether we wish to include Socrates among these legendary teachers, but at the very least we know that if the guardians were to be ready to reach initiation—for that was the goal—then it required that they have teachers who had already attained that higher state of consciousness themselves. It was for this indescribable *experience of initiation* that the guardians were ready to sacrifice everything connected to the material world and to dedicate themselves over the course of their lives, from the cradle to the grave, to this highest of all human endeavors. One assumes that Plato counts Glaucon among this rarefied group.

In setting the stage for what will follow, it is important to highlight (in Book IV) the re-introduction of the analogy, from the *Phaedrus*, of the soul as a charioteer who has control over two steeds, one white and good, and the other black and evil. In the *Republic* Socrates gives a deeper explanation of this analogy. He describes the soul as tripartite: the charioteer represents the faculty of reason; the good steed represents the high-spirited nature of the warrior, and the evil steed represents the appetitive nature of human beings, whose desires can drag the whole chariot down to destruction. As Socrates explains, just as each person had a specific function in the external city, so each of these parts of the soul has its own function, and that the soul will be good and harmonious when each part does its own job. The problem is when one of the steeds, particularly the evil one, starts to think it should have a different function from the one assigned to it. For example, if the evil steed wishes to overrule the function of reason, the chariot will be overthrown because if human desires are what lead people, they will fall into wrongdoing and disaster.

Glaucon's real education begins in Book V, after Socrates has affirmed that his city has been established, and that it remains for them to discover where justice and injustice are to be found within it (*Republic* 427). What is justice? And what is *ideal* justice? Socrates begins by stating that *philosophers* must be rulers because they are lovers of wisdom—lovers of the *whole* of wisdom and not just a part. The true philosopher loves truth. In what sense do you mean? questions Glaucon. Here Plato introduces a major development with regard to the Forms, because Socrates replies that just as the fair and honorable is opposite to the base and ugly, and that each is one, so "in respect of the just and unjust, the good and the bad, and all the ideas or forms, the same statement holds, that *in itself each is one,* but by virtue of their communion with actions and bodies and with one another they present themselves everywhere as a *multiplicity of aspects*" (*Republic* 476).

Socrates elaborates by distinguishing those who live in the realm of sensible things, "of sights and sounds," declaring that they are incapable of apprehending *things in themselves*. One who believes in beautiful things but cannot apprehend the Form of beauty is as a person who is asleep and mistakes semblance for reality. On the other hand, those who are able to recognize Beauty itself and all of the other forms are considered to be those who are awake, those who understand *things in themselves*. They are people of knowledge compared to the sense-oriented person, who has only an *opinion* of the truth. As Socrates reveals, between wisdom and ignorance lies opinion, but the knowledge of the lover of wisdom is not opinion, but *science*.

In Book VI Socrates begins by affirming that he has just given a definition as to who is a lover of wisdom—those who are capable of apprehending what is eternal and unchanging. Those who merely opine are described as "those who have no vivid pattern in their souls and so cannot, as painters look to their models, fix their eyes on the absolute truth...or "establish in this world the laws of the beautiful, the just, and the good" (*Republic* 484). Lovers of truth are those who live ever with the patterns before them and who "would always derive their judgments from what Homer had called 'the image and likeness of God'" (*Republic* 501). Socrates reiterates (*Republic* 494) that such a love of wisdom is impossible for the multitude, and here Socrates drops a hint of his own experience. "My own case, the divine sign is hardly worth mentioning—for I suppose it has happened to few or none before me. And those who have been of this little company and have tasted the sweetness and blessedness of this possession... have come to see that there is nothing sound or right in any present politics" (*Republic* 496).

But the current rulers are not such individuals; they are tyrants, or people haughty of mien and stuffed with empty pride and void of sense (*Republic* 494-d), and people of this type do the greatest harm to the entire community (or city) as well as well as to individuals. Against such people, Socrates compares the guardians, that elite group of worthy souls who would have mastered all the virtues, have great facility in learning, and have harmonized within themselves both the gentle and the brave temperaments. These are the *true* rulers, and they would prove the more worthy rulers precisely because their goal was the pursuit of philosophy and the sublime state of divine initiation and not the power of rulership. Nevertheless, warns Socrates, students would be tested in the *most difficult subjects*. Glaucon wonders what these difficult studies are.

In order to understand Socrates's reply Glaucon will need to summon all of his faculties of inspiration, understanding, and reason. Let us pause with him before he attempts the final ascent upon the mountaintop, and consider the fact that Socrates is about to bring together, both literally and metaphorically, not only all of the arguments found in the *Republic* dealing with justice and injustice, but, in fact, the theme and conclusion of every single dialogue that was written *prior to the Republic.*

It is also crucial to bear in mind that the teachings that Socrates will give to Glaucon take place against the framework and guide of the curriculum taught over a century before him by the legendary Pythagoras. This curriculum is known as the Pythagorean quadrivium, and it comprises four main disciplines: number (mathematics), geometry, astronomy, and music. It is highly significant, therefore, that although Plato only mentions Pythagoras by name once or twice in all of the dialogues, it is here in the *Republic* that he does so, and at the most significant place for the would-be guardians—what will bestow understanding of the true nature of higher knowledge and, indeed, of existence itself. Along with Glaucon we too must gather all of our faculties together because Socrates is about to pitch his arguments, if we were to use musical terms, two or three octaves higher than any prior paean. We will, therefore, follow Socrates's arguments very closely.

The question Glaucon asked was what counted as "the most difficult studies."

Socrates begins by stating that while he had distinguished the three aspects of the soul (from the analogy of the charioteer) as reason, high spirit and appetitive, he had also established the definitions of justice, sobriety, bravery and wisdom severally. Now he adds an all-important statement that will change everything. "But there is still something greater than justice and the other virtues we described [*Republic* 504-d] and that is the study of the good [*Republic* 504-d] a study he had characterized earlier as that by which all other things become useful and beneficial, but which now includes the qualifying statement that "we have no adequate knowledge of it" (*Republic 505*). This is indeed a mysterious statement but Socrates does not pursue it further at this juncture.

Instead, Socrates explains that the multitude believes *pleasure* to be the *Good* but that is merely semblance of the Good, because their conclusions are sense-oriented. The finer spirits believe the Good *to be knowledge*—knowledge of the *reality of the Good* (*Republic* 506).

Glaucon implores Socrates to explain the nature of the Good just as he had set forth the nature of justice, sobriety and the other virtues. Socrates balks and replies, "Nay my beloved, let us dismiss for the time being the *nature of the good in itself*, for to attain to my present surmise of that seems a pitch above the impulse that wings my flight today. But of what seems to be the *offspring of the good* and most nearly made in its likeness I am willing to speak" (*Republic* 506-d).

Socrates's distinction needs to be underscored. He is distinguishing between the *Good in itself* and the *offspring of the Good Itself*. He is unable to speak to Glaucon of *the Good in itself* but he is able and willing to speak of *the Form of the Good*. Thus, like Socrates, we leave aside the topic of the *Good in itself*—for the time being—and turn our attention to its offspring. Here Glaucon meets his first challenge. Socrates brings to his attention that up until now they have been discussing the virtues such as beauty and piety and justice as each individually and that when one approaches them that way they can be construed as many different virtues, but Socrates is now saying that those things which had been hitherto "posited as many, we turn about and posit each as a *single idea or aspect*, assuming it to be a unity and call it that which each really is" (*Republic* 507- b). By way of explanation Socrates reminds Glaucon that while things of sense can be seen but not thought, the Ideas, the Forms, can be thought but not seen.

The Sun Analogy

In order to approach an understanding of the Good, Socrates gives an example from the world of sense: a man may use his eyes in order to apprehend a sense object, but without the presence of a third factor, light, the perceiver will see nothing. Which of the divinities in the heavens is the cause of light? The Sun, replies Glaucon. Well then, replies Socrates, just as the Sun is not vision itself, but is the *cause* of vision taking place, so in the intelligible world, the Good stands in the same relation to objects of reason as the sun stands to objects of sense. Then Socrates makes his famous statement. "This reality, then, that gives their truth to the objects of knowledge, and the power of knowing to the knower, you must say is the idea of good, and you must conceive it as being the cause of knowledge, and of truth, in so far as known" (*Republic* 508-e). He warns Glaucon that as for knowledge and truth, like the perceiver and the object of sense, one must not think they *are* the sun. In the intelligible realm, great honor belong to knowledge and truth, but "still higher honor belongs to the possession and habit of the good." Socrates presses his point further by declaring, "The objects of knowledge not only receive from the presence of the good their being known, but their *very existence and essence* is derived to them from it, *though the good itself is not essence but still transcends essence in dignity and surpassing power*" (*Republic* 509-b).

Socrates's intention is clear. He is saying that the intelligible Forms of truth and knowledge—as well as all the other forms, of beauty, courage, piety, justice—all derive their *existence* and their *essence* from the Good. Of that part he is able to speak. But he has hinted in passing that the *Good Itself* is not essence. It *transcends essence*. Of this part Socrates cannot speak to Glaucon. One surmises that Socrates *could* speak about it—*if* Glaucon had reached the point of having the experience of the Good for himself. He would then understand what Socrates was speaking about.

The implication, however, is that Socrates *does* have an understanding and experience of the Good Itself, otherwise he would not be able to demarcate it from its *offspring,* the *form* of the Good. Here we may ponder anew whether Alcibiades was not near the truth when he said that Socrates was like the seleni that, when opened up, revealed a god inside.

Glaucon recoils from Socrates's statements about the Good transcending essence, thinking Socrates was engaging in hyperbole! Socrates must therefore provide Glaucon with another analogy by which he can understand the offspring of the Good. We will continue referring to the offspring of the Good as the *form of the Good*, for that is what Socrates intends when he uses the term.

The Divided Line Analogy

Socrates begins by distinguishing the intelligible and sensible realms from one another. As he tells Glaucon, "Represent them... by a line divided into two unequal sections, and cut each section again in the same ratio—the section, that is, of the visible and that of the intelligible order—and then as an expression of the ratio of their comparative clearness and obscurity you will have, as one of the sections of the visible world, images, shadows, reflections in water and other surfaces" (*Republic* 509-d). These belong at the first, the lowest level. The corresponding faculty of apprehension at this level is conjecture, or image making. The second level includes all actual sensible objects, and the corresponding faculty that apprehends these objects is designated as that of belief. In the third section the individual arrives at the realm of intelligible objects, and the faculty employed at this third level is that of the understanding. Those who dwell here are scientists, mathematicians, logicians, and the like, and their objects are theories relating to their particular disciplines that, according to Plato, argue down to conclusions that rely on visible proofs in the sensible world. The fourth and highest level has as its objects the Forms and *things in themselves*, and reason is the faculty that corresponds to such objects.

It is at this juncture that Socrates comes up with one of his most radical hypotheses yet. And Glaucon will need to get a hold of it! Socrates argues that those theoreticians at the third level, those who employ understanding in their investigations, may think they have discovered the truth, but for Socrates it is only a relative truth, not one that will stand comparison in context of the Good. Socrates argues that their investigations may give rise to *theoretical pictures* describing the truth, but for Socrates as long as you are relying on *anything visible* to support your theories, you have failed to adequately or completely explain them. As he says, when you are at the third level of understanding you are offered two choices: either you can take your assumptions and argue *downward to a conclusion* that relies on *visible* proof, or if you are using reason you will "advance from its assumptions to a *beginning or principle that transcends assumption,* and in which it makes no use of the images employed by the other section, *relying on ideas only* and progressing systematically through ideas" (*Republic* 510-c).

Basically, Socrates is saying that theoreticians, using the faculty of understanding, treat their theories as absolute assumptions and therefore do not question them further. But one who uses reason will treat theories *as a starting point* and will argue backward or upward from those assumptions until, using pure thought, detached from the senses, he apprehends the *source* of all theories

> that which reason itself lays hold of by the power of dialectic, treating its assumptions not as absolute beginnings but literally as hypotheses, underpinnings, footings, and springboards so to speak, to enable it to rise to that which requires no assumption and is the starting point of all, and after attaining to that again taking hold of the first dependencies from it, so to proceed downward to the conclusion, making no use whatever of any object of sense but only pure ideas, moving on through ideas (Forms) to ideas (Forms) and ending with ideas [Forms]. (*Republic* 511-b)

Glaucon is unable to comprehend all that Socrates has said, but offers that he does understand that applying the power of dialectic to the intelligible world will give truer and more exact answers than objects from the arts and sciences whose assumptions are arbitrary starting points. He also understands Socrates's charge that those theoreticians who are at the level of understanding do not possess true intelligence, and that only those who use reason, or dialectic, can understand the *things in themselves* "when apprehended in conjunction with a first principle."

We have taken note of what Glaucon understands, and what he has admitted he does not yet know. We notice that, so far, Socrates has made no attempt to give full definitions of the Good, or dialectic; the "beginning of all" or the "first principle." For that, we, like Glaucon, will have to wait. In the meantime Socrates will offer a third way of understanding the Good.

Parenthetically, scholars like Ross and others have tried to insist that the Divided Line be interpreted in terms of logical deductions providing the key between the various levels of consciousness. However, since Socrates begins the discussion by saying that Glaucon take a piece of thread and divide it into two unequal sections, and then divide them again in the same *ratio*, I think it much more likely that Socrates is relying on Pythagorean mathematics in describing his divided line, perhaps even the golden mean. That mysterious mathematical equation is described by Priya Hemenway in her book *Divine Proportion: Phi in Art, Nature and Science* as follows: "The whole is to the larger in exactly the same proportion as the larger is to the smaller" (3). What we do know about the Divided Line is that the four levels of consciousness—and their corresponding faculties and objects—include the entire spectrum of human experience.

THE CAVE ANALOGY

This is the more pictorial of the analogies. Socrates says Glaucon is to picture people dwelling in a cave, which has a long entrance open to the light on its width. The men have been chained in the same spot since childhood, able to look only forward. Furthermore, Glaucon is to picture the light from a fire burning higher up and at a distance behind them, and in between, a road with a low wall. When men move along that road, carrying implements of all kinds, they will be perceived as puppets above a stage, and what the prisoner in the cave sees is "the shadows cast from the fire on the wall of the cave" (*Republic* 515). Here Socrates is making a reference to the lowest level of the divided line, characterized by reflections and shadows.

Socrates's point is that those in the cave who are suddenly unfettered and turn toward the light would feel pain in their eyes. But as their eyes gradually adjust to the light, they would first see shadows and reflections;

Second, they would see sensible objects; third, they would contemplate the appearances in the heavens (in other words, create theories from their contemplations of sensible objects), as do the scientists and astronomers at the third level of the divided line. Fourth and last, they would be able to "look upon the Sun itself and see its true nature" (*Republic* 516-b). When they did so, they would understand that it is the Sun that creates the movement through the seasons and all the visible things in the sensible world and would see that the Sun "is, in some sort, the cause of all these things that they had seen" (*Republic* 516-c).

Socrates then applies the Sun analogy to the intelligible world, showing that as the sun stands to visible objects, the Good stands in relation to intelligible, invisible objects, and that as he had stated earlier (*Republic* 509-c) the objects of knowledge "not only receive from the presence of the Good their being known, but their very existence and essence is derived to them from it...." Finally, Socrates asks Glaucon to join him in his dream "that in the region of the known, the last thing to be seen, and *hardly* seen, is the idea of the Good," and that *when seen* it "must point us to the conclusion that it is indeed the cause of all things, of all that is right and beautiful," that it gives birth to light in the visible world, and in the intelligible world is the authentic source of truth and reason.

Socrates has now taught Glaucon three different ways to apprehend the "offspring" of the *Good Itself*. In order to contemplate this offspring, what we have called the Form of the Good, one must turn one's soul away from the world of becoming and toward the realm of true being. Why is this? Plato tells us that it is the duty of the best natures, worthy disciples, including the guardians, to attain to the *vision* of the Good. Glaucon is concerned that if the guardians attained to such a vision, they would want to linger there and refuse to go back down into the world. Socrates reminds Glaucon that they are seeking the happiness of the whole city, and not just a part, and it is their duty to take the fruits of their vision of the Good back to their cities so that they will rule with justice and peace. In fact, the guardians will be the best rulers for the precise reason that they have no *desire* to rule.

Now that Socrates has given Glaucon an understanding of the *offspring* of the Good, the *form* of the Good, he asks him what studies would draw the soul away from the world of becoming and toward the realm of pure being. Gymnastics, music and the arts are cited, but then Socrates explains that there is one intellectual discipline that applies to all other areas of the arts and sciences—and that is the science of *number*, but not just the mundane, visible application of it such as a soldier might use it in order to count his battalions, but the higher, intelligible application of it—what will draw the mind toward essence and reality. Socrates then asks to which *class* of things numbers belong, arguing that when the mind is challenged by contradiction, it requires something *else* in order to judge between the two opposites, and to ask: "Whatever then is the one *as such*, and thus the study of *unity* will be one of the studies that guide and convert the soul to the contemplation of true being" (*Rep.* 525). This requires contemplating number not in its visible and mundane applications, but grasping it by pure thought in order to arrive at the *essence* and *nature* of number, and in this endeavor Socrates warns against "the discussion (of) numbers attached to physical and tangible bodies" (*Republic* 525-d-e).

Socrates then takes the argument to a deeper and even more difficult level to understand, asking, "What numbers are these you are talking about in which the one is such as you postulate, *each unity equal to every other* without the slightest difference and admitting no division into parts?" (*Republic* 526). Glaucon responds that such units can *only* be conceived by pure thought and not by any practical application. Socrates agrees that the higher, intelligible numbers do in fact require pure thought, and pure thought is indispensable for an understanding or experience of the truth. An association with Pythagorean number spontaneously arises here. The parallels are quite plain, and as we recall, scholars such as A. E. Taylor in his book *Plato: The Man and His Work* have claimed that perhaps Plato borrowed from or was influenced by Pythagorean ideas, especially in his later dialogues.

The next subject to be examined is geometry, and the essential point of Socrates's teaching is that it, too, must be approached in a way that will transcend the visible world and turn the soul to the contemplation of essence, and toward the Good. Socrates is critical of the contemporary "adepts" of geometry, charging that they do not take the higher road in order to contemplate truth or being, but drag it down into the world of genesis and destruction, the world of becoming. He insists "the real object of the entire study is pure knowledge" (*Republic* 527-b).

The subject of different dimensions is then raised. Mention is made of plane surfaces, the tri-dimensionality of cubes and other solid objects that have depth. Socrates then turns to astronomy because it deals with the *movement* of solids. The discipline of astronomy also troubles Socrates, because he holds astronomers have either passed over its ultimate questions or used it in mundane applications that, once again, draw the soul back to the world of becoming and not upward into the arena of pure thought.

Socrates is adamant that astronomy would have to be approached in a way completely different from that used by his contemporary astronomers if it was to lead to truth, and to the realm of being. He emphasizes it by stating that the visible movement of the planets "fall far short of the truth, the movements, namely of *real* speed and *real* slowness in *true* number.... These can be apprehended only by reason and thought, but not by sight" (*Republic* 529-d). Socrates therefore thinks it would be absurd to examine the visible movements of the planets with the expectation of finding absolute truth in them. For him, they are *patterns*, illustrations of a deeper, intelligible truth, one where the humble astronomer, in contemplating the mystery and wonders of such planetary movements would "concede that the *artisan of heaven* fashioned it and all that it contains" (*Republic* 530). Such an astronomer would then understand that while the *source* of planetary movements is *eternal*, the planets themselves, being but illustrations of that deeper truth, have movements and orbits that are rooted in the world of becoming, of change. This is the reason why Socrates dismisses the astronomy of his time. It is oriented toward the earthly world and supported by calculations of merely the *visible* aspect of the planets, thereby missing the import of the deeper truth of *being* that they represent.

In moving ahead to music, the following significant statement is made by Socrates: "As the eyes are framed for astronomy so the ears are framed for the movements of harmony, and these are in some sort *kindred sciences*, as the Pythagoreans affirm and we admit" (*Republic* 530-d). Here we are being asked to find the parallels and concordances between astronomy and music—something no self-respecting twenty-first-century Western philosopher would care to be seen tackling! Socrates makes the same charge against the musicians as he does against the astronomers. They expend useless labor on hearing and measuring the *audible* aspect of sounds against one another, but do not proceed to the realm of pure thought where they could examine its *intelligible* aspects. This means, in effect, music must be examined from a point *transcending* audible sound, and would seem to indicate that in the intelligible realm there are aspects of sound that exist but are inaudible to the outer senses, and that the ultimate meaning of sound is to be found in its opposite, and source, namely silence.

Socrates is quite specific in his charges. "Their method exactly corresponds to that of the astronomer, for the numbers they seek are those found in these heard concords, but they do not ascend to generalized problems and the consideration which numbers are inherently concordant and which not and why in each case" (*Republic* 531-c). The concordances between astronomy and music are entirely understandable when we remember that the Forms and all higher inquiries into truth and being ultimately are unified in the one eternal, transcendental, unhypothesized principle, the *Good Itself*.

Replying to Glaucon's recognition that the study of the deeper meaning of astronomy and music, and especially the *numbers* underpinning both disciplines, is a superhuman task, Socrates indicates that rather than being a superhuman task, it is in fact a *useful* task, highlighting his own familiarity with it. He teaches that it is "useful...for the investigation of the *beautiful* and the *Good*, but if otherwise pursued, useless" (*Republic* 531-c). Last, he underscores his point about the purpose of such studies: "I take it that if the investigation of all these studies goes far enough to bring out their community and kinship with one another, and to infer their affinities, then to busy ourselves with them contributes to our desired end, and the labor taken is not lost, but otherwise it is vain" (*Republic* 531-d).

Parenthetically, since it is transcendental affinities and concordances that are the subject material here, it becomes clear that the form of dialectic to be applied to these concordances must be a dialectic of inclusion and union (in the One, the Good) and not the earlier form of elenchus dialectic in which by a process of *division*—namely, repeatedly choosing between two possibilities—a *definition* was being sought.

Socrates's criticism of astronomy and music needs no explanation. As he saw it, the study of these disciplines should be pursued in such a way "that their *affinities* and *kinship* will be revealed, and will be useless if not devoted to both the beautiful and the Good. Not only that, they are a *"preamble* to the law itself" (*Republic* 531-d), indicating that these studies have even farther to go if they are to help one reach their ultimate goal.

For this reason, Socrates renews his charges against the astronomers, and now the musicians, that they are content to believe they have apprehended truth in the visible or audible aspect of the world. He asks Glaucon to agree with him that such experts are surely not reasoners or dialecticians, precisely because they have not been able to detach themselves from the visible world and proceed to the examination of the *essence* of each thing in the intelligible world. And because they cannot rise into the intelligible world they cannot give an exact account, namely of the essence of each thing; they are barred from knowing the kinds of things that for Socrates fall under the categories of reason and dialectic.

The paradox is that for those experts—Socrates will not call them *scientists*—who remain in the visible aspect of things, the truth is not attainable, whereas the one who *is* a true dialectician—having apprehended the kinship and affinities in various disciplines and penetrated to the Good, the beauty, and the truth of essences—is then easily able to find in those very disciplines of astronomy and music an *imitation* of the eternal world. In short, they *represent* the eternal world, but the eternal world is not fully revealed by the merely *visible* aspects of them. This is why Plato calls time the moving image of eternity.

And, in case we, like Glaucon, might want to rest from faintheartedness at this daunting task—that of understanding the relationship of time to eternity—Socrates makes a statement even more difficult to apprehend: "When anyone by dialectic attempts through discourse of reason and apart from all perceptions of sense to find his way to the very essence of each thing and does not desist till he apprehends by thought itself the nature of the *Good in itself, he arrives at the limit of the intelligible"* (*Republic* 532-c).

Socrates does not beat about the bush. The statements he makes are clear. Whether we can follow him is another matter. What he says is that in the same way extensive study of the visible world can lead to a partial understanding of the intelligible world, but that the visible world has a limit beyond which it cannot pass, an extensive apprehension of the *intelligible* world will, in time, yield the knowledge that we have indeed reached the *limit* of the intelligible world, and that *something else* lies beyond it, namely *the Good Itself.*

But we are not at that stage yet. Glaucon is still at the point where he needs to understand the nature of dialectic. He asks Socrates to explain it to him. Socrates replies: "You will not be able, dear Glaucon, to follow me further, though on my part there will be no lack of good will. And, if I could, I would show you no longer an image and symbol of my meaning, but the very truth, *as it appears to me*...and nothing less than the power of dialectic could reveal this, and that only to one experienced in the studies we have described" (*Republic* 533). Here Socrates tells Glaucon quite plainly that dialectic is the only way to the truth of things. But, more important, he does more than hint to Glaucon that he has had the *direct* experience of the truth, and that the direct experience is not communicable to another other than by way of images and symbols. And that direct experience of the truth, we suspect, is precisely what makes Socrates unique among his fellow Athenians and is the real reason the Oracle pronounced him as the wisest man in Greece.

If Glaucon wants to follow Socrates beyond the intelligible world, he must do so by his *own efforts*. He must move beyond the images and symbols and attain the direct experience *for himself*. This is merely a continuation of Socrates's method of teaching in the early dialogues where no final definition is given of the topic at hand, but it is left for the student to use his own efforts to arrive at it. We might think this is a harsh or cruel method. Quite the contrary! Socrates has shown us that because our soul is immortal and *akin* to the divine, man is able to know all things. Use of the faculty of recollection, if applied with persistence, will lead eventually to true knowledge.

Dialectic is the key to that knowledge and experience. Glaucon asks Socrates to explain the nature of dialectic. Socrates points out to him that it is a method "of inquiry that attempts systematically and in all cases to determine what each thing really is" (*Republic* 533-b). In other words, it is the study of *essences*.

He returns to his criticism of those "experts" who examine things with mere opinions or desires as their guide, or who view all things through the prism of generation in the material world. And he rejects the objects of their inquiry when examined from the visible viewpoint. Socrates wishes to concentrate on those topics that rise above the visible world and belong in the intelligible world. Even there, as he states, these topics have only *some* hold on reality, but not all truth. What is the *source* of the movements of the planets and their mathematical ratios? What is the *true source* of number? What is the *source* of musical harmonies? These questions, for Socrates, are not to be answered by theories emanating from the visible aspect of things, but only by penetrating deeper to the essence of each thing, at which time its true relationship to other things and to the truth itself may be determined.

Socrates tries to make his meaning crystal clear. He asks, "Is not dialectic the only process of inquiry that advances in this manner doing away with hypotheses, up to the first principle itself in order to find confirmation there?" (*Republic* 533-d). *Dialectic* is the thread through the disciplines they have discussed—numbers, geometry, astronomy, music—what leads to the truth. In fact, as Socrates points out, the way these studies are usually approached doesn't really deserve the name of science, because for him the only *true* science is dialectic—what arrives at the truth of essences and not of visible things.

It is here, in Book VII, Socrates reiterates the teaching of the Divided Line, where he demarcates the four levels of human consciousness and their corresponding objects. The highest division of inquiry is to be called science, by which he means reason, the third understanding, the second belief, and the first conjecture. He then ascribes science and understanding to the realm of the intelligible, while belief and conjecture fall within the category of opinion. He states, "Opinion deal[s] with generation, and intellection with essence, and this relation being expressed in the proportion: as essence is to generation, so is intellection to opinion, and as intellection is to opinion, so is science to belief and understanding" (*Republic* 534). (We sense the Pythagorean connection here.)

Socrates returns to his point that the dialectician can give an exact account of the essence of each thing, and that most other investigators can not do so, and then he adds that a parallel can be made regarding the investigation of the Good: "that man who is unable to define in his discourse and distinguish and abstract from all other things the aspect or idea of the Good...does not really know the Good Itself or any particular good...and his contact with it is by opinion and not by knowledge" (*Republic* 534-c-d).

This is a highly significant statement, and we must pause and examine its implications. Earlier Socrates had claimed that using dialectic would, ultimately, lead to the *unhypothesized* first principle. Now he is saying that we must place the Good in that same relation, namely that our investigations of the Forms and things in themselves must lead to the *Good Itself*. The unhypothesized principle is nameless, and the Good has a name, but we cannot escape the implication here that Socrates means to *equate* the unhypothesized first principle with the *Good Itself*. The reason why this parallel is so significant is because, as Socrates reiterates, dialectic (or true science) is the *coping stone* of all other studies. The question arises: Why is dialectic the coping stone or foundation of all other disciplines and investigations? The answer is: because it alone can lead to an apprehension of essences and the truth of things.

What, in fact, the science of dialectic accomplishes is twofold. In the early form of dialectic, referred to as negative elenchus, dialectic is what continually performs the function of division until it arrives at a *definition* that will distinguish that object from all other objects.

But in the later form of dialectic, where it is the coping stone of all other studies, Socrates has already shown us that it is the study of *unity*. Here dialectic performs the systematic division *of essences from all sensible objects* found in the visible world. Dialectic, then, is the actual *demarcation point* between the sensible world and the intelligible world. However, what is it that is *signified* when we divide essences away from composite visible objects? The answer is that we have crossed the threshold of the *transcendental* world!

We are no longer in the world of composite objects that can delude us if we view them from the perspective of conjecture, opinion, or even belief. And let us be quite clear—all those twenty-first-century disciplines such as logic, science, and theoretical studies belong at the level of understanding and not true science as Socrates defines it. The reason for this is precise and clear. Scientists, logicians, theoretical thinkers do not "do away" with their hypotheses in order to arise to the "first principle itself," meaning that their theories always remain strongly attached to things of the world of *becoming* and not of true *being*. They do not take that further and vital step—that of *examining* the hypotheses themselves, or more important, the *assumptions* behind their hypotheses. What Socrates states is that they fall short of the science of dialectic, for only the true *dialectician* has the faculties needed to take that next, crucial, step.

The true dialectician examines his hypotheses and assumptions. That is easier to do when one has crossed the threshold into the world of pure thought, into the intelligible world. What the true dialectician accomplishes, then, in "doing away" with his hypotheses is not to actually *dispose* of them as though he sawed off the lower rungs of a ladder as he progressed upward. No, the true dialectician discovers that those very hypotheses are ultimately *subsumed* by higher and higher hypotheses, until they come to rest in something higher—and that something higher is, ultimately, the unhypothesized first principle. This may sound like scientific talk, but as Socrates points out, the true dialectician will find *confirmation* of his process of inquiry. And the first thing that the true dialectician discovers is that the world of the intelligible is a world of *unity*. Although I hold that Plato would see the intelligible and sensible world as a continuum, for the sake of the argument the intelligible world stands in diametrical opposition, as it were, to the world of multiplicity signified by the visible, sensible world.

Dialectic reveals the great divide between the world of becoming and the world of true being. It *demonstrates* that all things that are designated in the intelligible world are—by definition—part of that unity. This is the reason why Socrates is so insistent that students learn to detach from the senses in order to enter into the realm of pure thought—it allows them to apprehend the Forms, the eternal patterns, the *essences* of things.

But successfully applying dialectic accomplishes another significant breakthrough of understanding. It shows the student that those sensible objects that *appear* to be separate in the world of becoming can, in fact, be reconciled into a higher *unity* in the intelligible world. And it reveals, like a bolt of lightning, that while the world of becoming exemplifies the multiplicity of things in the material world, the unity discovered in the intelligible world is finally illuminated by the unhypothesized first principle. And if it's a first principle, could its *unity* signify anything else but that the unhypothesized first principle's true name is the *One?* Thus, the true dialectician, in crossing the threshold into the world of unity in the intelligible world, is shown the true significance of the old philosophical argument between the One and the Many—that the One is truly apprehended when perceived from the side of the intelligible world, the world of true being, but commonly misunderstood when perceived from the vantage point of the sensible world. The world of becoming is composite, and therefore designated as the Many.

The true dialectician understands Socrates's statement that time is the moving image of eternity. He sees it for himself. He understands that those astronomers, geometers, so-called scientists who do not examine their assumptions *are* barred from apprehending the world of unity in the intelligible world, and are therefore not to be called true scientists of dialectic, but are called scientists from habit. They are operating from the level of understanding and not true science.

While Socrates speaks in scientific, rational terms about the world of true being and the unhypothesized first principle he has, so far, only *hinted* at it its true nature. For the moment he is content for the student to understand that if he reaches the unhypothesized first principle by way of dialectic, his process of inquiry will be confirmed, and as a result he will be able to descend once again through those same realms of essences with yet another confirmation of their veracity. It should be underscored, however, that by having had this apprehension of unity, the student will forever have a changed perspective of the world and his place in it. In short, he will never be the same.

In light of this, a word should be said about the modern view of dialectic. Much speculation exists about it, and many commentators have interpreted Plato's concept of dialectic in strict logical terms. I mention Richard Robinson's book *Plato's Earlier Dialectic,* as the most detailed examination of this topic, but it can also be found in W.D. Ross's book, *Plato's Theory of Ideas,* as well as A. E. Taylor in his book, *Plato: The Man and His Work,* and many others too numerous to name. It is also found, it must be said, in *The Basic Works of Aristotle* (edited by Richard McKeon), because it is supposed that from Socrates's method of questioning—described as elenchus—Aristotle eventually derived the syllogism, which was to provide the first foundation for symbolic logic. When such commentators turn their attention to Plato's dialectic, they are usually referring to Plato's earlier dialectic, in which so many of his helpless victims find that Socrates has taken each of their beliefs and completely dislodged them from their moorings. In short, they feel numbed by the apocryphal sting ray of Socrates's questions. This has been called the Socratic elenchus, and apparently there were many critics who attacked Socrates for adopting this method. They described it as a negative form of dialectic, and argue that in the end Socrates never found his infernal definitions, did not put forth his own positive argument, and finally had to fall back on his own ignorance, a position they found quite untenable. In short, they assume it to be a process whereby one can start from a hypothesis and proceed by a series of negative arguments to a *logical* conclusion. Whole books could be written unraveling the minutiae of this view.

But, as Plato himself makes clear, his use of dialectic in the *Republic* and *Symposium* where he is pursuing the *mystic* teachings makes no use of such rules of deduction precisely because the deductions sought by logicians and scientists are *mechanical and "empty"* operations that rightly should be categorized at the level of understanding and not of true science. Why is this? The answer is: deduction is hypothesizing, but from "empty" premises. The conclusion will be the product of strict logical deduction, but such deductions cannot guarantee the *truth* either of the premises or the conclusion. The axioms are mere symbols, and the users thereof will stand rebuked by Plato because, once again, they did not question those basic hypotheses and assumptions to discover their source. So when we say that modern logicians *understand* Plato's later dialectic, a metaphysician must come to the definite conclusion that they are on the wrong track. It is true that the inquiry of the Socratic dialectician leads him to divide the world of visible things from the realm of essences, and that could be understood by some to be a negative procedure, but by the same token we must focus on the end result of such dialectic, which was to discover the *unity* inhering in that world of essences. And this revelation of the unity of essences is most clearly not derived from logic!

Regarding this issue of logic, we recall Guthrie's comments about it: "One must always remember that his (Plato's) concern with language, logic or method was only ancillary to a larger purpose. The end was *right living*."[7] And as F. M. Cornford so pithily added, "Dialectic is not what

---

7   Guthrie, *A History of Greek Philosophy*, vol. 4, 244.

is now known as "Formal Logic".... Formal Logic may be described as the study of 1) propositional forms—*not actual significant statements* but the patterns or types under which statements can be classified; 2) the constituents of these propositional forms (subjects, predicates, relations between terms, etc.); and 3) formal relations of inference between propositional forms. The beginning of Formal Logic is marked precisely by the introduction of symbols.... The introduction of symbols means that the attention is now fixed on the *form* of statements apart from their *content*... The science of Dialectic... does not study formal symbolic patterns to which our statements conform, nor yet to these statements themselves.... What it does study is the structure of the real world of Forms.... There is nothing to show that he (Plato) had ever conceived of such a science as Formal Logic."[8]

Let us return to the topic of dialectic and now consider its essential purpose. As Socrates has said, the student crosses the threshold to the transcendent world by employing the method of dialectic to separate all objects in the visible world from those in the intelligible world. But what is it that the student is contemplating when he crosses that threshold into the transcendent world—none other than the Forms, the patterns, the archetypes of existence, those divine and transcendental laws that govern not only the intelligible world, but the visible world as well.

We are acquainted with some of those Forms. They are the virtues—courage, piety, love, justice, beauty, and the others. As Plato has shown, to those we must add the Form of number because it lies behind not only the theories of geometry, astronomy, and music, but of every mathematical measurement made in the mundane world. And, to be fair, we must mention the *Parmenides* dialogue where Socrates is eventually forced to admit even such things as hair and mud are to be included as Forms.

We may have left the Forms unattended so far, but that is because in dealing with the studies undertaken by the guardians—number, geometry, astronomy, music, dialectic—Socrates has focused on the "scientific" side of the curriculum. We recall, however, that immediately prior to these studies, Socrates had gone through a lengthy explanation to Glaucon of the Good, and backed up his arguments by giving three ways to understand it—namely, the Sun, Divided Line, and Cave analogies. He

---

8 Cornford, *Plato's Theory of Knowledge*, 264–265.

had explained that the Forms, the virtues, were all parts of the Good, and that the Good was the cause of all knowledge and truth. Therefore, alongside the scientific studies outlined, the student was to bear always in mind the truth and reality of the Forms of the virtues. The Forms must be placed in their proper perspective. Without living by the ideals of the Forms man cannot make progress toward the Good, but remains stuck in the mundane world concentrating on food, procreation, and the fulfillment of his desires. For this reason Socrates tries to convince all people—regardless of work, rank or affluence, to look to higher things and to be guided by them. For him the Forms may be invisible and ideal, but he has tried to show others that they are what is most real.

While the Forms may have started out in the unassuming garb of virtues, and thereby seem familiar and understandable, they proceed, even in the early dialogues, through a stunning evolution—as is demonstrated by W. D. Ross in his book, *Plato's Theory of Ideas*. For example, even in one of the earliest dialogues, the *Laches*, Socrates is asking for a definition of *courage itself*. What is the *essence* of courage? Right here we notice that Socrates is pressing for a definition of essences, things he has later described as transcendental. In the *Hippias Major*, and later in the *Parmenides*, the question is raised as to whether one is participating in a Form in *whole or in part*. In the *Cratylus* Socrates says things have a being of their own, *independent* of us. Forms or archetypes are now seen as *unchanging*, non-sensible objects, and by the time of the *Phaedo* these Forms are shown as not known by the senses but only by pure thought. In the *Symposium* the Form of beauty is declared to be *a being apart from its embodiment in any particular beautiful thing*. The Forms are now seen as eternal and unchanging. And finally, in the *Republic* Socrates reveals that all the virtues that were originally defined as individual entities are, in fact, *a part of the Good*, although he distinguishes between the offspring of the Good, what we have called the Form of the Good, and the *Good Itself*. He has also shown that by studying number, geometry, astronomy, music and dialectic, the student comes to understand that all hypotheses ultimately are subsumed into *a unity* whose definition goes no further than to say it is an unhypothesized first principle. Finally, he has also made the remarkable statement that by using dialectic one eventually comes to the "limit of the intelligible world."

With the definition of the Good as *eternal and unchanging*, and as the *cause* of all truth and knowledge, and as the unity of the One, Socrates has moved directly into the realm of transcendence and mysticism. He may have held back thus far, and he even approaches it in the *Republic* in a somewhat "scientific" and "rational" manner, but his meaning is unequivocal—the Good is the source not only of intelligible things, but of *all* things—and that necessarily includes *visible, material* things.

Now we must ask the all-encompassing question: What is the true nature of the Good? Socrates has sidestepped that issue thus far by describing it as the unhypothesized first principle, and that may have been a useful way to approach it, until now. The paradox is that we are trying to define something that in fact eludes full definition. It lies beyond the "limit of the intelligible" realm.

It helps our cause to place our final investigation in the light of Socrates's method of pedagogy. As we saw in the early dialogues, the participants were set on the road to contemplation of the virtues, but in each case, fell short of a definition. We must put that failure down to the level of understanding exhibited by the participant himself during the discussion. The implication is that if his consciousness *were* on the level of reason—and not understanding, belief or opinion, he would have been able to use the method of dialectic to separate the essence of the virtue from its immanent instantiations. What is clear is that it was not Socrates—as the great teacher—who would fill the student with his knowledge. Quite the opposite! Socrates provides some questions that prompt the student to contemplate these questions *for himself*, with the understanding that because a man has an immortal soul, capable of recollection, he therefore has the capacity, indeed the duty, to reach the full definitions *for himself*.

The early dialogues turn out to be an exercise in the separation of essence from immanent instantiation, but the students are not yet ready for it, so they fail. But as Socrates tells us it was not his appointed task to be a teacher of students in public, for money, but to be a *midwife* to their birth, by which we mean he was assisting the students to bring forth the birth of higher knowledge in themselves. As we recall, there were many students who failed to prove themselves worthy, chief among them Alcibiades, and we may add, all those young men who came under Socrates's charismatic influence, misunderstood his motives, and by irresponsibly mimicking his method of inquiry, stirred up discontent among their fellow Athenians—acts for which Socrates was blamed.

In the same way as the students were guided, but left in the end to discover the definitions of the virtues for themselves, so it may be seen as a parallel that in the final understanding of the Good in the *Republic,* Glaucon is assisted by Socrates, the midwife, but ultimately the experience must be won by his own efforts. What the Good *is* each student must unconceal and experience for himself.

But, being the kind midwife that he is, Socrates has left the student *clues* about the nature of the Good scattered throughout the dialogues. These are clues that we may have passed over superfluously or considered as inessential to our understanding at the time. When we add these clues together, however, their cumulative value can be almost revelatory.

Starting with the *Apology* we find Socrates affirming: "A man has only one thing to consider when performing any action—that is, whether he is acting rightly or wrongly, like a good man or a bad man" (*Apology* 28-b). At the very end of his life, Socrates tells those few gathered around him: "Make yourselves as good men as you can. This is my last message to you who voted for my condemnation" (*Apology* 39-d). In the *Laches,* Nicias says to Socrates, "I have often heard you say that every man is good in that in which he is wise, and bad in that in which he is unwise" (*Laches* 194-d). And again, "All knowledge appears to be a good. And, if as the teachers of the art affirm, this use of arms [in discussion of courage] is really a *species* of knowledge" (*Laches* 182-d-e).

In the *Charmides* Socrates states, "Wisdom alone is a science of other sciences and of itself" (*Charmides* 166-c), but he will not designate temperance as wisdom until "I can also see whether such a science would not do us any good" (*Charmides* 169-b). In the *Meno,* Socrates asks: "Does anyone know what a part of virtue is without knowing the whole?" (*Meno* 79-c). He asks his students to ponder why it is that prominent men of virtue in Athens do not have the capacity to pass on their own virtue to their sons. He adds that "if the Good were *knowledge,* there would be teachers of it, but since there are not teachers of it, virtue cannot be taught and in fact, is given by *divine dispensation*" (*Meno* 100). And in the *Euthyphro,* Socrates says, "There's no good that we possess but is given by them [the gods]" (*Euthyphro* 15-b). In the *Republic* Socrates reiterates that "justice, temperance, and the like, are all of them *parts* of virtue" (*Republic* 611-612). He then makes the same argument for the Forms—that they may each have their own task and function, but in reality are *parts* of virtue, parts in fact of the Good. He confirms this by declaring, "In the case of all the things that we then posited as many, we turn about and posit each as a *single idea or aspect*, assuming it to be a *unity* and *call it that which it really is*" (*Republic* 507-b). And again, "And in respect of the just and the unjust, the Good and the bad, and all the ideas or forms, the same statement holds, that in itself each is one, but that by virtue of their communion with actions and bodies and with one another they present themselves everywhere each as multiplicity of aspects" (*Republic* 476). And last, from the *Republic*: "This reality then, that gives their truth to the objects of knowledge and the power of knowing to the knower, you must say is the idea of Good and you must conceive it as being the *cause* of knowledge, and of truth, in so far as known.... In like manner, then, you are to say that the objects of knowledge not only receive from the presence of the Good their being known, but their very existence and essence is derived to them from it, though the Good Itself is not essence, but still transcends essence in dignity and surpassing power" (*Republic* 508-e).

When we contemplate Socrates's statements about the Good, two things begin to become clear. First, the notion of the Good has informed even the earliest dialogues, though it might have been misinterpreted as the mundane good from its designation as an immanent instantiation of a virtue. Second, when we understand that each virtue is in fact a *part* of virtue, we see that Plato has already crossed the threshold into the realm of transcendence where all things, having been separated from the visible and composite aspects of their nature, have been determined to be essences, and not merely individual essences, but a part of the Good. This, then, can provide a possible clue as to the reason why no concrete definitions of individual virtues could be attained in the early dialogues. The virtues had in the final analysis to be seen as parts or aspects of the Good, and the participants in the early dialogues were not ready to understand the all-encompassing, eternal nature of the Good. Therefore, Socrates abandoned the inquiry at the place where their minds failed in that daunting task, as any definition arrived at would have been provisional and subject to later review.

This also raises the question as to whether Plato did, in fact, write the dialogues with foreknowledge of the Good. That will no doubt be debated for a long time to come. Many commentators suppose that after revealing the barrier to knowledge at the end of the early dialogues, Socrates was unable to form the definitions for himself. But the overwhelming evidence of the continuity of the theme of the Good throughout the dialogues is much more likely to reveal a conscious intention on the part of Plato because it is the underlying theme of the dialogues up to and including the *Republic*. The alternative would be to suggest that the notion of the Good "spontaneously" and "unconsciously" appeared at the strategic point of each dialogue of its own volition. Such an idea flies in the face of common sense. In fact, as it evolves through the dialogues the Good presents itself almost as an ascending spiral of ever higher and higher definitions of the Good until in the *Republic* it is seen as the cause of all knowledge and of all truth as far as known. Surely this evolution is beyond coincidence.

There are many in the western philosophical tradition who reject statements found in Plato that are purely metaphysical. They prefer to hoe to a more scientific method of inquiry that demands proof of a scientific nature to prove Plato's assertions. Among that number are philosophers of science, others who hold to a material explanation of the origin of our world, those involved in mathematics and science generally, who argue down to conclusions in the sensible world, and logicians bound up with syllogisms and logical deductions. Notwithstanding that for Plato they are operating at the level of *understanding and not of reason*, they reject as unreal the existence of the Forms, the immortality of the soul, and the very notion of any form of transcendence. We shall not find ourselves among that number, but will pursue our inquiry to its inevitable metaphysical conclusion.

As we have seen, clues have been *continually* presented to us about the nature of the Good. And here, again, we are relying on Plato's own statements, found in the *Symposium* and the *Republic* that actually *tell us about* the ultimate nature of the Good. We have seen that the Good was the *guiding principle* behind the search for definitions in the early dialogues, and that no virtue was of any benefit unless it had *Good* as its purpose. And while Aristotle would have argued for a teleological purpose for the Good, Plato assigns it an ontological status that is central to his entire philosophical project. It may have been slipped into the discussion in a rather unassuming way in the earlier dialogues, and possibly escaped our attention, but Plato is already hinting that virtues are *essences* (*Laches*), and by the time of the *Republic* Plato states unequivocally that virtues may have been seen as individual, but in fact, they are parts of the Good. He goes still further, telling Glaucon that *any inquiry* of a theoretical nature—whether it is mathematics, geometry, science, etc.—is wasted labor if it argues down to conclusions that root it in the visible world, and not up to the unhypothesized first principle. Dialectic, or pure thought, is what is employed to separate essences from the things of the sensible world. That is its unique function, and why it is referred to by Socrates as the coping stone of all other sciences. Only dialectic, which takes all theoretical assumptions as mere *beginning* hypotheses and a *springboard to the ultimate inquiry* into the *Good,* has this capacity to separate sensible things from the world of essences. And when true seekers pass across the threshold of essences, they receive the rewards of their search—they discover that the world of essences is a *unity,* and thus they confirm *for themselves* that all the virtues are *part* of the Good. However, they also recall Socrates's statement that, for all its wisdom and power, dialectic has a limit, *and the limit is the end of the intelligible world*. They understand therefore, that they are still not at the end of their quest!

Now the momentous task presents itself—to try to arrive at an *understanding* of the Good. Up to this point dialectic has brought the disciple to the end of the intelligible world, but not beyond it. As Socrates has said, intelligible world objects can be thought but not seen, and sensible world objects can be seen but not thought. The Sun is the analogy used to explain the cause and relationship of the objects in the sensible world. The perceiver and the object perceived are not in relationship unless a third factor—the light of the Sun—reveals the object to the subject, to the perceiver. In the intelligible world the good is equivalent to the Sun, and the intelligible objects such as the Forms—justice, beauty, courage, piety and the like stand in relation to the perceiver as the sensible objects do to the Sun—namely, they derive their light, their meaning, their *reality* from the Good. In fact, *without the Good*, as Socrates has been emphasizing throughout the dialogues, *there is no* adequate meaning for the intelligible objects.

Only from the point of view of the world of essences, of transcendence, can the seeker understand Socrates's statement in the *Republic*: "This reality, then, that gives their truth to the objects of knowledge and the power of knowing to the knower, you must say is the idea of the Good, and you must conceive it as being the cause of knowledge and truth so far as known" (*Republic* 508-e). What is Plato saying here? He is saying that the Good is the cause of knowledge and truth. Good is the *cause,* and knowledge and truth are its offspring, its manifestations, its effects. Plato also states: "In like manner then, you are to say that the objects of knowledge not only receive from the Good their being known, but their very existence and essence is derived to them from it, though the Good Itself is not essence, but still transcends essence in dignity and surpassing power" (*Republic* 508-e).

We shall concentrate on the first part of that statement, namely that the essence of the objects of knowledge, namely the Forms, are derived from the Good. We know that the Good encompasses the objects from the intelligible and sensible worlds. But we must stretch our minds to encompass the full import of these ideas. What Plato is saying quite unequivocally is that *everything existing is a part of the unity that is the Good*. And if such is the case, then a definite conclusion begins to present itself.

As Socrates has shown us, he is the midwife, but each seeker must give birth to his own transcendence. Now that the conclusion becomes more and more clear, *we* must finally utter what Socrates does not directly disclose. And what *would* Socrates disclose to us *if he could*? The truth that illuminates once and for all that the Good is **God!** There is only *one* universe, *one* unhypothesized first principle. God is the creator of our world! God is the Form of the Good! God is the creator of the heavens and earth, astronomy and mathematics, intelligible objects and visible things, even hair and mud. There is no second universal principle! And there is no regress argument!

Plato has demonstrated that if the Good is the *cause of everything that exists,* it must be equivalent, or in fact *be,* what is the Creator or Artificer of all in the universe. The final inference, left unspoken, confirms for the seeker that the Good *is* none other than God! *God* is the creator of man's immortal soul—and God's messenger, Socrates, has led us to where philosophy will never usually take us—to the contemplation of God! He may have concealed his great secret until the last possible moment; he may have moved his project along in relative obscurity; he may have guided us to the point where we must take that leap beyond dialectic and into the Good by ourselves; he may have left unstated the *definition* of the unhypothesized first principle, but what the seeker understands in that penultimate contemplation of the Good is that the Good is *God!*

Perhaps Plato has startled us by this conclusion, but, given his statements about the Good throughout the dialogues, it is the only conclusion that provides the authentic culmination of his teachings. The Good is God! God is Creator! God is Nous! God is the Absolute! And why can Plato not say it directly? First, his method of pedagogy would not allow it, because the student had to come to the realization for himself in order for it to hold the weight of true understanding. And second, Plato's ideas about God were not understood by the authorities in fifth-century-BCE Athens, as is underscored by Socrates's execution (*Apology*) for believing in divinities other than those recognized by the state.

Perhaps we have imagined we have completed our task, but such is still not the case! Plato leaves yet a *further* mystery to solve. We must understand what Plato meant by the second part of his sentence in the *Republic*, where he states that although the intelligible objects owe their very existence and essence to the Good, "*the Good Itself is not essence, but still transcends essence in dignity and surpassing power.*" What puzzle has Plato now set us? How does Plato mean us to understand the *Good Itself*? As we have seen, Plato has distinguished the *Form of the Good* from *the Good Itself*. In contemplating this distinction we understand that if the *Good Itself were a Form* it could be understood merely as an essence, but Plato has clearly stated that the "Good Itself is not essence, but *transcends* essence in dignity and surpassing power" (*Republic* 508-e). If the Good Itself were an essence, Plato's critics might have argued that an essence is a quasi-material substance, notwithstanding its highly rarefied and ethereal nature. Plato's vision of the truth will not allow that! To reiterate: Plato is telling us that while the Good is a Form, *the Good Itself is not a Form*. The Good Itself is the *cause of the existence of the Form of the Good, but the Good Itself is not a Form*. What a paradox! What does Plato mean to imply?

As Plato has himself stated, the *Good Itself* is beyond reason, beyond dialectic and beyond the end of the intelligible world. He means us to understand that the Good Itself is *beyond any* kind of Form. In fact it is the *opposite* of a Form, even of the Form of the Good that allows us to *comprehend* its relation to all of existence. To reiterate: The Good Itself is not a Form, and it is not apprehended by reason or dialectic. The Good Itself is the *opposite* of a Form. And what is the opposite of Form? *It is what is Form-less!* The transcendent source of the universe, that eternal and unchanging first principle, the *unhypothesized* first principle, the Good Itself—cannot be spoken of except in the most halting terms because the ineffable and surpassing power of its utter transcendent *presence* shocks the mind into silence and awe. The transcendent first principle is *formless* and eternal, unchanging and divine, the cause of all things. We can only apprehend it because we have an immortal soul, which is *akin* to it, and because the faculty of recollection helps us to unconceal its truth. Plato has shown us that when we contemplate the *Form of the Good* the mind can, in some fashion, still use reason and dialectic to understand the unity inherent in the Good. This is confirmed in Plato's statement that dialectic is the coping stone of knowledge and its focus is precisely on discovering transcendental unity in its journey through the Forms. In fact, we might say that in our investigations of the *Form of the Good,* the subject-object relationship still obtains, in that the seeker can still have an *idea* about God.

But when it comes to the Good Itself, no such rational supports are left to the seeker. The subject-object relationship must *fall away* in the moment of divine illumination, namely a *direct experience* of the transcendent such that, as A. E. Taylor describes it, "science here passes in the end into direct 'contact,' or as the schoolmen say, 'vision,' an apprehension of an object which is no longer 'knowing about' it, knowing propositions which can be predicated of it, but an actual possession of it and being possessed by it" (Taylor, *PMW* 230–231).

If they were able, the students would communicate to us that they now understand, from their own experience, those baffling statements made by Socrates—that dialectic has a limit, that the limit reveals the end of the intelligible world, and that the Good is the last thing seen, and *hardly* seen— because they have been swept into the transcendental realm of illumination. Even from the realm of dialectic, such final realizations are not possible! That sudden and *direct experience shatters all former assumptions.*

It explodes the myth that the realm of the sensible world, the realm of "appearances," is separate from the transcendental world. From the standpoint of the sensible world there is no clear view into the world of transcendence, but from the standpoint of the transcendent world all of existence is understood and *experienced* as part of the cosmic unity of the One! The realizations that come from transcendence are known by *direct experience of God*, and not by thinking or even through the divine faculty of dialectic. The direct experience of God is the experience of the divine nature of the *Good Itself* that is formless, eternal, and unchanging. That is why Socrates could not *communicate* it to Glaucon.

And there is another realization that is bestowed upon the seeker. Socrates has taught him of the immortal nature of the human soul, and the fact that the use of recollection can help the soul recover its lost memory of the divine world. Socrates has shown him that this is possible because his immortal soul is *akin* to the Good. But there is a secret concealed in that statement, and it has a parallel in the *Republic* where Socrates explains that he had examined each of the virtues individually, but that now he has to say how things *really are* among the virtues, and unconceal the truth that all the virtues are *part of the Good*, and *depend* upon the Good for their existence.

In the final realization of the nature of the *Good Itself*, of God, the seeker becomes *possessed* by God and, in that state of bliss and rapture has the revelation that not only is his soul *akin to God, it is a part, a spark of God.* **It is God! This** is the final revelation of divine initiation—the experience of the soul's divine re-union with God. The human soul is part of God! This is the truth that humans may not utter! *This* is the great secret taught in the mystery schools! This is the truth that led to persecution and execution!

And to underscore our point, let us not forget that Plato provides an *actual experience* of divine illumination in the *Symposium*, described by Diotima to Socrates as follows:

> And now, Socrates, there bursts upon him that wondrous vision which is the very soul of the beauty he toiled so long for. It is an everlasting loveliness which neither comes nor goes, which neither flowers nor fades, for such beauty is the same on every hand, the same then as now, here as there, this way and that way, the same

> to every worshiper as it is to every other. Nor will his vision of the beautiful take the form of a face, or of hands or anything that is of the flesh. It will be neither words, nor knowledge, nor a something that exists in something else, such as a living creature, or upon the earth, or the heavens, or anything that is—but *subsisting of itself and by itself in an eternal oneness,* while every lovely thing partakes of it in such sort that, however much the parts may wax and wane, it will be neither more nor less, but still the same inviolable whole. (*Symposium* 210-211)

And so it is that Plato's dialogues ultimately reveal the transcendental nature of God in the dialogues, and confirm that Socrates is his divine messenger. In fact, Socrates was quite straightforward about his role, but he was not believed, at least not by those in power, those who were most threatened by his unusual "theories" and unwelcome influence upon the youth of Athens.

Socrates himself tells us of his mission, and it is highlighted in three important places. In the *Symposium*, Socrates tells Agathon that it was Diotima, the wise woman of Mantinea, who taught him the philosophy of Love. It was Diotima who bequeathed to Socrates her method of inquiry using questions and answers that he employed ever afterward. It was Diotima who taught Socrates that all men really seek is the Good. It was Diotima who recounted to Socrates the transcendental experience of mystical illumination, and it was she who taught Socrates that this experience was considered a supreme *initiation*. After his education by Diotima, Socrates says to Phaedrus, "I was convinced, and in that conviction I try to bring others to the same creed, and to convince them that, if we are to make this gift our own, Love will help our mortal nature more than all the world. And this is why I say that every man of us should worship the god of love, and this is why I cultivate and worship all the elements of Love myself, and bid others to do the same. And all my life I shall pay the power and the might of Love such homage as I can" (*Symposium* 212-b).

No more needs to be said about the power of Love upon Socrates, nor of Diotima's crucial influence in the formation of Socrates's philosophical project, except to point out what is obvious—God is *Love*. God may be interpreted as the source of the order in the heavens and the earth, but God may not be confined in a logical deduction or dry abstraction, because God is Love, and **Love** is ***alive***.

The second place where we find a clue to Socrates's divine mission is in the *Apology*. He is telling his accusers that he has been brought into the court to answer charges because he has a reputation for a certain kind of wisdom, and he says he will call as his witness none other than Apollo, the god at Delphi. He explains that his friend Chaerephon went to Delphi and asked the Oracle whether there was anyone wiser than Socrates. The Oracle replied that there was no one wiser. When Chaerephon told him of the Oracle's pronouncement, Socrates wondered what the god (Apollo) meant, and he immediately set out to check the truth of it. He interviewed prominent Athenians—politicians, poets, artisans—and discovered that they thought they knew things that they did not. During these dialogues Socrates discovered his own wisdom lay in the fact that he was *aware* of his own ignorance, and the others were not. Socrates says, "I pursued my investigation *at the god's command*," and felt "*compelled to put my religious duty first*" (*Apology* 22). Socrates carried out the god's command, even though it was already provoking resentment against him.

Later on Socrates tells his accusers, "It is literally true, even if it sounds rather comical, that God has specially appointed me to this city, as though it were a large thoroughbred horse that because of its great size is inclined to be lazy and needs the stimulation of some stinging fly. It seems to me that God has attached me to this city to perform the office of such a fly" (*Apology* 30-e). Socrates then points out to those assembled at his trial that he questions his fellow Athenians because it "is what my God commands, and it is my belief that no greater good has ever befallen you in this city than my service to my God…for I spend all my time trying to persuade you to make your first and chief concern not for your bodies nor for your possessions, but for the highest welfare of your souls" (*Apology* 30). And finally Socrates tells his accusers, "I am your very grateful and devoted servant, but I owe a greater obedience to God than to you" (*Apology* 19).

In making his defense Socrates says he is quite aware of the difficulty of his task, but as he says, "However, let that turn out as God wills. I must obey the law and make my defense" (*Apology* 29-d). Finally, Socrates declares: "I have a more sincere belief, gentlemen, than any of my accusers, and I leave it to you and to God to judge me as it shall be best for me and for yourselves" (*Apology* 35-d). It hardly needs to be said that Socrates was to suffer the martyrdom that often befalls great teachers who threaten those in power when they introduce new ways of understanding the human condition.

The *Apology* is the *first* of Plato's dialogues, and yet during the course of this short work, Socrates invokes the name of *God* at least thirteen times! What is interesting, perhaps, is that in making those thirteen invocations he is not referring to the single god Apollo from the Oracle at Delphi—one among the plurality of the gods of Greece, but to the single, unified concept of God—a concept quite foreign in fifth-century-BCE Greece. There is no doubt that Socrates stands in the dock because he is accused of having belief in gods *different* from those of the state. Socrates was charged with investigations of things above and below the heavens, similar to those of the scientific inquiries of Anaxagoras and other Pre-Socratics. Many of his accusers thus took him for an atheist, but that was likely the result of political expediency, as they could count on a guilty verdict for those charges. More elusive are Socrates's invocations to a *different* God from those gods believed in by average Athenians. That single unified concept of God was unknown to Athenians of the time, and it would have been considered blasphemy to have publicly acknowledged such a view.

It echoes the story of Akhenaton, the Egyptian Pharoah of the XVIIIth dynasty who broke with Egyptian concepts of multiple gods and worshipped the single God—the Sun God Ra—during his short reign. The fact that when he died the old gods were restored did not alter the importance of his project. For, that single, unified concept of God, monotheism, would not only be found in the Athens of Socrates's time, but would reappear in full force in Christianity with the teachings of Jesus, and also in Judaism with those of Moses.

No one can deny that the unified concept of a single God has come to dominate western civilization for the last two thousand years. And if we take the statements provided by Plato in the *Apology* as a truthful testament of Socrates's divine mission to educate his fellow Athenians for the "care of their souls," then his role in the history of *religion*—not merely philosophy—needs to be revised. It might explain why Plato, the son of an aristocratic family in Athens, who was embarking on a distinguished career as a playwright, and perhaps an even more distinguished *political* career, could be so bewitched by the aura, wisdom—and mystery—surrounding Socrates that he gave up everything, burned all of his plays, and set out to be his follower. Were it not for Plato's dramatic conversion, the divine mission of Socrates in the fifth century BCE, Athens might have been completely erased or, at best, remain as a minor footnote to history!

Transcendence and Immanence

No investigation of Plato would be complete without discussing the issues of transcendence and immanence. Starting with transcendence, Plato's own statements about it are our best evidence for his claims about it. But four main comments may be made about them. First, that the inspiring passage in the *Symposium* is an actual record of someone's *experience* of the transcendental could hardly be doubted. You simply could not make that up! In addition, as Taylor and others tell us, it falls into line with similar passages in religious and mystical literature. What does this transcendental experience reveal? It reveals that there is Something—Something Unnameable—that is beyond time and space, the *same in all times and all places, that it's not objects, nor knowledge, nor even the heavens. While everything in existence participates in this unhypothesized first principle, it cannot be identified with any one particular thing.* The *Symposium* passage shows that, paradoxically, it must be identified with *all things*.

Second, it may be hard for those in the western scientific tradition to accept what Plato says here—that transcendental experience is *not knowledge*. Even dialectic, strictly speaking, is merely a preparation for the transcendental *experience* which is said to be a "sudden" and "direct revelation." Taylor unequivocally states that in experiencing the final realization, the soul is described as having got *beyond* "science" itself. It *possesses* and *is possessed* by the transcendental principle, God. In order to do justice to this transcendental experience, it should be stated that the mystical literature reveals—and there is such literature—that the experience is suffused by, indeed, *characterized by* states of bliss and ecstasy. See, for example, St. Theresa of Avila, *The Interior Castle*, where she describes her many experiences of religious ecstasy. The sculptor Bernini has captured this religious ecstasy in his remarkable statue, *The Ecstasy of St Theresa*, located in the Vatican in Rome. Christopher Isherwood's book, *Ramakrishna and His Disciples*, is a biography of the legendary nineteenth-century Indian incarnation, who experienced states of religious ecstasy throughout his life. These states of ecstasy were witnessed by his disciples on countless occasions. Because ineffable bliss characterizes the moment of illumination, or enlightenment, is precisely why the transcendental experience falls in the *Symposium*, the dialogue on Love. That Plato *placed* it there is evidence that he was well aware that bliss and ecstasy were at the heart of this spiritual illumination, and in order to appreciate *this* fact, a philosopher has to step outside of the parameters of his own discipline. Most western philosophers would balk at the idea that the Transcendental Principle, whatever *else* it may be, is also *Love*!

Third, the fact that the *Symposium* passage is an *actual record* of a transcendental experience proves that it *can happen*, and happen *while a person is in an earthly body*. So when scholars like Ross or Gaye want to claim that by the time of the *Phaedo* and *Republic,* Plato was already experiencing dissatisfaction with the theory of Ideas *because Ideas could not be fully known*, they are clearly mistaken. When we consider the ineffable nature of the experience, we can begin to understand why, in the *Republic,* the guardians were prepared to spend their whole lives in a long and arduous toil in pursuit of this most elusive and transcendental state. Moreover, it is obvious not only that the Ideas or Forms *could, in fact, be known*, but they could be known *only in the transcendental experience*. As Taylor reminds us, that state deals with "an apprehension of an object which is no longer 'knowing about' it, knowing propositions which can be predicated of it, but *an actual possession of and being possessed by it* [note the language of *participation* here].... You cannot properly predicate anything of it, because it does not 'participate' in good or any other 'form'; it is its own So-sein. Consequently, the apprehension of it is strictly 'incommunicable' since all communication takes the form of predication" (Taylor, *PMW* 231).

Where I differ with Taylor is when he states that the transcendental principle, God, doesn't participate in the Forms, because Taylor has just spoken of the individual who has the transcendental experience of possessing It and being possessed *by* It. From Plato's description of the Good Itself it is clear that the God does not only *participate* in the Forms but indeed it is the very *source of the Forms and all else that exists*, as long as we understand it in the context of the paradox that the Good, God—because it is *eternal*—doesn't in the act of such participation *change Itself* in any way.

As I have indicated earlier, when God projects himself/herself/itself into matter, it is understood that the manifested universe only comprises *part of* God. There is always another part of God *as Absolute*, which remains *beyond* and *above* in eternal stillness and repose, while the universe exists and moves within the parameters of time and space. Plato confirms this statement in his account of the mystical experience in the *Symposium* where he describes the Good (or God) as "subsisting *of itself and by itself in an eternal oneness,* while every lovely thing partakes of it in such sort that, *however much the parts may wax and wane, It will be neither more nor less, but still the same inviolable whole*" *(Symposium* 210-d-22b).

He also clearly delineates the experience from anything known by reason or any other faculty designated by the divided line: "It is an everlasting loveliness which neither comes nor goes, which neither flowers nor fades, for such beauty is the *same on every hand, the same then as now, here as there, this way as that way, the same to every worshiper as it is to every other" (Symposium* 210d-22b). These are statements that defy all human logic. If we *were* to understand them in the context of our world of time and space, everything would be the same—all the time—and yet it is contradicted by the statement that lovely things participate and move within It. These things can only be understood in the transcendent experience itself. That is why it is so rare an occurrence.

The single thing that Socrates and Plato omit from this description is that the transcendent principle—the Good, God—has no Form (not even the Form of the Good), but is in fact *Form-less*. That is the last inference Plato leaves for the student to make in order to attain his or her own transcendence. However, he gives another clue to this transcendence in Book X of the *Republic* where, in order to determine what things are *real*, he is discussing the question of three different couches. As he says, there is first the *Form* of the couch—what is transcendentally real; second, a pictorial image of a couch, which is a *representation* of a couch, an appearance of the couch, but not its true reality; and third, there is the mundane couch itself, which is a copy, an imitation, a *material couch*. This object is a material instantiation of the Form of the couch.

He applies this analogy to the relation existing between the transcendent realm and the sensible world of objects. The image he uses is unassuming, but deceptively profound. He tells Glaucon that if he wants to understand that there is a *creator* of things: "You could do it most quickly if you should choose to take a mirror and carry it about everywhere. You will speedily produce the sun and all the things in the sky, and the plants and all the objects of which we just now spoke" (*Republic* 596-e). By this statement Socrates means to imply that the manifested world is an image, a pattern, a reflection of the transcendental world, and that if you had a mirror that could stand "objectively" between the transcendental and sensible worlds, the patterns from the transcendent world would appear reflected on the mirror surface as images—images that people in the sensible world take to be real—but that are mere *appearances* and not the *reality* of the transcendental world.

Another way to understand this relation of the transcendent God to our three-dimensional world is found in the Indian scriptures of Vedanta that tell us that the whole world of appearances is merely a *projection of the divine into matter.* For the Hindus, there is no Big Bang. A process of *emanation* accounts for the unfoldment of the universe from God, while the transcendental principle exists eternally—formless, Absolute, and unchanging. Eventually, due to cosmic law, God allows part of Himself/Herself to flow into, to *become*, and to *shape* the three-dimensional cosmos governed by time and space, while retaining *a part* of Itself in the transcendental realm. Once God, the transcendental principle, unfolds the many levels of Itself until it finally arrives at matter, you may call it by many names. God is the unhypothesized first principle, the Good, the Formless Absolute, the Source, Nous—but once it is *in matter, it is immanent in* the world of appearances. However, the *divine Source* remains changeless, transcendental, and in eternal repose.

Even for Plato, who has argued throughout the dialogues for the supremacy of the divine world, the final revelation shows that the Good, which is also reflected in the mirror *as the world of appearances*, is in fact **All That Is**. What this says is that hair and mud and stones and worms—things that are recognized as sensible objects of *appearances*—are, in fact, permeated and saturated by the divine, and that everything mundane *can ultimately be traced back to the transcendental source.*

The divine is in fact **All That is**, it *saturates* the sensible world, but is concealed from consciousness until students start to seek their own transcendent nature. Perhaps *that* is why, having fully explicated the spiritual journey from immanent instantiations of virtues all the way up to a transcendental experience of the Good, of God, Plato left it until much later in his life to focus his attention on *how* the divine pervades the material world; he provides an explication of his cosmology in the *Timaeus*.

Fourth, the transcendent principle, God, the Absolute Being, can be approached in two different ways: morally and aesthetically as the Good, and mathematically as the One. Although I did not have occasion earlier to bring up this topic, in examining the dialogues I concluded that while the moral virtues provided an opportunity for *"participation"* in the Good, the mathematical objects do not give an opportunity for *participation*, but of *"knowing."* For example, you cannot *participate* in a geometrical diagram, but you can *know* it. I take these statements to mean that Plato was well aware that some individuals were scientifically oriented, and that others more morally and ethically oriented. Therefore, in the *Republic* Plato has a rational and scientific explanation of the unhypothesized first principle (*Republic* 532–533-d), and in the *Symposium* (210d-22-b) he describes an actual experience of the Good.

However, when Plato says that dialectic reaches the end of the intelligible world, he is making it clear that even scientists *must go beyond thought* and *possess* the transcendental principle and allow It to possess them in a "sudden" and " direct" revelation. Thus, in the end, whether approached scientifically, or morally and ethically, the different seekers will arrive at the same final mystic experience of divine illumination and will experience the Good, the One, as unchanging and eternal, and paradoxically as the source of movement or change behind all things.

On this point, I must confess that Taylor, who seemed so reliable a source for information on the transcendent experience in the *Symposium*, seems to contradict himself throughout the whole second chapter of his book, *Plato's Mind*, in which he argues that "Plato's conception [of the ultimate principle governing the universe] is closely akin to the ideal of the growing school of mathematicians who maintain that the whole of pure mathematical science *is a body of deductions from a few ultimate premises* which are all of a purely logical kind, and require for their statement no primary notions except those of formal logic" (Taylor, *PM,* 57).

This statement cannot be maintained on at least five grounds. First, Plato explicitly states that there is One unhypothesized first principle, not several ultimate premises. Second, that principle is the *Good Itself,* which is the *cause* of all knowledge, including logic and mathematics. Third, the transcendental passage from the *Symposium* explicitly states that the Good Itself is *not knowledge.* Fourth, Taylor cavalierly argues that because measure, order, and proportion are characteristics of the morally good, it (the morally good) can be subsumed into the strictly *logical* deduction of universal principles. In other words, the Good (aesthetic/ moral) can be subsumed into the One (logic/math). Fifth, Taylor ignores even Aristotle's comments about Plato's Forms, "that in the last resort, the concepts or defineables of science all *presuppose two primarily indefinable notions,* that of Unity...and Multitude" (Taylor, *PM,* 68). These statements clearly contradict Taylor's claim that Plato's ultimate principle can be equated to "a body of deductions" from a few ultimate premises that are all of a purely logical kind and require for their statement no primary notion except those of formal logic." In fact, it would appear he was on the right track regarding the *Symposium* where he stated that "the *sudden* and *direct* moment of final realization is no longer 'knowing about' it, knowing *propositions* which can be *predicated* of it, but an actual *possession* of it and *being possessed* by it" (Taylor, PMW, 230–31).

My other point is technical, but also relates to what Taylor interprets as Aristotle's comments about the Forms. Aristotle rejects what he calls Plato's "'reification of concepts' as a fallacious attribution of substantive existence to universal predicates, and condenses his objection to the statement that what science requires is not that there should be 'Ideas, or a One which is something over and above the Many,' but merely that one attribute should be predicated of many subjects" (Taylor, *PM,* 48). What Taylor says next is quite astonishing. "The difficulty has been felt so strongly by modern interpreters that many of them have endeavored, *in the face of Plato's declarations, to explain it away,* and *thus to bring Plato's theory of predication into accord with that of his great disciple*" (ibid.). I am stunned at this comment because, as we know Aristotle, being primarily a scientist and also a logician, stands diametrically *in opposition* to

Plato on the question of the metaphysical (and transcendent) nature of the Forms. He simply doesn't believe in them. He *is* dealing with substantive predicates. Judging from this comment and what we know about Aristotle, we should expect him to have a quite distorted view of Plato's "logic." As Cornford has shown, *there is no symbolic logic in Plato*. As for the many modern interpreters who did not take Plato's metaphysical statements at face value, but attempted to bring them into line with *Aristotle's logic*, shame on them for conveniently avoiding a difficult metaphysical problem!

Suffice to say that I concur with Cornford when he says the transcendental principle can be approached in these two different ways—the moral/aesthetic and the mathematical. (The theory of light is similarly elusive—it can be interpreted both by the wave theory, and by the particle theory.) However, despite these two different approaches, the divine revelation would show even these two perspectives will ultimately be subsumed, not in logical deductions, but in that *incommunicable, ineffable* transcendent *experience of unity*.

What can we say about this experience? It is incommunicable, and ineffable. It happens as a sudden revelation. It happens in a moment in time, but that moment takes on the aura of transcendence because the consciousness of the participant transcends time and space and enters the eternal world. Thus, the moment becomes permeated, saturated with eternity; it is *transformed* into the *transcendental* moment. In that eternal moment the participant can see the world, all objects and, indeed, *its own self* in the light of the transcendental principle—God. The account in the *Symposium* tells us the transcendental experience contains *all forms*—objects, knowledge, and the heavens themselves. When we consider all of this, the most enchanting image that arises to express it is the little *mirror* mentioned in the *Republic, the* mirror that shows us the *appearance* of all things but not the *reality*. But it reveals, as does the passage of illumination in the *Symposium*, that on a single mirror surface, *all possible objects* are reflected—in a *unity*. Who would have thought a little mirror could do all that!

What the transcendental experience does is shatter all our former assumptions! First and foremost, it *explodes the myth that the realm of appearances is separate from the transcendental world*. And, for Plato and Socrates, it confirms their belief in the immortality of the soul.

Furthermore, if we include the whole world of *appearances* within the horizon of the transcendental illumination, we must also include *ourselves*. In the spiritual illumination of the final revelation, in which the soul possesses and is possessed by the transcendent itself, *the soul knows*—by *personal experience*—that it has *forever been* a part of the Good, God, indeed, **that it is** God. *This* is the truth that cannot be uttered! This is the transcendent truth, for which, tragically, great beings such as Socrates sacrificed their lives. And finally the all-encompassing understanding dawns that man's source, destination, and very identity are forever rooted and nurtured by the divine world.

Immanence

We have seen that the transcendental experience happens in time, but confers on all sensible things the invisible cloak of transcendence. It allows, says Socrates, a person to know that they are awake whereas most other people in the sensible world are merely dreaming. But let us approach this experience from the opposite pole of immanence. The only place where immanence might seem to be vulnerable to challenge is when Socrates declares the Forms can only be contemplated by pure thought. Here, however, Plato tells us that while *contemplation* of the Forms necessarily involves approaching them as completely non-sensible objects with the use of *reason*, on the fourth level of the divided line, particular *instantiations* of a Form occur in the sensible world at the second level of the divided line, whose mental objects are governed by *belief or opinion*.

We have seen that the immanent instantiations of the virtues and even sense objects, through recollection, lead eventually to the eternal and unchanging Forms. We know from the *Republic* about the long and arduous program of study required for the guardians to be true rulers of the city (i.e., the city of the soul as well as the external city), and we have understood that dialectic alone reveals the principles upon which all other knowledge depends. Last, we have seen that the final step is a sudden and direct revelation of the transcendent nature of existence itself.

Our soul, says Plato, is immortal, *akin* to the eternal and unchanging Forms and, with effort, can recollect the divine knowledge it once had. What, therefore, is the soul touching, and seeking, in all of its *immanent* experiences? If we are to believe Plato, the soul is seeking—perhaps, at the early stages, *groping* its way toward—its own transcendence. If a person was not fully prepared, over a long period of time, to experience the unspeakable power of the divine revelation, it would probably shatter their body completely. Thus, a long process of purification of the soul takes place, and at the same time the soul refines its knowledge until it finally approaches closer and closer to the sought-for transcendent experience. When the sudden and direct revelation finally takes place, the mystical literature says it can approach like a tidal wave of divine power that engulfs the soul completely.

What role does the immanent play in this experience? First, the transcendental *experience* takes place outside of time and space, our normal frame of reference in the sensible world. Without long preparation and purification, as has been said, the experience would shatter our body and, indeed, be beyond the ability of our mind to recall it. The Good Itself is everything that is. The eternal principle has allowed itself to *become*, *in part*, the realm of appearances, including Mother Nature herself. It has also allowed itself to become time and space. *And* the mud and hair mentioned in the *Parmenides* dialogue.

The sensible world's discrete moments of time and place allow the soul to begin to experience the transcendental principle immanently, by way of the virtues, and later by way of sensible objects. Without the ability to gradually frame our increasing understandings in the light of our immanent experiences the *transcendental* experience and any knowledge of it would be completely beyond human comprehension. The immortality of the soul and recollection makes such connection possible, but our immanent experiences are *crucial*. When the soul has passed through the purifications and strengthening needed for the transcendent experience, the illumination of transcendence shatters the myth that the world of appearances is separate from the transcendental world. Indeed, it also shatters the myth that the *soul* is separate from the transcendental world. Therefore, one who has had the transcendent experience understands that his soul is a part of, is one with God—in fact, *is* God—but also understands, by direct and sudden insight, that transcendence and immanence are just two sides of the same coin in exactly the same way as appearances and transcendence are two sides of the same coin. What the transcendent experience reveals is that the transcendent has been present, is present, will be *forever* present. It just remains for us *to recognize* it. Without our immanent experiences such recognition would be impossible.

Plato does not make direct statements about the *relation* between the first immanent instantiations of the virtues and the final realization of the unity of the divine world with that of appearances, but as with the endings of the dialogues where no final definition is given for a specific virtue, I think we can use the same inferences to argue that if the divine world and that of appearances are unified in the transcendental experience, Plato would have no difficulty in saying that in parallel fashion transcendence and immanence are two sides of the same coin, in fact two sides of the cosmic nature itself. In fact, these two aspects—immanence and transcendence—are involved in an eternal play of consciousness.

Conclusions

My philosophical project has been to see Plato's dialogues in a way that I believe goes back to his true intention when he wrote them. And while I admire the brilliant and charismatic nature of the rational thought he brings to bear on the various topics under consideration, I have argued that he has other, more encompassing reasons than mere rational thought as the true goal of his life's work.

I have tried to demonstrate that *The Collected Dialogues of Plato* are not merely to be read and contemplated individually, but that in reality they are all connected together in a *grand design* in such a way that the individual dialogues are like separate chapters of a single book. In addition, my project has been to show, using either Socrates's or Plato's own words, that a thread runs through the dialogues—from the *Apology* all the way up to the *Republic*—which reveals a *system of spiritual/religious teachings* aimed at encouraging people from all walks of life to take "care for their soul."

I have laid out the plan for such a system by stating that it has three levels: the first level describes people seeking definitions of the various virtues: courage (*Laches*), piety (*Euthyphro*), love (*Symposium*), beauty (*Hippias Major*), knowledge (*Theaetetus*), justice *(Republic)*—and then putting such virtues *into action* in their everyday lives. This procedure follows a proscription found in most recognized *religions*, including Christianity, Judaism, Buddhism and Hinduism. It is precisely the attention placed on "care of the soul" that reveals how far Plato's philosophy is from mere rational thought or the practice of intellectual comparison of one philosophy with another. In emphasizing virtues, moral and ethical action, and the search for higher knowledge, Plato confirms that his intention is to encourage his readers to an active and ongoing life of commitment to spiritual and religious goals. As has been shown, such a commitment starts with a desire to live a virtuous life. We have followed Plato when he tells us that when an individual is instantiating a virtue, he or she is in fact "participating" in the *divine nature* of that virtue, and that by so doing the individual is demonstrating a desire to live a virtuous life and eventually to be worthy of entry into the next stage of the spiritual journey.

The second level of the spiritual/religious system consists of higher knowledge that is restricted to those who have proven worthy, over a period of time, in living an intentionally virtuous life. When such a person moves up to the second level, he or she is provided esoteric teachings—on the immortality of the soul, the process of recollection, and the twin doctrines of transmigration (reincarnation) and of necessity, and the impartial law of cause and effect (karma). Critics might wish to dismiss or reject such theories, which were certainly esoteric in fifth-century-BCE Athens, but Plato's carefully worded dialogues confirm *his* acceptance of such theories, and they cannot be dismissed or rejected without doing intentional violence to Plato's entire philosophical project.

The seeker who, through persistent effort, eventually makes his or her way up to the third level of the spiritual teachings is more than likely to be a rarefied individual, man or woman, who after many years of esoteric training may be capable and worthy of ruling his or her city (both the external city as well as the city of the soul). These are the guardians, who after many preliminary years of education are finally ready to be students of the Pythagorean curriculum—number, geometry, astronomy, and music. In terms of astronomy and music, the seeker will be required to find the natural concordances between these two disciplines as a test of dialectic, that coping stone of all the sciences, which can ultimately show the seeker a vast ocean of divine unity in the cosmos—providing he or she can detach themselves from all sense impressions and contemplate these truths by pure thought alone.

However, as Plato teaches, even dialectic has its limit, a startling limit—namely, the end of the intelligible world! From here the student must have the inner strength, courage, and spiritual purpose to go beyond all rational structures into the mystical realm of the Good. In the *Republic*, the Good is seen as the cause of all knowledge and truth, but the *Form of the Good* is distinguished from the *Good Itself*, which, it is inferred, is transcendental, eternal, and formless. Only in that sublime experience of divine initiation in which the soul is reunited with God in a mystical experience of direct revelation is the spiritual journey deemed to have been completed. This ultimate mystical experience is recounted in the *Symposium*, the dialogue on Love.

I have given a brief outline of Plato's philosophical purpose embodied in those dialogues from the *Apology* through to the *Republic*. However, I will suggest the following hypothesis: that just as Plato speaks in the *Republic* of arguing upward to the unhypothesized first principle and, having once attained it, descending *in the same way* through the Forms and thus confirming its truth, *as a proof of the ascending journey,* I hold that, in the dialogues *that follow* the *Republic* Plato *tests the transcendental truth of the Good, and the Good Itself* against the *institutions or ways of humankind*. And I would specifically draw attention to the *Sophist*, *Statesman*, and *Laws*. In the same way that seekers who "participate" in a divine virtue can do so only incompletely—because it is human nature to live in the sensible world, where the divine influence is somewhat diluted owing to humanity's physical embodiment and the distractions of mundane objects—Plato argues while human institutions do the best they can, given their nature and status in the sensible world, they can never quite capture the full divine nature that is their source. That alone rests with God. And that is why Plato and Socrates place God's law above human law and why, incidentally, Socrates is vindicated from that third charge against him—that he believed in gods of his own invention instead of those recognized by the state—because he was doing God's work! The *Timaeus*, Plato's cosmology, is in another category, but it also confirms that God, the Good, is the origin of the cosmos. Even the cosmology in the *Timaeus* confirms Plato's transcendental truth.

But, what of Plato's project in relation to philosophy proper? By definition this entails comparison with Homer, the Pre-Socratics, Heraclitus, Parmenides, and the Sophists. Starting with Homer, we recall that in the *Republic* where he is describing the early education of the guardians, Socrates criticizes the Homeric gods, charging that Homer has depicted them as warring and promiscuous—traits that Socrates not only finds offensive in the gods, but an untrue characterization of them. He is quite clear that the guardians should not be exposed to influences of such a questionable nature, and their education as guardians will not include such fanciful mythological thinking. In his criticism Socrates has therefore summarily dismissed approximately four hundred years of accepted religious doctrine!

The Pre-Socratics also come under the stern gaze of Socrates's judgment. We recall that in the *Phaedo* Socrates tells his companions that for a time he had studied the scientific explanations for the cosmos—those that assigned its beginning to one of the four elements of water, fire, air, earth—and eventually found them not just wanting, but as "absurdities." In hindsight we can see that this rejection of the Pre-Socratics was first and foremost because of Socrates's unshakeable belief, knowledge (and probable experience) of the creation of the universe by God. For Socrates it is God who orders the earth and the heavens, and it is God who nurtures and supports the immortal human soul. For this reason, Socrates sees the intention of the Pre-Socratics to assign *material* causes to the cosmos, as having profound and dangerous consequences. For Socrates and Plato, this means not only that the Pre-Socratics have focused their attention away from God, but at the same time their scientific explanations have exposed the average man to the dangers of skepticism or materialism that could undermine or destroy his faith. In fact, Socrates found the material explanations of the Pre-Socratics to be merely provisional and relative. He would have charged them of not contemplating their hypotheses and assumptions, of not using them as *springboards* for contemplation of the unhypothesized first principle. To *challenge* those suspect, Pre-Socratic theories of cosmology—ones that in Athens were judged as antithetical to the authority of religion or the state—were part of Socrates's philosophical enterprise. It is more than ironic, then, that he should have been accused of those selfsame charges by his accusers and eventual executioners.

Next, let us turn to the Sophists. Socrates has nothing but contempt for them and feels he stands on firm ground in rejecting their purposeful philosophical posturing. While he, Socrates, has his unshakeable foundation in God's will and purpose guiding human affairs, the Sophists start from the premise that "man is the measure of all things," a position that ultimately ignores God's authority in favor of the person's own ego-centered pronouncements on all matters. Furthermore, the Sophists hold that individuals each have their own truths—truth as they alone see it. Socrates rejects such nonsense because it makes of truth a merely subjective judgment on the part of each individual, and Socrates argues that, if human beings *were* the measure of all things, no consensus of opinion could ever be reached regarding the laws that govern the state, religion, or politics. Plato sees the danger in this approach, because it leaves each individual totally adrift, with the possible result that one could succumb to feelings of despair and alienation. It could also funnel into the uncertainty and instability that characterize the philosophy of Heraclitus. In the worst case scenario, it could lead to nihilism.

But Socrates's greatest charge against the Sophists is that in arguing that man is the measure of all things, they twist and distort the truth and charge their students fees for the lies they feed them. Because of Socrates's great faith in God, the immortal soul, and the universal nature of truth—namely, that it holds true in all times and all places—he treats the Sophists' treacherous trickery with scorn and mockery.

Next, Plato refutes the main thrust of the philosophy of Heraclitus, who held that, because of the constant flux inherent in the external world of change, people were unable to find a point of stability within themselves and that, as a result, no true knowledge was possible. Plato saw this philosophy as posing a great danger because, again, it seemed to encourage a materialistic explanation of the cosmos. It undermined human faith in God and in the immortal human soul, and it cut people off from their faculty of recollection, or what could help them reacquire true knowledge. Humankind would in fact be cut off from the divine world if it fell into the trap of accepting the scientific and materialist explanations of the cosmos. For this reason, Plato soundly rejects the ramifications of the philosophy of Heraclitus while accepting that he accurately *described* the sensible world as being ever in the process of motion and change.

Last, Plato takes on the formidable Parmenides, who held that all was the One, eternal and *changeless*. Parmenides stubbornly refuses to accept the existence of the material world and the obvious change that propels it. For him only the One was real, and the rest of existence was unreal, an illusion, an appearance. Plato—and Heraclitus—opposed that absolute position on the grounds that it was useless to negate the sensible world because it quite clearly existed.

Of great concern to Socrates and Plato is the fact that Parmenides claimed that the eternal and changeless One could be expressed in a series of dry, logical *deductions*. It is because of Parmenides's great authority, stature, and influence that Plato feels it necessary to confront him head-on and challenges his arguments in the *Parmenides* dialogue. I have dealt with that dialogue elsewhere, but suffice it here to state that, in my view, Plato successfully refutes Parmenides in that argument. Parmenides echoes those mathematicians Taylor spoke of who believed the world could be reduced to a few mathematical premises that were all of a logical kind and required no proof but that of formal logic. Plato is able to refute Parmenides's logical arguments precisely because they contain *the form* of the premises, but there is no specific *content*, and therefore he cannot arrive at a conclusion that contains truth. The premises are in the last analysis a *form* of an argument, but are therefore empty of specific truth. And it should be remembered that when waging his argument against Parmenides, Plato did not even use his most important weapon—that of the immortal soul! No, he fought Parmenides on his own territory and, in my view, soundly defeated him. Plato could refute Parmenides because he was buoyed by the knowledge that with the appropriate training and preparation, the immortal human soul could go beyond dry syllogisms, and even the opposites themselves, and attain to the supreme human experience—a spiritual illumination in which the soul is possessed by the ineffable presence of the living God.

Plato stands in the middle of all these surrounding forces—Homer, the Pre-Socratics, the Sophists, Heraclitus and Parmenides—and as a result his philosophical project comes more clearly into view. He rejects the mythical gods dreamed up by Homer, the science of the Pre-Socratics, the distortions of the Sophists, the total instability of the external world described by Heraclitus, and the equally untenable Parmenidean idea that there is no change in the material world. Parenthetically, we might note that viewed *from* the side of the external world, Heraclitus is right in his *material* assumptions that all is change. Viewed *from* the eternal and changeless world of the One, Parmenides is also correct that only the One exists and that it is eternal and changeless. However, Plato would say they each fail in their philosophical enterprise because they are showing only one half of the truth. If Heraclitus had the knowledge of the immortal soul, then he would have found that there was a still point in the midst of flux, a point where knowledge and truth *could* be acquired. If Parmenides had accepted the external world, he could have accepted the obvious—that change *does* occur in the external world and, moreover, that in the material world the One becomes Many.

It was Plato's great genius to reveal that *both* points of view were true, *from their own perspective*, but they needed to be reconciled into a new synthesis. And I believe it was the purpose of his *Collected Dialogues* to provide just such a synthesis, made possible by restoring the immortal human soul to the central focus of attention, with its faculty of recollecting knowledge of the divine world.

Plato, then, stands alone amidst all these opposing forces in fifth-century-BCE Athens and forges his dialogues as a way to point man in the direction of the transcendental truth of the Good, a truth that would sustain him when external social conditions were characterized by war or by brutal tyrants ruling the city-state. His dialogues, I have argued, are to be understood not only as brilliant rational philosophy but, more important, as providing a clear system of ethical, moral, and *spiritual/ religious* teachings intended to restore God to the center of the cosmos and to the human being's interior existence.

Plato's dialogues are *possible* because the Oracle of Delphi had proclaimed Socrates as the wisest man. And because of his divine mission, which he states quite clearly in the *Apology* was given to him by God, Socrates undertook as the work of his life to help each man "take care for his soul." A true seeker could thereby rediscover and confirm the eventual inclusion of the virtues into the unity of the Good, apprehend the eternal nature of the Forms, and finally experience the divine initiation that would demonstrate, by direct mystical revelation, that the human soul is not only reunited with the Good, with God, but, indeed, *is* God.

To reiterate, Plato's philosophy performs the crucial function of restoring God into a world that was on the brink of replacing Him with purely material explanations. This materialism was something that Plato could not let pass unchallenged. He took on that challenge and refuted not only the materialist views of the time, but replaced them by a glorious exposition of transcendent values such as have rarely been in evidence in philosophy proper since his own time. Though many may have mistaken his entire project for introducing rational thinking into Greece by way of those Socratic "definitions," I think Plato might measure his own success by the degree to which individuals reading the dialogues took up their simple encouragement to "take care for the soul," for, as we have seen, that spiritual journey, with its humble beginnings, leads to the most sublime and extraordinary mystical experience of the transcendent human soul.

Last, what were the effects of Socrates's teachings upon the people of Athens? As we know, he was brought to the court on various charges, underwent a trial, was found guilty, and was executed by drinking a poison made of hemlock. But what are we to make of those charges? *Was Socrates guilty as charged?* Socrates was brought to the court on three main charges: 1) corrupting the youth of Athens; 2) that he "has theories about the heavens and has investigated everything below the earth, and can make the weaker argument defeat the stronger" (*Apology* 18-b); and 3) of believing in deities of his own invention instead of the gods recognized by the state.

Let us take them in order. If we appreciate Socrates's intention in educating those around him as "care for the soul," he was clearly not guilty of intentionally corrupting the youth of Athens. On the contrary, the young men admired the question and answer method in which Socrates showed citizens from all walks of life that they did not, in fact, know what they professed to know. But the young men did not have his wisdom: they misunderstood and arrogantly misused his method and succeeded in making prominent citizens angry with them—acts for which Socrates was blamed. This first charge was, therefore, spurious.

The second charge against Socrates is a clear attempt on the part of his accusers to put him in the same category as the Pre-Socratics—those who investigate the heavens and earth with the intention of finding material causes for the cosmos. Socrates defends himself quite plainly, mentioning

Anaxagoras of Clazomenae as one who holds these ideas, but Socrates rejects the idea that he has beliefs in common with the Pre-Socratics. After all, it is their materialist theories that he has rejected as absurdities! This second charge, then, was also spurious.

The third charge is much more serious. It holds that Socrates believes in deities of his own invention instead of the gods recognized by the state. Although Socrates tries to defend himself by saying that "he believes in supernatural activities, and therefore must believe in supernatural beings, since supernatural beings are either gods or the children of gods" (*Apology* 27-c), he also states, significantly, that "it does not matter whether they are new or not."

It is clear that in the *Republic* Socrates criticized the ancient Greek poets, especially Homer and Hesiod, for painting pictures of the gods as warring and as engaging in promiscuous behavior. Socrates objected to the gods being depicted in this way because he held that the gods were *good and did not engage in such questionable behavior*. There are times in the dialogues where Socrates mentions, or calls upon a specific god, as for example in the *Phaedrus*, when he says he must cover his head while he makes a (wrongful) speech against the god of Love. But when we pay close attention to the wording in the dialogues, we find that there are innumerable references to *God*. God understood as singular, all-encompassing and, ultimately, transcendental. Why else would Socrates argue that all the singular virtues—courage, piety, beauty, justice—are *a part* of virtue, part of the Good? Why else would Socrates have the guardians learn dialectic, which would gather into a unity those intelligible, transcendental objects, understood by pure thought, from the multiplicity of discrete objects in the sensible world? Why else would Socrates acknowledge in the *Republic* that the Good was the source of all knowledge and truth, so far as known? And why would Socrates make the distinction between the *Form of the Good*, which could be contemplated and studied—both transcendentally and by its reflections in the sensible world—from *the Good Itself*, which could only be finally approached when all subject-object relations had fallen away and the soul *possessed and was possessed by* the Good Itself—eternal, unchangeable, and formless.

Our conclusion in this matter is that from a *legal* point of view Socrates is guilty of believing in other gods than those recognized by the state. Perhaps it is understandable that those representing the state were unsettled by such theories. After all, so far as we know *they* were not directly guided by God and had no way to judge the goodness and truth of Socrates's deities. More important, they found Socrates's new ideas a threat to their entrenched power, and therefore wanted to be rid of him.

The sad part about Socrates's trial is that he could not communicate his own knowledge or experience of a unified, transcendental God. It was an ineffable experience, and therefore incommunicable, not only to his accusers, but even to those near to him such as Glaucon, who, in the *Republic*, was his primary student in the investigation of the Good. Even more tragic is the fact that if he *had* shared his transcendental experience with his accusers, they simply would not have been able to understand what he was talking about anyway.

We cannot doubt that it was Socrates's intention to honor this new, all encompassing idea not only of a transcendental God, but of an all-encompassing *monotheistic* God, because even in the *Apology* Socrates specifically mentions the word God (singular) at least thirteen times. And the word God (capitalized) is scattered throughout the other dialogues on innumerable occasions. This is not a coincidence.

Thus, even though Socrates may have been found guilty from a legal point of view, there is no doubt that in the last analysis he was unfairly sentenced because, as he clearly states, in teaching the citizens of Athens he was fulfilling a mission given to him *by God*. Socrates's introduction of a monotheistic God into Greece was, of course, a concept that was reintroduced and expanded in the public consciousness by Jesus as the spiritual leader of Christianity, and by Moses as the spiritual leader of Judaism. And, as we all know, that idea has dominated western civilization for over two thousand years. It was Socrates's fate to be a martyr for that Idea.

When some scholars sum up Socrates's contribution to philosophy as being the one who sought "definitions," the inference is present that Plato took up *from that point* and that it is his philosophy alone that we have honored throughout the ages. But the telltale signs, in the dialogues themselves, are that *Socrates* was the mystic, the mentor, the charismatic disarmer of citizens who thought they knew more than they did. It was *Socrates* who was told by the Oracle at Delphi that he was the wisest man, who said his mission was given to him by God, who experienced trances and had his daemon; it was *Socrates* who was impervious to hot and cold, fearless in battle, and honorable in politics; *Socrates,* whom Alcibiades astutely described as being like the statue of the seleni, who, when you opened it up, revealed *a god* inside. These are the hallmark traits of a great charismatic mystic, and it was precisely the charismatic, and ultimately mysterious, influence of Socrates upon Plato that caused the latter to disavow his formerly comfortable, affluent Athenian life, and to follow him as a disciple. For, in the end, it was Socrates's *experiences of God* that are the basis for his charismatic influence, but also for the wisdom and the knowledge of the divine world that he was able to communicate not only to Plato and his contemporaries, but through Plato to world history. In fact, one could argue that Socrates's transcendental, mystical experience is the underlying *basis* for the Platonic dialogues, and that in encouraging his fellow Athenians to take "care for their soul" and to arrive at "definitions" that provided the basis for rational discourse, Socrates was in the most unassuming fashion possible, ushering in a revolution in consciousness that would reverberate throughout history. The idea of One transcendental, monotheistic God ultimately overthrew the old Homeric gods. And the "definitions" not only challenged the individual to *think for himself*, and not depend on collective, state doctrine, they also freed the Greeks once and for all from mythological thinking and ushered in that focus on reason that was ever after to be the glory of Greece.

If I seem to be unduly honoring Socrates, it is because I believe his true contribution has been under-appreciated. At the same time there is no doubt that Plato was his most brilliant student, and that the dialogues represent not only his great skill as a playwright, but his profound understanding and exposition of philosophy in fifth-century-BCE Athens. In his various dialogues, he dethrones the Homeric gods from their long reign, he exposes the treachery of the Sophists, and reveals the relative nature of Pre-Socratic, materialistic interpretations of cosmology. In countering the flux of Heraclitus he preserves the existence of the immortal human soul and a transcendent God, and in dueling with Parmenides he reveals that dry logical formulae are no match for the sublime experience of divine initiation in which one's soul has a direct revelation of the living God. Last, in introducing and honoring the faculty of reason into Athens in the fifth century BCE, Socrates and Plato may be credited as the evolutionary forces behind the next two thousand years of western civilization. And great though the honor be for that achievement, the underlying theme that runs through the dialogues is the spiritual/religious impulse that compels human beings to seek their better angels in living virtuously, and to discover their ultimate origins.

There have been some who have claimed that religion belongs to the mythological past, and that when reason became king, philosophy actually supplanted religion. What Plato reveals, however, is that reason is not an end in itself, but the very tool by which human beings can rediscover their relation to God! At the very moment when human beings might have judged religion as outmoded or dead, Plato shows us that no matter what new faculties people may discover within themselves, they, too, can and ever *will* reveal the transcendent God, for as Socrates says in the *Republic,* the Good is the cause of *all* knowledge and truth, as far as known. The dialogues ultimately reveal themselves as a philosophical/spiritual/religious system, a grand design, that gradually unconceals the inevitable truth that God is forever present in our world, and that human souls can experience that sacred truth any time they open their minds to that possibility.

PART TWO

Plato and Pythagoras

We still marvel today at the Platonic dialogues. They appear incomparable in the field of philosophy. The later dialogues are not the focus of this project, but in the early, transitional, and middle dialogues the intellectual rigor and the profundity of thought is matched only by the soaring heights and seemingly artless expression of dialectic and mystical illumination.

But what, we may ask ourselves, made such a philosophy *possible* in fifth-century-BCE Athens? That is still today something of a mystery. Over the centuries we may have come to accept the dialogues as a familiar part of the history of philosophy, but on closer examination it is clear that completely "foreign" spiritual/religious doctrines are embodied in Plato's philosophy that have only a tangential connection with his contemporary Greek culture and religion. Those doctrines are the ones exemplified in the *Meno, Phaedo, Phaedrus, Symposium,* and *Republic*—namely, the doctrines of 1) immortality of the soul, 2) transmigration of the soul (reincarnation), 3) the law of cause and effect (karma), and 4) recollection.

But these are not the doctrines that were encompassed in the charge against Socrates, namely that he believed in gods and doctrines not recognized by the state. The doctrines sought by Socrates's accusers were those that could be seen as akin to those of the Pre-Socratics. Leaving aside the fact that Socrates defended himself by demonstrating that *God* had given him the mission to encourage his fellow Athenians to put the "care of their soul" before the more mundane aspects of life, there is definite truth in the charge that he believed in gods of his own invention and not those of the state.

Greek religion at the time of Socrates and Plato was still governed by a strong belief in the imaginative power of the Homeric gods, in the cult centers dedicated to the various gods of the Olympian pantheon, and in the Oracles at Delphi and Eleusis. The pan-hellenic religious festivals exemplified by the Athenian Panathenaea were under the control of the state, and the populace was expected to be in collective conformity to all state doctrines. Nevertheless, the mystery religions, under the auspices of Demeter and Dionysus, were in full sway, and many individuals, including well-known philosophers, had participated in their secret initiations. During this time period the focus of Greek life was very much on the here and now, and people did not trouble themselves unduly about what happened after death. If anything, they thought that they would be barred from the vivid life they had lived on earth. Any belief in the soul was inherited from Homer, who had taught that after death the soul assumed the shape of a wraith, or a ghostly presence that, over time, dispersed into the atmosphere.

But cracks were beginning to appear in the old Homeric paradigm. The Pre-Socratics had begun speculating—and disagreeing—upon the possible *material* causes for the cosmos. Because of these inquiries, philosophers such as Anaxagoras came under official scrutiny for formulating supposedly dangerous scientific theories that undermined the state. In hindsight, Plato's doctrines of the immortality of the soul, of recollection, of the soul's transmigration and the law of cause and effect (karma) pushed even wider cracks in the Homeric paradigm. Let us emphasize that such doctrines were quite "foreign" in fifth century-BCE Athens. As the example of Socrates shows, it was against state political authority to utter such beliefs in public.

As we recall, Socrates taught that the immortal soul had dwelt before its birth in the divine worlds, and prior to its transmigrations into different human bodies, had *experienced all things*. Socrates taught that when humankind entered the human body people tended to forget their divine origins, and they became subject to the law of necessity, the objective and sometimes implacable law stating that good and moral actions would reap beneficial conditions in one's future life, and that bad or ignorant actions would also bring their inevitable corresponding effects. Unless human beings came to know and understand the law of cause and effect, or karma, they would continue, life after life, to make the same mistakes and their soul would not make progress. However, by understanding the virtues and the doctrine that the immortal human soul was *akin* to God.

By using their faculty of recollection and its associations, people could thus come to know the invisible and intelligible part of human existence that led back to their origin in the divine world.

We thus return to our initial question. What could have given rise to Plato's philosophical/spiritual/religious system when considered against the backdrop of the historical times in which he lived? Where did it come from? What was its origin? Did he create it?

I am suggesting that we take as a point of reference the educational quadrivium, mentioned in the *Republic*, that was taught to worthy disciples and to the guardians. These guardians, we may recall, were those who would eventually rule their cities (both external and internal) with justice and wisdom. Furthermore, Plato gives us to understand that these guardians were really philosophers who were best qualified to rule because they had *no ambition* to do so. In fact, they had sacrificed everything in their lives to the quest of divine initiation, mystical illumination and enlightenment.

The education of the guardians—comprising the quadrivium of number (mathematics), geometry, astronomy and music—is, perhaps, the central focus of the *Republic*, because it appears to be the required course of study that preceded *initiation* of the philosopher-rulers. As Plato clearly states, that system of education was inherited from Pythagoras, a legendary sage of the sixth century BCE. For that reason, when we consider possible precedents to Socrates and Plato, our first and most obvious choice is Pythagoras. It will therefore be necessary to undertake a close examination of the life and teachings of Pythagoras to determine whether those "foreign" doctrines found in Plato's dialogues originated with him. Five areas comprise our examination of Pythagoras:

1. Did he hold that two opposing principles governed existence?
2. Did he assert that things *were* numbers?
3. Did he hold that number was immanent?
4. What is the Tetrad? How is it to be understood?
5. Is there a parallel between his philosophy and that of Plato?

Before we consider possible connections between these two great philosophers, it is important to review the outline of Pythagoras's life because he is a legendary figure who is still controversial in modern scholarship, and some of the details of his life have great significance for an understanding of his philosophical/spiritual/religious doctrines.

We are indebted to the great historian W. K. C. Guthrie for the most detailed compilation of Pythagorean information known up until 1962, the year his seminal work, *A History of Greek Philosophy*, was published. According to Guthrie, Pythagoras was born around 570 BCE on the island of Samos, in Ionia, now part of Turkey. Guthrie says he heard about travels in Egypt and Babylonia but questions those sources. He concedes that a man like Pythagoras might well have been interested in seeking enlightenment in Egypt, and that he probably did so. In that connection, Guthrie mentions that according to Diogenes Laertius (VIII, 3) the tyrant Polycrates gave Pythagoras a letter of introduction to Amasis, the Egyptian Pharoah. Nothing further is said of that period in his life.

Guthrie picks up the thread by telling us that later on Pythagoras emigrated to Croton in Southern Italy to escape the yoke of tyranny under Polycrates, and not only set up his mystery school in Croton, but took a leading part in politics, possessing a great zeal for reforming society according to his moral ideas. Apparently the Pythagoreans wielded great power across Southern Italy for over twenty years, but eventually revolts incurred due, in all likelihood, to suspicion about their secret doctrines or resistance to their particular form of spiritual/political rule. Guthrie believed Pythagoras was banished from Croton and eventually reached Metapontum where, according to information from Dicaearchus, one of the students of Aristotle, "he was forced to take refuge in a temple of the muses, where he starved to death."[1]

According to Guthrie an eventual revolt against them ended up with their meeting houses being destroyed and led to their dispersal from Southern Italy. The Pythagorean influence lasted another forty or fifty years, but of the remaining Pythagoreans, a few escaped to the mainland of Greece where they established Pythagorean centers at Phlius and Thebes. The Pythagorean disciple Philolaus is said to have been part of one these communities in Thebes while another disciple, Archippus, is said to have remained in Tarentum, Southern Italy. It is well to note the name of Philolaus as he will reappear in the scholarly debate about Pythagorean principles.

---

1 Guthrie, *HGP*, vol. 1., 173–181 (hereafter, "*HGP*").

This is the brief history of Pythagoras as outlined by W. K. C. Guthrie in 1962. Apart from the number-cosmology that some scholars have found either in part or whole in Plato's *Timaeus*, not much else about Pythagoras seems to have interested philosophical researchers. Guthrie synopsizes the general scholarly direction in Pythagorean scholarship and touches on some points of contention among scholars.

It is now fifty years since Guthrie's history was published. Since that time many world-historical documents from antiquity have become public knowledge; among the most significant are the discovery of the Dead Sea Scrolls and the Nag Hammadi Library. Would that we could say that among them were manuscripts attributed to Pythagoras himself, but such is not the case. However, a recent book about Pythagoras written by Charles Kahn, *Pythagoras and the Early Pythagoreans,* expands our knowledge of Pythagoras's life by mentioning his legendary semi-divine status at the time he lived, his ability to recollect some of his former lifetimes, and the supernatural powers he was said to possess. Kahn tells us:

> His learning was universal. He first studied geometry and astronomy with Anaximander, then hieroglyphic symbolism with the priests of Egypt and the science of dreams with Hebrew masters. He studied also with the Arabs, with the Chaldeans of Babylon, and finally with Zoroaster, who taught him the ritual of purification and the nature of things. In the late tradition, Pythagoras's life thus assumes mythic form; he becomes the paradigm of the *theos aner*, the "divine man" who absorbs all forms of wisdom in order to become a sage, a seer, and a benefactor of the human race.[2]

The information from Kahn has broadened our picture of Pythagoras considerably. We now know that Pythagoras studied with some of the best minds in the known world, and that his prodigious learning was amassed from almost every significant culture of his time. We would like to know more specifically what Pythagoras studied. Unfortunately, Kahn does not provide those essential details but says they are mentioned by Herodotus and Isocrates who lived in the early fourth century BCE.

---

2 Kahn, *Pythagoras and the Pythagoreans,* 5–6.

Kahn continues that Pythagoras was born at a time when natural philosophy was developing in Miletus, and that in all likelihood he would have been familiar with it. Nonetheless, he left Ionia in the middle of the sixth century BCE and settled in Croton, in Southern Italy where he founded a sect or community that was known as a cult because of its ritual practices of purification, abstention from some kinds of meat, and its custom of ritual burial. According to Dicaearchus, a student of Aristotle, Pythagoras taught immortality of the soul, the concept of transmigration, that human beings are akin to all living beings, that everything happens according to recurring cycles, and that there is nothing that is absolutely new. Those in the community were known as initiates, or students of initiation, and they were forbidden, by a vow of absolute silence, from divulging their secret knowledge to those in the outside world.

Kahn points out that the community was said to have exerted a powerful influence in the political life of Croton and, indeed, in Southern Italy for at least two or three generations. Reports seem to suggest that eventually there was a violent uprising against Pythagorean rule, resulting in the murder of the students, and their meeting houses being burned to the ground. Pythagoras apparently escaped to Metapontum, where, says Kahn, he died as a refugee. A few of his students may also have escaped, because Philolaus went to mainland Greece and settled in Thebes, while Archytas was said to have remained living in Tarentum, Southern Italy.

According to Kahn, Pythagoras was known as a fabulous personality, a sage and religious teacher, even a charlatan during the fifth and early fourth centuries BCE, but that by the time of Plato and his school he was revered as the creator of the mathematical interpretation of the cosmos, a novel and strange idea at the time. Kahn wonders whether there is truth to this latter description of Pythagoras, or whether it might have been a Platonic projection onto Pythagoras of the ideas of Philolaus, the Pythagorean, in the later fifth century and then developed by Archytas, a contemporary of Plato. Kahn mentions Walter Burkert as allowing that Pythagoras taught religious principles of immortality of the soul, reincarnation, and the like, but rejected the idea that Pythagoras could at the same time have been the source of the scientific ideas. This view is furthered by Carl Huffman, who sees Philolaus as the first Pythagorean to be associated with the Pre-Socratic tradition, and claims that he has no debt to Pythagoras. Since the earliest dated writings are from Philolaus, his role between the Pythagoreans and Pre-Socratics is pivotal. This is a question to which we shall return shortly.

In the meantime, let us return to what we know of Pythagoras's life. What we have so far is a few historical facts and a few philosophical references. Of the purported Pythagorean studies in Egypt, Chaldea, and under Zoroaster—perhaps the most tantalizing of clues—Kahn makes no further mention. But if Pythagoras was studying with the priests of Egypt and Zoroaster, there is every reason to suppose that Pythagoras was actually studying in *mystery schools* in those countries. In fact, it is impossible to confine our investigation of Pythagoras solely to philosophy because, as a leader of a religious cult, he clearly straddles the fence into the realm of religion.

The works we have mentioned so far, by Guthrie and Kahn, come out of the western philosophical tradition, with its emphasis on historical evidence and testimony, scant though that may be where Pythagoras—and most of the ancients—were concerned. But there are other more modern sources in the mystery tradition whose information comes from direct apprehension of the truth. Because the historical evidence is so flimsy, and interpretations are based on possibly questionable testimony, or on doxographic inferences that may themselves be overreaching or inaccurate, it seems worthwhile to be open minded about other, mystery school sources if they can throw more light on the topic at hand and may possibly spur investigation in new directions.

One such direction is provided by a Frenchman, Édouard Schuré, whose book, *The Great Initiates: A Study of the Secret History of Religions*, was first published in 1889. The information in that book was gained from a direct apprehension of the truth and we will examine this work to see how Schuré's words compare to those of Guthrie and Kahn. Schuré's book contains a section devoted to Pythagoras, which includes biographical information and his philosophical doctrines. Because his information adds considerably to what is already known, I shall quote at length from Schuré's book in order to present what he says without the veil of yet another interpretation.

According to Schuré, around the seventh century BCE the spiritual and moral level in Greece had fallen to a very low level, resulting not only in forms of government that were tyrannical, of military aristocracy, or based on an anarchical form of democracy, but the spiritual principles of Greece had also been violated, such that the oracles of Delphi were no longer honored, the priests were seduced by political power, and even the mysteries began to be corrupted.

Into such a world Pythagoras was born at the beginning of the sixth century BCE on the island of Samos in Ionia—birthplace of so many of the Pre-Socratic philosophers. At the time Samos was ruled by the tyrant Polycrates, who had forced Asiatic culture upon the island. According to Schuré, the parents of Pythagoras, Mnesarchus, and Parthenis went to the Oracle of Delphi to ask about the destiny of their future son. The Oracle replied that they would have "a son who will be useful to all men for all time," and sent them to Sidon in Phoenicia in order for the child to be born in less tumultuous surroundings than obtained in Samos. When Pythagoras was a year old he was taken by his mother to the temple of Adonai in Lebanon, where he was blessed by the high priest, and after this event the family returned to Samos.

His parents encouraged Pythagoras in his search for wisdom, and he came into contact with the physicists of Ionia, where he studied under Hermodamas of Samos, and at age twenty was under the tutelage of Pherecydes at Syros. He had sought knowledge from Thales and Anaximander at Miletus, but still his soul was not satisfied. Eventually Pythagoras found himself in a crisis. For solace he visited a temple of Diana to ponder his situation. He was torn asunder by conflicting interpretations: philosophy gave one answer, science gave a second answer, and human nature yet another possibility. "All these voices spoke the truth: each was triumphant in its own sphere, but not one revealed to him his *reason for being*."[3]

At that moment Pythagoras had a startling illumination. It appeared to him in the form of a vision:

> The three worlds (divine, natural and human) existed, eternal as the heart of Demeter, as the light of the stars and as the human heart. But only one who could find their agreement and the law of their

---

3 Schuré, *The Great Initiates*, 275.

balance would be a true sage; he alone would possess divine knowledge and would also be able to help men. In the synthesis of the three worlds was to be found the secret of the cosmos!⁴

At that moment his gaze fixed itself upon the Dorian façade of the temple. The severe building seemed transfigured by the ideal image of the world and the solution he was seeking. The base, columns, and architrave suddenly represented for him the threefold nature of the human being and universe, microcosm and macrocosm, crowned with a triangular pediment, which represented the divine trinity. *Cosmos,* dominated and penetrated by God, formed

> The holy Tetrad, vast and pure symbol,
> Origin of Nature and model of the gods.

Yes, it was there, hidden in those geometric lines—the key to the universe, the science of numbers. In a tremendous vision Pythagoras saw the world move according to the rhythm and harmony of the sacred numbers.... He saw all this, and his life and work in an instantaneous and clear illumination, with that irrefutable certainty of spirit that feels itself in the presence of the truth. It was seen as if in a flash of lightning. Now it was a question of proving through reason what his pure intelligence had grasped in the Absolute; in order to do this, a lifetime and a Herculean effort were needed."⁵

Pythagoras wondered where he could find such knowledge as would fulfill his destiny, and, at that moment, the memory arose of the day in Lebanon when he was presented at age one year to the priests of the temple of Adonai. At that time the hierophant had said to the mother of Pythagoras: "O woman of Iona, your son will be great in knowledge, but remember that if the Greeks still possess the *wisdom of the gods,* the *science of God* is to be found only in Egypt."⁶ Ah! In that moment, so many years later, Pythagoras finally understood the meaning of the hierophant's words. Now his decision was made. He would go to Egypt to be initiated!

---

4   Ibid., 275.

5   Ibid., 274–276.

6   Ibid., 276.

How would that be accomplished? Help came from an unexpected quarter. The tyrant Polycrates gave Pythagoras a letter of recommendation to the Pharoah, Amasis, who in turn introduced Pythagoras to the high priests of Memphis, who apparently were unwilling to share their secret knowledge with Pythagoras because they considered Greeks to be superficial and undependable. But Pythagoras would not be turned aside. For *twenty-two long years* Pythagoras submitted himself to the extreme, and often life-threatening trials and tests of initiation with immense patience, perseverance, and effort of the will, absolutely determined to achieve his goal of total control of all the faculties of his being.

One of the major tests of initiation was to experience what happens at the death of the physical body, where, if one survived the ordeal, the disciple would be granted the experience of the mystery of resurrection "into the light of Osiris...this divine insight which allows one to see the spheres of life and of the sciences in a concentric order, to understand the involution of the mind in matter through universal creation, and its evolution, or its re-ascent to unity through this individual creation, which is called the development of consciousness."[7] According to Schuré, once Pythagoras had reached the pinnacle of initiation, the Egyptian high priests were finally able to reveal their treasured secret knowledge to him. He was thus able to "delve deeply into sacred mathematics, the science of numbers, or the universal principles, which he made the center of his system and formulated them in a new way."[8]

It was in Egypt then, that Pythagoras became an initiate. What does that really entail? It means that by rigorous purification of his body, emotions, mind and soul, Pythagoras had acquired such a high level of consciousness that the people of the time deemed him a demigod. For example, it gave him the ability to recollect his prior lifetimes, gave him direct insight into other human souls, as well as secret knowledge of the intelligible world that lay beyond the visible, sensible world. It also bestowed upon him superhuman powers to manipulate the energies of nature in ways that humanity would describe as miraculous, but that the initiate knows are merely *the laws* of the higher order of consciousness under which they operate. As Jesus shows, an initiate had the ability to perform

---

7   Ibid., 277.

8   Ibid, 280.

Plato and Pythagoras

miracles—to heal the sick, to change water into wine, to produce food for the five thousand from five loaves and two fishes, and to raise Lazarus from the dead. He also had power over nature, stilling the winds in a terrible storm and walking upon the water.

As an initiate Pythagoras would have had similar powers under his control. This is the reason why the mysteries taught in Egypt were both sacred and secret. Acquiring them meant having totally purified one's consciousness of all ego, because if such powers fell into the hands of the immature, or those with tyrannical ambition, it could have led to real catastrophe in the world. (One recalls that Hipparsus was supposedly banished from the Pythagorean school because he revealed some of the secret knowledge in public places. By such action he broke his oath of silence, and not only endangered the secret knowledge itself, but also those who taught it.) Last, the initiates not only had the vision of the inner workings of the divine world and of nature; it was the destiny of some to be the force behind a major new impulse—each in their own time and place—of humankind's evolution.

When one ponders the awesome power and charismatic personalities of adepts such as Pythagoras or Jesus, it becomes easier to accept some of the miraculous things that are attributed to them. It becomes understandable that they assumed legendary status in the eyes of the general populace and why their inexplicable, legendary powers and great moral force were revered as semi-divine or, in the case of Jesus, as *actually* divine. The many miracles attributed to him made him appear as a wonder-worker, but in the case of Pythagoras there were unbelievers, those who maligned him as a sorcerer or charlatan. Some today question that such initiates ever lived, and judge all the marvellous stories about them as fanciful fairy tales. There are scholars who doubt that Jesus existed in a human body just as they doubt the existence of Pythagoras. It is said that similar initiates exist today, but they keep their presence secret from the people because public knowledge would interfere with their great work in assisting humanity in its forward evolution.

It was in Egypt, then, that Pythagoras became a great initiate, and it was in Egypt that Pythagoras learned the mysteries of sacred mathematics. As we recall, it took him twenty-two arduous years to reach his final goal. Ironically, then, at the very moment when Pythagoras might have considered returning to Greece, invasion came over the horizon in the form of Camybses the Persian conqueror, headquartered in Babylon, who invaded Egypt, sacked the temples of Memphis and Thebes, and humiliated the Pharoah Psammetichus by forcing him to watch the slaughter of his high priests and members of powerful Egyptian families. Pythagoras watched this scene of despotism with horror, was himself captured and removed to Babylon where, along with some members of the Egyptian priesthood, he was imprisoned.

Schuré informs us that Pythagoras spent twelve years in Babylon. Despite the fact that Persian despots had conquered Chaldea, Assyria, Judaea, Syria, and Babylon, the latter was still a colossal city where "representatives of three different religions rubbed elbows with each other: the high priesthood of Babylon; the ancient Chaldean priests, survivors of the Persian Magi; and the elite of the Jewish captivity."[9] In Babylon, therefore, Pythagoras studied under the Persian Magi in order to further advance in those powers that gave manipulation over the secret powers of nature, and other knowledge that represented the mysteries of ancient magic. He was able to "compare the advantages and disadvantages of Jewish monotheism, of Greek polytheism, Hindu trinitarianism and Persian dualism. *He knew that all these religions were rays of the one truth,* filtered by different degrees of intelligence, and intended for various social conditions. He held the key, that is, the synthesis of all these doctrines of esoteric science" (Schuré 282).

After twelve years in Babylon perfecting his universal knowledge of the mysteries, Pythagoras was finally freed from captivity. Armed with his divine knowledge, and after an absence of thirty-four years, Pythagoras finally was ready to begin his mission, and to this end he returned to Samos at around age fifty-six, where he found his island crushed and broken by the Persian invasion. As Schuré tells us, Pythagoras reached Samos in time to be present at the death of his first teacher, Hermodamas, and to be reunited with his mother. It was impossible to remain in crushed and oppressed Samos, so Pythagoras and his mother set sail for Greece—there to accomplish his great mission: "to awaken the sleeping soul of the gods in the sanctuaries, to give back power and prestige to the temple of Apollo and to establish a school of knowledge and life from which would

---

9 Ibid., 280.

come not politicians and sophists, but initiated men and women, true mothers and pure heroes!"[10]

Pythagoras eventually settled at Croton on the Gulf of Tarentum in Southern Italy, and after a few years the Pythagorean Institute was built, surrounded by broad porticoes and beautiful gardens. There he set up his school, where "his aim was not only to teach esoteric doctrine to a circle of chosen disciples, but also to apply these principles to the education of youth and to the life of the state" (Schuré 298). Pythagoras wanted to extend his spiritual and religious ideas and he therefore set up an institute in which the laity could be initiated and where their service to the state would emanate from the highest principles of truth and knowledge. (An echo here in Plato's *Republic*?) In fact, Pythagoras can be understood as a political reformer of the highest order, for the charismatic power of his presence and ideas influenced many of the cities of Southern Italy—such as Tarente, Heraclea, Metapontus, Sybaris, and, if we are to believe Aristoxenus, even the Estruscans. His prodigious knowledge and spiritual power had acquired for him in people's eyes the legendary status of a demigod.

As Schuré recounts, the very character of a great spirit had also the power to stir up hatred and persecution against him. Pythagoras was no exception. After twenty-five years in power, and (arguably) at the age of ninety, an uprising took place in Sybaris, a rival city, in which Pythagoras attempted but failed to intervene. However, all of the consequences were laid at Pythagoras's feet, and this tragic situation led to a revolt of the people in which a mob apparently besieged and set fire to the house in which Pythagoras and many of his disciples were barricaded. Schuré states that Pythagoras and thirty-eight of his disciples died in the fire. Other disciples were put to death by the mob, but two students, Archippus and Lysis, escaped. The death of Pythagoras led to a general uprising against Pythagorean rule in the cities of Italy, and the remnants of the Order were dispersed into Sicily and Greece. Although the Pythagoreans were eventually allowed back into Italy, it was only on condition that their activities excluded politics.

The Pythagorean Order, it is said, survived for over two hundred and fifty years, and, as Schuré reveals, "the later writings of the Pythagoreans,

---

10 Ibid., 282–83.

by Philolaus, by Archytas, and by Hierocles, the *Dialogues* of Plato, the treatises of Aristotle, as well as those of Porphyrus and Iamblichus, have made the principles [of Pythagoras] known."[11]

The Pythagorean influence extended into Roman times, and then into the early Christian period of the second and third centuries CE where the Neoplatonists were chief among its adherents. Threads no doubt exist in subterranean form throughout the succeeding centuries, but Pythagorean ideas did not re-surface until the fourteenth century in Italy when Marcilis Ficino translated Plato's works into Latin. In fact, it is stated that Ficino was a follower of Pythagoras and translated at least one of his treatises into Latin. The great astronomers Copernicus and Kepler claimed their astonishing new astronomical theories actually owed inspiration to the great genius of Pythagoras and Philolaus who had lived over two thousand years earlier!

There is no doubt that scholarship has been seriously hindered by lack of evidence about Pythagoras's life and teachings. According to Aristotle, by his own time some two hundred years later, all the works of Pythagoras were lost, and Aristotle is sufficiently removed to omit Pythagoras by name and to attribute all evidence to "the Pythagoreans." The evidence is sketchy, but it is essential to mention the information that did find its way into public life. A succinct and methodical synopsis of this material is provided by W. K. C. Guthrie in his book, *A History of Greek Philosophy* (HGP, vol. 1, 269). According to Guthrie, three sources of the sixth and fifth centuries BCE were Xenophanes of Colophon, Heraclitus, and Ion of Chios. However, these fragments were not original statements, but only reported by Diogenes Laertius. The fourth source is Herodotus, but more modern information reveals that there are questions as to his reliability. However, he is one of the main sources of ancient commentary.

As to the sources of the fourth century BCE, excluding for the moment Aristotle and his pupils, these include Plato, for his reference to Pythagoreans found in the *Republic,* Book VII. This is, however, a significant reference because Plato is adopting the esoteric Pythagorean curriculum of arithmetic, geometry, astronomy and music as the course of studies to be undertaken by those who would become the guardians of the

---

11 Ibid., 269.

state. The second source of the fourth century BCE is said to be Isocrates, a rival of Plato, who reportedly claimed that Pythagoras had derived all his wisdom from Egypt, and was the first to introduce philosophy to Greece. A third source is Heraclides of Pontus, a pupil of Plato whose works are lost, but whose statements are quoted by later writers. One of these quotations refers to Pythagoras sharing his previous incarnations with students—namely, as Aethalides, son of the god Hermes; Euphorbus, a Homeric hero wounded by Menelaus; Hermontimus, who recognized the rotting shield of Menelaus in the Temple of Apollo at Branchidae, thus authenticating his own life as Euphorbus; a Delian fisherman named Phyrrus; and finally Pythagoras.

The Post-Platonic sources are subjects of greater controversy. They include Aristoxenus and Dicaearchus, two pupils of Aristotle, whose quotations are not original but are to be found in two lives of Pythagoras written by the Neoplatonists in the second and third centuries CE—i.e., nearly eight hundred years after the birth of Pythagoras. The first of these was Porphyry's *Life of Pythagoras*[12] and the other, *Iamblichus: On the Pythagorean Life*.[13] It is mentioned that Iamblichus received his information from Apollonius of Tyana, a Neopythagorean sage in his own right, as well as Nichomachus of Gerasa.

As we can see from the foregoing, the sources are scanty and often involve only minor contributions. The dispute and the controversy, however, are great, and the conclusions uncertain. To that we must add another possible problem. As Guthrie says, use has been made of the "a priori" method to test and possibly expand positive testimony. This method entails researchers arguing "*a priori or from circumstantial evidence, what they* [i.e., various ancient philosophers] *are likely to have said*" (*HGP*, vol. 1, 171). Considering the fragmentary nature of the evidence and the mystery in which Pythagoras is shrouded, it would appear somewhat cavalier to assume that modern-day philosophers, often carved in the scientific/logical Aristotelian mold, could make true inferences as to what *Pythagoras* is likely to have said, especially if his philosophy, science, mathematics and spirituality/religion were esoteric and secret. In this particular a priori situation there is enormous room for error.

---

12 Hadas and Smith, *Heroes and Gods*, no. 12, 105.
13 Clark, *Iamblichus*.

In addition to the dearth of evidence, Guthrie mentions other difficulties when dealing with Pythagoras. He reminds us that Pythagoras was not only a philosopher, but a religious and political teacher, who founded his school as a religious sect and not as a school of philosophy. It was the custom to venerate and perhaps deify the Teacher of such a school, and to attribute all doctrine to the founder, a view shared with the mystery religions. Another difficulty was the oath of secrecy sworn by disciples, a secrecy and silence that barred the way to a true representation or understanding of Pythagorean teachings unless you were a disciple. Last, there is the problem of Aristotle, and in this connection Guthrie admits that "when we come to the 'fragments' of Aristotle, it is advisable to be cautious, since most of them are not represented in his actual words, and some in late compilers are doubtless at second or third hand" (*HGP*, vol. 1, 154). Aristotle had plenty of explanation and criticism of Pythagorean philosophy, but Guthrie admits that only the contradictory statements of later men give us any perspective upon Pythagoras. In addition, as Guthrie also admits, Aristotle was so committed to his own system of the four causes that he interpreted all other philosophies by its yardstick, an interpretation that might be open to question if you do not happen to be of the Aristotelian persuasion.

In the end, it comes down to the fact that there are apparently no *known* fragments of Pythagorean writings extant before the time of Philolaus who, at the end of the fifth century BCE, after Pythagoras was dead and the South Italian schools had been dispersed, became head of the Pythagorean school at Thebes. Since Philolaus was born circa 470 BCE, we are talking approximately one hundred years after the birth of Pythagoras (in 570 BCE). Diogenes Laertius[14] is said to have claimed that any knowledge of Pythagorean beliefs before the time of Philolaus was impossible, and Guthrie credits Iamblichus as stating the same thing in his book, *On the Pythagorean Life*.

This is the information we had on Pythagoras when Guthrie wrote his book in 1962. In *Pythagoras and the Pythagoreans: A Brief History* by Charles Kahn, we see him quoting from mainly the same historical sources as Guthrie and coming to many of the same conclusions. He mentions

---

14 Laertius, *Lives of Eminent Philosophers*, VIII.

some important analysis done by Walter Burkert,[15] Carl Huffman,[16] and Zeller, stating that these fragments reflect essentially the same world view that is attributed to the Pythagoreans by Aristotle and ascribed to Philolaus and the Pythagoreans in the later doxography deriving from Theophrastus, "so it will be convenient to refer to this, the oldest attested version of Pythagorean theory, as the *system of Philolaus*, without prejudging the question of its originality."[17] This is a remarkable statement. He also states that these efforts have been conducted within the context of the cosmological theories put forth in the fifth century BCE. We shall return to this point later on.

> The briefest sketch of Pythagoras's doctrines and beliefs, following Guthrie will enable us to frame the debate about his philosophical positions which are still controversial today. Let us start from Guthrie's observation that "for Pythagoras religious and moral motives were dominant, so that his philosophical inquiries were destined from the start...to be first and foremost the basis for a way of life...for a way of eternal salvation." (*HGP*, vol. 1, 173–257, 182–83)

The doctrines of immortality of the soul and transmigration were a central part of the spiritual/religious Pythagorean system, along with the belief that the universe was animate, and that there was, therefore, a kinship between all life forms. The Pythagorean ideal was to purify the soul and to this end they engaged in ritual practices, such as not being buried in wool, the avoidance of beans, and abstaining from meat or killing of animals because they, too, had a soul.

There were two kinds of Pythagorean students—the *acusmatici*, who received the teachings in a simpler, more summarized form, and the *mathematici*, who were able to receive in a fully worked-out form the highest secrets of his wisdom. As Guthrie astutely comments, "The genius of Pythagoras must have possessed both a rational *and* religious quality such as are rarely united in the same man" (*HGP*, vol. 1, 192), and that, as a result, Pythagoras attracted two different types of disciples—those who wished to live the Pythagorean religious life (the *acusmatici*) and other

---

[15] Burkert, *Lore and Science in Ancient Pythagoreanism*.

[16] Huffman, *Philolaus of Croton*.

[17] Kahn, 23.

more mature students (the mathematici) who had, in addition, a gift for mathematical philosophy.

The soul was of paramount importance, and Pythagoras's understanding of it marks a sharp divergence from the Homeric notion that death was a separation from the vividness of the life of the body. As Socrates puts it, Homer's view was that after death the soul was considered a wraith, or a ghostlike entity that eventually dissolved into the atmosphere. For Pythagoras the soul was immortal, and regaining one's immortality was the essential purpose of human life. It involved a strenuous toil, lasting over many lifetimes, and was achieved by purification, elevation of the divine element in man, and eventual initiation into the mysteries.

As Guthrie shows, the Orphics shared with the Pythagoreans the belief "that the essential part of man, his soul, was not mortal...it was neither more nor less than a small fragment or spark of the divine and universal soul, cut off and imprisoned in a perishable body."[18] This belief gave a student the incentive to purify his soul in order that it could eventually attain salvation, meaning the divine initiation, union with God.

What was perhaps new was that Pythagoras advocated using *reason* and *observation* in order to gain understanding of the divine world, the cosmos and the human being's place it. The cosmos—a word that Pythagoras is said to have introduced into Greek thought—represented order, structure, and beauty such that all things were in proper proportion.

According to Guthrie, as far as an interpretation of the cosmos was concerned, Pythagoreans set "at the very beginning of things...two contrasting principles by which the world evolved. Limit (peras) seen as good, and the Unlimited (apeiron) seen as evil.[19] These are the principles that have vexed many generations of scholars, and we shall later on have to deal with them. For the present, however, we are reminded that active intellectual study—especially in the field of number-theory, geometry, astronomy and music—is what will reveal the order present in the heavens, in external nature, and in our own human nature. Let us underscore that these scientific pursuits were undertaken with the aim of eventual assimilation of the soul with God, and by understanding that, for the Pythagoreans,

---

18 Ibid., 202.

19 Ibid., 206.

numbers "had, and retained, a mystical significance, *an independent reality*. Phenomena, though they professed to explain them, were secondary, for the only significant thing about phenomena was the way in which they reflected number. Number was responsible for 'harmony,' the divine principle that governed the structure of the whole world."[20]

In addition Guthrie affirms that mathematics have a metaphysical as well as a purely mathematical significance, and that because "the objects of geometrical knowledge" are "eternal, not subject to change or decay, they draw the soul upward to truth."[21] This is true of the objects of mathematics proper, geometry, astronomy, and music—all draw the soul upward to the intelligible world and to truth.

If we wish to understand Pythagorean "numbers," we must therefore be vigilant in remembering that these studies were meant to help disciples understand the eternal unchanging laws that govern the cosmos and their own souls. This inferred the relation of microcosm to macrocosm.

> Although he had predecessors in the East and among the Ionians, Pythagoras is generally considered to have laid the *foundations* of Greek mathematics. We must, therefore, take seriously Aristotle's claim that, for the Pythagoreans, "things themselves are numbers," or that they "imitate" or "represent" numbers...and that the whole heaven [is] a harmonia and a number"[22]

Guthrie explains that the word *harmonia* usually meant fitting things together, but that it also had a musical meaning by which the harmony of the numbers could be established in terms of proportions and ratios, hence the musical intervals of the octave, fourth and fifth, that were to play such an important role in Pythagorean cosmogony. In fact, it is the musical relationships between the octave, 1:2; those of the fifth, 3:2; and the fourth, 4:3 that "made it appear that cosmos—order and beauty—was imposed on the chaotic range of sounds by means of the first four integers 1, 2, 3, and 4, which were the source of the

---

20 Ibid., 212.

21 Ibid., 213.

22 Ibid., 220 (*Meta.* 987 b28 II 986 a I).

Pythagorean belief that the number ten was a perfect number and was represented by the Tetrad.

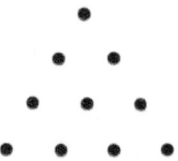

There are various interpretations of the Tetrad, including logical, scientific, mythological, and symbolic, but most, if not all of them are considered to be conjecture. It is said that perhaps in a flash of insight Pythagoras understood that this musical system of ratios, proportions, and harmony had a *mathematical* application to the universe, and that is why number is so intrinsic to his system. Within this mathematical/musical/cosmological system, there is another important doctrine—namely, that the numerical basis of the universe expresses itself in multiples of three, which some say gave rise to Plato's theory in the *Timaeus* that objects are composed of triangles. Guthrie reminds us (*HGP,* vol. 1, 230) that, for the Greeks, numbers served as *both ideal and as real principles*. In fact, for Pythagoreans the triad came to assume such central significance, that they believed the universe "had a numerical basis, being expressed in multiples of three" (*HGP,* vol. 1, 218).

Guthrie sums up the achievements of the Pythagorean "all-embracing cosmic philosophia" by accepting that "the fundamentals of the system—the numerical explanation of reality as well as transmigration, universal kinship, and the assimilation of man to god—all belong to it in its original form as taught by the Master himself" (*HGP,* vol. 1, 220).

Did Pythagoras Accept the Two-Principle Theory?

Historians have told us that nothing of Pythagoras's doctrines or teachings remain extant, and they point to Philolaus as the likely author of writings first attributed to the Pythagoreans. Some assume that means Pythagoras himself wrote nothing. However, it is extremely unlikely that a scientist, sage, and the originator of Western mathematics and music, would have omitted writing down his important doctrines, teachings, and treatises, even if they were in code or symbolic form.

This view is corroborated by Diogenes Laertius: "There are some who insist, absurdly enough, that Pythagoras left no writings whatever."[23] But Diogenes adds, "Down to the time of Philolaus it was not possible to acquire knowledge of any Pythagorean doctrine, and Philolaus alone brought out those three celebrated books which Plato sent a hundred minas to purchase." Parenthetically, Schuré notes it was *Archytas,* another disciple of Pythagoras and a contemporary of Plato, from whom Plato acquired one manuscript by Pythagoras himself.

We also note that the *Golden Verses of Pythagoras,* by Lysis, a direct disciple of Pythagoras, may at the time of Diogenes Laertius have been lost, but there are at least two versions currently in published form today. One of them has a commentary by Hierocles, whom Schuré included as among those making the principles of Pythagoras known to later generations after his death. While that book refers mainly to Pythagorean moral teachings, it does raise a question as to whether it is true that there was no knowledge of Pythagorean thought until the time of Philolaus, who was born one hundred years after the birth of Pythagoras. It is more likely that all such knowledge was secret and remained, via the oath of silence, with the trusted inner circle.

Nevertheless, Philolaus is significant because it is said that he was taught by Lysis, one of the two students who survived the terrible massacre of the Pythagoreans and who escaped to Greece. Indeed, Philolaus assumes a singularly pivotal and significant position in this debate because as Charles Kahn (in *Pythagoras and the Pythagoreans*) and Carl A. Huffman (in *Philolaus of Croton*) explain, Philolaus was at the same time a Pythagorean *and* a Pre-Socratic. It does not seem feasible, to me, to hold both those positions simultaneously—namely, to use mathematical principles *to interpret* the cosmos and, at the same time, engage in the Pre-Socratic search for the *origins* of the cosmos in material things, such as the elements of fire, air, earth or water. While I concede that it is possible to hold such positions consecutively, this places a searchlight of examination upon Philolaus, as his allegiance is unclear.

---

23 Laertius, *Lives of Eminent Philosophers,* VIII, 14–17 (335) (325).

In evaluating the contributions of Philolaus against what we know about Pythagoras, we need to know: 1) Did he accept the two-principle theory of the origin of the cosmos? 2) Did Pythagorean mathematics play a major role in his fragments? 3) Did he accept the doctrine of the immortality of the soul? If it should turn out that, in fact, he mixed Pythagorean doctrines with Pre-Socratic investigations, such that the latter predominated, I might conclude that he was a "second-generation" Pythagorean who no longer embodied the original teachings. That would place much of his testimony in a questionable light. And that in turn might place similar views of Aristotle in the same questionable light.

Guthrie tells us that Aristotle's knowledge of the Pythagoreans went back to the time before the atomists and to the middle of the fifth century when Philolaus was a leading representative of Pythagorean doctrines that dated back to an even earlier period. We shall now turn to such evidence as we have and investigate each topic in turn.

Did Pythagoras Posit Two Ultimate Material Principles?

In posing the question, we hope to bring to light whether Philolaus is in alignment with Pythagoras, the Pre-Socratics, or both. We shall, therefore, approach this crucial issue by laying out the general cosmological positions maintained by Philolaus, Aristotle, Plato, and by Pythagoras, and provide commentary afterward.

Philolaus

One of the best-known fragments of Philolaus, as found in his book *On Nature* (or *On the Nature of Things*), is claimed by Diogenes Laertius to run as follows:

> Nature in the world order [cosmos] was fitted together harmoniously...from unlimited things [*apeira*] and also from limiting ones [*perain-onta*], both the world order as a whole and all things within it." (Fr. 1; Kahn, 24)

Philolaus is stating here that the cosmos was "fitted together" from two different principles, the unlimited and the limited; that the cosmos and everything in it are included in his description; and that all things were fitted together harmoniously.

Kahn explains:

> The Unlimited is of course the starting point from which the world develops in Milesian cosmology. The contrasting notion of the limit is emphasized by Parmenides [Fr. 8.30,42] as a mark of the perfection of Being. Thus Philolaus's two principles combine Ionian natural philosophy with Eleatic ontology, and they are joined together here by means of the concept of harmonia, or consonance. (Kahn 24)

Here, Kahn is telling us that the Unlimited is the starting point of Milesian cosmology. The implication is that, if Philolaus used the term *Unlimited*, he accepted the Milesian definition of the term, as a *material, originating* principle. But then Kahn mentions Parmenides, the Eleatic, as emphasizing that the contrasting principle, Limit, is a mark of the perfection of Being. Thus, the "starting point" of Milesian cosmology, the Unlimited, is said to be an originating, *material* principle, and the opposing, or second principle, *Limit,* is to be equated with Parmenidean Being, a rigidly *transcendental* view of Being that does not recognize the reality of the sensible world or of change. In addition, Kahn tells us that these two principles are joined together by means of the concept of a harmonia.

Kahn continues that *harmonia* is known as a principle of cosmic union, which he, Kahn, connects to Empedocles and Heraclitus but states that Philolaus gave it an "unprecedented, specifically *Pythagorean* development in terms of numerical ratios and musical scales" (Kahn 24). "The first consonance, the scale, one octave long, is called precisely by this name, *harmonia;* it corresponds to the ratio 2:1. The other two consonances, the fifth (3:2) and the fourth (4:3) are also specified by Philolaus in fragment 6a. Now if we add these four integers together, their sum is the number that (according to Aristotle, *Meta.* A.5, 986 a8) the Pythagoreans regard as perfect: $1 + 2 + 3 + 4 = 10$" (Kahn 25).

Kahn is telling us that the two principles, Unlimited and Limit, were joined together by a cosmic harmonia, Pythagorean in origin, that its structure relied on numerical ratios and musical scales, and that if we were to add all the integers together constituting the intervals of the harmonia, we would arrive at the number ten, which the Pythagoreans regard as perfect.

Adding this all together, we have the Unlimited, a Milesian, material, originating principle, opposed by Limit, equated with transcendental Parmenidean Being, joined together by a Pythagorean harmonia, with its numerical ratios and musical intervals.

Returning to Philolaus, his cosmological statement that is most often quoted is found in fragment 2:

> Concerning nature and harmony, things are as follows: the Being (*esto*) of things, which is eternal, and Nature itself (*physis*) admit divine but not human knowledge (gnosis) except that of the things-that-are (*ta-onta*) and that are known by us, it was impossible for any of them to have come into being if there was not already the Being (*esto*) of those things from which the world order is composed: both the limiting and the unlimited. (Fr. 6; trans. after Burkert, Kahn 25)

The interpretation of Fragment 6 by Huffman states it slightly differently: "It was impossible for any of the things that are and are known by us to have come to be, if the being of the things from which the world order came together, both the limiting things and the unlimited things, *did not pre-exist*" (Huffman 123).

Here Philolaus tells us that the Being of things and Nature are divine and therefore beyond human knowledge, but that of the things that *are* known to human beings, they could not have come into being without the prior existence of the Being of things. (Notice that Philolaus uses a capital letter in the word *Being*.) He declares that everything is *dependent* upon Being, including the world order, the Unlimited and Limit, and all else that exists. Some may view the "being of things" existing materially, but eternally. But due to the fact that *Being* is capitalized, and that *Being* had a traditional transcendental interpretation, I view Philolaus's reference to *Being* in context of its transcendental status as creator of the cosmos.

There are a few, less-well-known fragments attributed to Philolaus. One of these is Testimonium A.10 (from *Theo*), which states, "Archytas and Philolaus without making a distinction call the one also monad and the monad one" (Huffman 339).

This testimonium refers to the Pythagorean originating transcendental principle, the Monad, and it says that both Philolaus and Archytas, another Pythagorean disciple, accepted that the originating Pythagorean principle was unitary, One, and that the Monad and the One could each be substituted for the other since they carried the same truth. This is clearly a transcendental statement, and on the face of it reveals solely Pythagorean allegiances.

Of the Spurious or Doubtful fragments and testimonia is Fragment 21 (Stobaeus) from *On the Soul* by Philolaus: "But this cosmos existed from eternity and it will endure for eternity, one governed by one which is akin to it, most powerful and incomparable" (Huffman 342).

This fragment tells us that the cosmos existed from eternity, is governed by one *in* eternity, powerful and incomparable, and *akin* to the cosmos, namely the One, the Monad. This position is emphasized more clearly in Fragment 8a attributed to Syrianus:

> As a whole these men did not begin from opposites, but recognized what is beyond the two orders of opposites. Witness Philolaus who says that *god established limit and unlimited.* He indicated the whole order that is most related to the one by the [term] *limit,* and the order opposite to this by the (term) unlimited, and still ranked the cause that is unitary and transcends all things before these two principles. Archainetos calls it the cause before cause, but Philolaus maintains that *it is the first principle, starting point of all things.* (Huffman 345)

Syrianus is reporting that Pythagoreans, including Philolaus, understood that there was a principle *beyond* Unlimited and Limit, that it was transcendental, the first principle, the starting point of all things. Although he did not mention it by name, there is little doubt that he is referring to the Monad, to the One. In addition, Syrianus reports *Philolau*s as stating that *god established limit and unlimited.*

From these few fragments, which Carl Huffman made available in his book, *Philolaus of Croton,* which was published as recently as 1993, it appears that the predominating themes have allegiance to Pythagoras and the Pythagoreans. Mention of the "first principle," the interchange of Monad and One, the statement that the first principle was beyond the opposites, and that god established unlimited and limit confirm this point of view.

For the scientifically minded, Philolaus's statement that Nature and the whole world order was fitted together from Unlimited and Limited things convey, perhaps, the Milesian view that they are indeed originating, *material* principles, and since Kahn and Huffman refer to Philolaus as both a Pythagorean *and* a Pre-Socratic, we must examine their positions on this crucial issue. We will take up these issues in more depth in the commentary.

Aristotle

Aristotle does not provide many comments about the Pythagoreans in his voluminous writings, but his interpretation of Pythagorean doctrine, especially on metaphysical matters, is crucial because his influence on philosophy predominates even today. In *Metaphysics*, book 1, chapter 5, 986a 17, he makes the most succinct and yet all-encompassing analysis of the *so-called Pythagoreans:*

> They hold that the elements of number are the even and the odd, and that of these the latter is limited, and the former unlimited; and that the One proceeds from both of these (for it is both even and odd) and number from the One; and that the whole heaven, as has been said, is numbers. (McKeon 699)

Although Aristotle has already conflated the idea of the odd and even with Unlimited and Limit, he has nevertheless corroborated the basic notion of them as two material principles that govern our cosmos. Aristotle goes further:

> Other members of this same school say there are ten principles which they arrange in two columns of cognates—limit and unlimited, odd and even, one and plurality, right and left, male and female, resting and moving, straight and curved, light and darkness, good and bad, square and oblong...the contraries are the principles of things. (Meta. 986b 2; McKeon 699)

I note, however, the omission of life/death, as well as eternal/temporal, contraries that might have had great significance for true Pythagoreans.

In *Metaphysics,* book I (ch. 1, 987a5), Aristotle sets out the ancient knowledge about originating principles as follows:

On the one hand from the earliest philosophers, who regard the first principle as corporeal [for water and fire and such things are bodies]... some suppose that there is one corporeal principle, others that there are more than one, but both put these under the head of matter.

Aristotle continues in *Metaphysics* (book I, ch. 5 987a 15) as follows:

The Pythagoreans have said... there are two principles, but added this much, which is peculiar to them, that they thought that finitude and infinity were not attributes of certain other things (e.g., of fire or earth or anything else of this kind), but that infinity itself and unity itself were the substances of things of which they are predicated. This is why number was the substance of all things. (McKeon 700)

Aristotle says that the Pythagoreans recognize two principles, but he doesn't state what they are. Does he mean them to be Unlimited and Limit? He then introduces a different pair of Pythagorean principles, the infinite and the finite (which do not necessarily have the same correlation as unlimited and limit) and says the Pythagoreans do not consider finitude or the infinite as attributes of other things such as fire or earth *(a scientific interpretation)* but as *infinity itself and unity itself,* namely as substances. Aristotle concludes that *because* the Pythagoreans saw them as substances, they said *number was the substance of all things.*

Aristotle is clearly puzzled by the way the Pythagoreans define substances because for the Pythagoreans substances such as infinity itself and unity itself are transcendental in definition, and Aristotle rejects such transcendental definitions. We will examine, later on, the Pythagorean position from their own point of view in order to determine whether Aristotle has described their doctrines accurately.

Aristotle nevertheless feels he is on firm ground in his analysis about the way Pythagoreans define essences:

Regarding the *question of essence,* they began to make statements and definitions, but treated the matter too simply. For they defined both superficially, and thought that the first subject of which a given definition was predicable was the substance of the thing defined, as if one supposed that "double" and "2" were the same, because 2 is the first thing of which "double" is predicable. But surely to be double and to be 2 are not the same; if they are, one thing will be many—a consequence which they actually drew. (*Meta.* 987a20–25; McKeon, p. 700)

Once again Aristotle is puzzled by Pythagorean definitions. For him, as a scientist, double and the number 2 are not the same. He cannot conceive how the Pythagoreans can in all rationality assume that one thing can be many. We recall he makes the same claim regarding Plato's Forms. Aristotle simply rejects the idea that Forms are intelligible objects. And to conceive of Plato's individual Forms all being subsumed in the Good, must have seemed to Aristotle sheer irrationality.

Aristotle also examines the historical knowledge of first principles. In *Physics* 203a 1–10 he makes the following statement:

> "All physical philosophers of repute have discussed the *apeiron* (unlimited) and all have treated it as a first principle. Some, as for example the Pythagoreans and Plato, regard it as a first principle *per se* and itself a substance, not an attribute of some other thing. But the Pythagoreans regard it as present in sensibles (for them number is not a separate substance) and hold that what is outside the universe is infinite. Plato on the other hand holds that there is neither body nor ideas outside the universe (ideas are not in place) but that the *apeiron* is present in sensibles and ideas."[24]

Guthrie explains that the *apeiron*, the Unlimited, was thought of *"as a particularly tenuous form of matter,"* identified with the void and with breath (*HGP*, vol. 1, 278–280).

Here Aristotle is saying that the *apeiron*, as a first principle, is accepted by the physical philosophers—namely, the scientists. But he includes Plato and Pythagoras in the group of those physical philosophers, as if they *did* accept the *apeiron* as a first principle, when that is precisely the issue in question. Aristotle states quite clearly that for Plato the *apeiron* is present in sensibles *and* ideas, whereas for the Pythagoreans, the *apeiron* is present only in sensibles. The inference made is that because the Pythagoreans hold that "everything is number" and the *apeiron* is in sensibles, therefore number is in the sensibles. This may be the reason that Aristotle conflated *odd* with Limit and even with Unlimited, *apeiron*.

---

24 Philip, *Pythagoras and Early Pythagoreanism*, 64.

For Aristotle, the *Pythagorean* cosmos includes Unlimited and Limit as the two primary principles, or opposites, which are material, or quasi-material in nature. The odd is conflated with Limit, and the even with Unlimited, and they are included in the ten pairs of opposites which Aristotle has defined as the "principles of things." Aristotle has also interpreted the relation between Unlimited and Limit as generating a "One" that includes both odd and even.

> From the One come numbers, and the whole universe is seen as number. But then, there is the problem of exactly *how* things are generated in this world: "The inquiry that is both the hardest of all and the most necessary for knowledge of the truth is whether being and unity are the substances of things...whether each of them, without being anything else...is being or unity respectively...or whether they have some other underlying nature.... Plato and the Pythagoreans thought being and unity were nothing else, but this was their nature, their essence being just unity and being. But the natural philosophers take a different line....Empedocles...says unity is love. Others say...it is fire, and others say it is air. (*Meta.* book 3, ch. 4, 1001a5–15)

Aristotle here is laying out the doctrine of essences, whether being and unity are the ultimate definitions, or whether they rely on some other underlying nature. He states clearly that Plato and Pythagoras conceived of being and unity as essences, namely with no other underlying nature, which implies that they are transcendental definitions. But the natural philosophers found unity in the material elements of fire, or air, or even love.

This issue is a crucial one because it deals with how things are generated in the sensible world and whether such generation is to be assigned a transcendental or material cause. Questioning the origin of essences, as a scientist, Aristotle will align himself with those natural philosophers who advocate for material origins of the universe. But he understands that Plato and Pythagoras are saying that being and unity as essences are nevertheless the cause for the generation of the sensible world. It is little wonder, then, that James A Philip in his book *Pythagoras and Early Pythagoreanism* tells us that Aristotle comments upon these difficulties as follows: "It is absurd and indeed impossible to erect a theory ascribing coming-to-be (genesis) to eternal things. Yet without a doubt the Pythagoreans do so" (Philip 50). These issues will be discussed further in the commentary.

Plato

As to Plato's views on whether there are two ultimate principles governing the universe, there are some who point to the statement in the *Philebus* (16-c), where Socrates says: "All things that are said to be, are always derived from the One and the Many, having Limit and Unlimitedness inherent in their nature." They see in Plato a claim that Limit and Unlimited are the ultimate principles governing the cosmos. However, this is a lone statement that loses its influence when considered against Plato's whole philosophical enterprise up to the *Republic*, and also including the *Timaeus*.

Those dialogues demonstrate that he separated the objects of the sensible world from those of the intelligible world, in terms of how they were *perceived*, and I have argued that they emphasize the central doctrine of the *Good* as the sole universal originating principle. As we recall from the *Republic*, Plato referred to the Good as "the cause of all knowledge and truth as far as known" and declared that "the Good Itself is not essence, but still transcends essence in dignity and power" (*Republic* 508-e). Thus, whether or not one is willing to make the crucial inference that the Good is God, Plato affirms that a single universal principle presides over the universe, encompassing both the intelligible world and the sensible world.

However, that single universal principle can only be approached by *detaching the senses* from the external objects of the world, and by contemplating the Forms—ideal, intelligible objects—which are subsumed ultimately into one overarching cause, namely the Good. Eventually, divine initiation affords an apprehension of *the unitary nature* of the entire cosmos. On the other hand the person who *does not detach* from their senses lives in the sensible world and perceives the manifold objects *by way of the senses*. The divided line analogy shows this quite clearly.

The implication here is that the individuals on the lower two levels of the divided line are inhabiting *a world of duality*—one that reflects their limited level of consciousness. The relation of the subject to the external object is the crucial determining factor as to whether an individual exists in the world of the senses or in the intelligible world, and that relation depends on their level of consciousness as determined by the divided line.

In short, everyone who lives in the world of the senses lives in a world of duality. That world, after all, *may* be described as governed by the two material principles of Limit and Unlimited mentioned in the *Philebus*, but we must hasten to add that *this duality does not apply to the unitary nature of the intelligible world*. It applies solely to the sensible world, and it confirms why the philosopher desires to be free of the sensible world—namely, to contemplate *things-in-themselves*. Thus, the statement in the *Philebus*—that "all things that are said to be are always derived from the One and the Many, having Limit and Unlimitedness inherent in their nature"—is now found to be true, but only *in a relative sense*.

Plato confirms his cosmological views in the *Timaeus* but presents them in a form that is at times baffling and incomprehensible. We will focus only on the question of whether that dialogue subscribes to the notion of Limit and Unlimited as the ultimate original principles of the cosmos. The question is settled relatively early, for in the beginning of the dialogue *Timaeus* the astronomer gives a definition of God as what always is and has no becoming, that it is always in the same state, that it was always in existence, and had no beginning (a statement echoing the mystic vision in the *Symposium*). In contrast our world was created by a cause, it had a beginning and it has a visible and tangible body. Socrates identifies that cause with a maker, an artificer, who created the world using patterns that were eternal in origin and that applied to our world as a copy of that eternal world. The creator made the world of generation because God was good and desired that all things should be good (*Timaeus* 28–30).

Thus, in the *Timaeus* we find the first set of opposites: God, who is eternal and unchanging, creates using a cause and a maker, the visible, sensible, corporeal world that had a beginning and thus is subject to time and space and the laws of becoming.

Plato describes God's universe as a sphere, one that had no need of any senses because there was nothing outside of it. Plato also tells us that "in the center he put the soul, which he diffused throughout the body" (the cosmos), making it also to be the exterior envelopment of it (*Timaeus* 34-b). He adds that God made the soul *prior to the body*, describing the act as follows: "From the being which is indivisible and unchangeable, and from that kind of being which is distributed among the bodies, he compounded a third kind of being" (which after many analogous alchemical shakings, created the heavens, the planets and the earth).

"Now when the creator had framed the soul according to his will he formed within her the corporeal universe...with the soul interfused everywhere from the center to the circumference of heaven, of which also she is the external envelopment" (*Timaeus* 36-d). "The body of heaven is visible, but the *soul is invisible* and partakes of reason and harmony, and being made of the best intellectual and everlasting natures, is the best of things created."

Plato also tells us (*Tim.* 31-b) that the world is corporeal, visible and tangible but that in the beginning God made the body of the universe to consist of fire and earth. "But two things cannot rightly be put together without a *third*, there must be a bond of union between them" (*Timaeus* 31-c). And it is the principle of proportion that effects such a union. *Timaeus* tells us that when there are any three numbers—whether cube or square—there is a proportion (Pythagoras) between them that he calls the mean, and he states, "God placed water and air in the mean between fire and earth, and made them to have the same proportion as far as possible...out of these elements which are in number four, the body of the world was created, and it was harmonized by proportion" (*Timaeus* 32-c).

However, much later in the dialogue Plato tells us that he has not rightly explained himself so far, and that in fact a *third kind exists (as well as God and the corporeal world)* that he has not spoken of. Plato synopsizes this situation (*Timaeus* 48-e), where he states: "We made two classes, now a third must be revealed. The two sufficed for the former discussion. One, which we assumed, was a pattern intelligible and always the same, and the second was only the imitation of the pattern, generated and visible." (Note here that Plato is referring to *the second principle* as what God created.) Now Socrates mentions a third kind, which he describes as "the nurse of all generation." Socrates emphasizes that while all the elements are changeable, often into one another, the "universal nature" that "receives" these changeable things "must always be called the same, for inasmuch as she receives all things, she never departs at all from her own nature and never, in any way or at any time, assumes a form like that of any of the things which enter into her" (*Timaeus* 50-a-b).

Plato describes this receiving principle as a "mother" but states, "The matter in which the model is fashioned will not be duly prepared unless it is *formless*...wherefore that which is to receive all forms should have no form" (*Timaeus* 50-e). She is "invisible" and "formless" (*Timaeus* 51) and in a mysterious way partakes of the intelligible and as such is most incomprehensible (*Timaeus* 51-b).

These statements support my point that in the *Republic* the Good Itself is also formless. To complete this all-too-brief examination, Plato tells us (*Timaeus* 53-c) that God fashioned the elements by form and number. And then comes the statement that has baffled and mystified practically all commentators on Plato: "And every sort of body possesses volume, and every volume must necessarily be bounded by surfaces, and every rectilinear surface is *composed of triangles,* and all triangles are originally of two kinds" (which he goes on to describe further). Finally he says, "These (triangles), then,... we assume to be the original elements of fire and other bodies, but the principles which are prior to these God only knows" (*Timaeus* 53-c-e).

These few statements from the *Timaeus* do confirm that for Plato a single transcendent principle, God, who, using an Artificer, created the manifested universe with a visible corporeal body, and it had a beginning and was subject to time and change. As stated before, this is the first duality—that of eternal God on the one hand and the temporal universe on the other hand, which is subject to time and space and to becoming, and thus, if Plato is consistent with his statement in the *Philebus*, will be governed by the Limit and Unlimited, those laws that rule in the manifested world of duality. However, I note that Plato speaks not of two principles, but of *three principles* that create our cosmos.

Pythagoras

Let us now turn back to the account of Pythagorean teachings in Édouard Schuré's book, *The Great Initiates*. Schuré is certain to startle modern philosophers when he starts out by saying that the Pythagorean school was not only the model, or mother, of the Platonic school, but of *all* other idealist schools. Thus Schuré verifies that Pythagoras was, indeed, a great initiate—one who had regained his immortality and taught his disciples how to attain that transcendental state. In fact, as an initiate of the highest order:

> Pythagoras lifted his disciples from the world of forms and realities; he erased time and space, causing them to descend with him into the *Great Monad*, into the essence of the Uncreated Being. Pythagoras called this "the first One...the Unique, the Eternal, the Unchangeable, hidden under the many things which pass away and change." (Schuré 314)

"God, indivisible Substance, therefore has as a number the Unity which contains Infinity.... [It is] the symbol of the Spirit, the essence of Everything. This is the first principle" (Schuré, 315).

This statement could not be more clear. Pythagoras had the power to lift his disciples into a higher state of consciousness where they experienced the divine union of the soul with Uncreated Being, which Pythagoras terms the First One, the Monad. When the soul was in the transcendental state, it was filled with the awareness of God as indivisible substance and of the unity of all things.

In order to set cosmogenesis into motion, the Monad, the One, eternal and unchanging, brought forth *from Himself* a generative and reproductive faculty, the creative Dyad, who, in her role as the temporal and feminine aspect of God, generates the entire cosmos, including the corporeal world. The Monad and creative Dyad are not seen as mere abstract, scientific principles, but are *complementary* divine faculties, of which the former remains eternal and changeless while the latter symbolizes temporality and change. This means that even Nature would be regarded as divine and, if rightly understood, revered as such, which is probably the reason why Pythagoras stressed the kinship of all life. However, there is a mystery in this process of differentiation:

> Pythagoras said the Great Monad *acts as* a creative Dyad. *From the moment God is manifest, He is double, indivisible Essence/ divisible Substance, masculine, active, animating/passive feminine principles.* "The Monad represents the essence of God: the Dyad, His generative and reproductive faculty. The latter generates the world; it is the visible unfolding of God in space and

time.... The perfect image of God is not Man alone, but Man and Woman." (Schuré 315–316)

The union between Monad and creative Dyad is not, as with the materialists, a necessary "fitting together" of opposing forces by means of a harmonia, however that is construed. For Pythagoras it is a union of *complementary divine faculties* that generate a third divine faculty, what in Christianity would be termed the Son, child of the Father and the Mother. And so it is here. The three faculties complete a Divine Triad in this next step of the process of differentiation. As Pythagoras explains:

> The real world is threefold. Man is composed of three elements, distinct yet blended into one another: body, soul and spirit. The universe likewise is divided into three concentric spheres: the natural world, the human world, and the divine world. The Triad of the threefold law, therefore, is the essential law of things and the actual key to life.

The Triad of the threefold law does involve a harmonia, but we will deal with it under the section on number. For the present, it is sufficient to emphasize the importance of the threefold law because, according to Pythagoras, it affects all things:

> For this law is found at all stages of the ladder of life, from the constitution of the organic cell [all the way through]...the constitution of man, universe and God. It can be said that it forms the cornerstone of esoteric science. All the great religious initiators were aware of it: all spiritual leaders felt it.... The great accomplishment of Pythagoras is that he formulated the threefold law with the clarity of Greek genius. He made it the center of his theogony and the foundation of the sciences.... [It was] concealed in Plato's exoteric writings, but completely misunderstood by later philosophers....
>
> Plato replaced the doctrine of the three worlds with three concepts which in the absence of organized initiation, remained for two thousand years as three roads leading to the supreme goal.... [These were] the True, the Beautiful and the Good. (Schuré 316–318; 389–390)

We might speculate that when Plato tells us in the *Timaeus* that all things come from triangles, this threefold law is what Plato is probably referring to, albeit in a symbolic and veiled expression.

For Pythagoras, then, the threefold law affects all things. As we have seen, the Monad brings forth the creative Dyad, his temporal, feminine and generative faculty, and their union produces the third faculty that completes the Divine Triad. From the permutations of the manifold relations between these three divine faculties are generated not only the corporeal world itself, but all the subjects and objects that inhabit that cosmos.

Although we might not have noticed it, this process of differentiation occurred in four major stages. And these stages are represented in the mysterious Tetrad of Pythagoras, which has been the subject of so much speculation. In fact, the explanation is, on the one hand, deceptively simple to recognize:

> The single dot at the apex of the triangle is a Point.
> The two dots below represent the extension of the point into a Line.
> The three dots represent a triangle, a three-sided geometrical form, which has surface.
> The four dots represent the tetrahedron, or pyramid, a four-sided figure, the first solid.

However, this deceptively simple diagram, which even Meno could understand, represents the entire cosmic process of differentiation. In short, the Tetrad is a symbolic representation, in which Point, Line, Surface, Solid reveal successive states of material differentiation, as processes of a cosmogenesis that involves *eons* of time as the Monad makes its incomprehensible journey from formlessness into matter. We recall Schuré's explanation that Pythagoras turned to numbers to symbolize cosmic processes that otherwise were hard to understand.

In cosmic terms:

> The single dot, the Point, represents the undifferentiated Monad, the One, the first principle, eternal, unchanging, and formless.
> The two dots represents the manifestation of the Monad into its generative and reproductive aspect, the creative Dyad, and the pairs of contraries that begin to structure the emerging, material cosmos.

> The three dots represent the union, or relation between the divine faculties that completes the Divine Triad, the threefold law, whose manifold permutations bring about the actual manifestation of the material cosmos.
> The four dots, the pyramid, represent the completion of the differentiation of the One into the corporeal cosmos. The One has become Many.

This is a vastly more sophisticated cosmology than that of the Pre-Socratics, and scholars like Burkert—who found it impossible to believe that Pythagoras could be a scientist while at the same time leader of a religious school—clearly failed to see the universal genius in the erudite cosmological and scientific hypotheses of Pythagoras.

A case in point, still controversial and one that must be included as it relates directly to the question of cosmology, is mentioned by Kahn (26) in the course of the discussion of the central fire, that principle that was considered to be at the center of the universe. Aristotle is known to be specifically referring here to the Pythagoreans.

> As Aristotle reports...it is not expressly stated but clearly assumed that the periodic motions of these bodies around the central Hearth (fire) somehow instantiate the ratios of musical concord, so that their revolutions produce the cosmic music of the spheres.
>
> In this peculiar world system the earth is, as it were, a heavenly body, revolving around the central fire and producing night and day by its position relative to the sun. (DK 58B.37)
>
> This permitted Copernicus to name "Philolaus the Pythagorean" as his predecessor, and in fact the Copernican system was originally known as *astronomia Pythagorica,* or *Philolaica.* (Meta. A5, 986a3; DK 58B.4)

What Kahn is referring to, perhaps rather obliquely, is that "in this peculiar world system" the motion of the planets around the central fire amounted to a *heliocentric theory* of cosmology, a hypothesis that would not be validated until two thousand years later by Copernicus and Kepler. It is perhaps odd that Copernicus names his predecessor as Philolaus the Pythagorean when the Copernican system was originally known as *astronimia **Pythagorica**,* or Philolaica.

Is there some confusion as to whether this astronomical treatise originated with Pythagoras *or* Philolaus? We recall that Philolaus was interested in how mathematics related to the cosmos and was involved in medicine, but he was not a physicist or a scientist, and it stretches the imagination to assume that he could have arrived at the heliocentric theory. It would require a man of universal genius to arrive at the heliocentric theory of the cosmos, when everyone else, for the next two thousand years, still held firm to the belief that the *earth* was the center of the universe. (Parenthetically, there are indications that the ancient Maya were also aware of the heliocentric theory, and that it was symbolically represented in the temple complex of Teotihuacan in Mexico.)

In the end, whether Pythagoras (or his indirect student, Philolaus) was rightly credited as the originator of the heliocentric theory, Copernicus and Kepler traced their sources directly back to Pythagorean doctrines (and not to those of the Pre-Socratics) when scientifically validating the heliocentric theory in the sixteenth century. That crucial fact cannot be disputed.

The Central Fire

Another issue that falls under the rubric of cosmology is that of the mysterious "central fire." The ancients, in trying to understand the origins of the material world, felt that the cosmos had a "center," what came to be called the "central fire." They wanted to locate it in relation to earth, and differing attempts were made to correlate it to the origination of number.

These investigations, praiseworthy as they were, led to vexing assertions and obscure theories. Perhaps the easiest way to approach the *Pythagorean* approach is through Guthrie, bearing in mind that for him Aristotle is his primary authority. First of all Guthrie tells us:

> The most remarkable feature of the Pythagorean cosmology recorded by Aristotle is that it displaced the earth from the center of the universe and made it into a planet circling the center like the others. This idea was unparalleled in pre-Platonic thought;...it was not, however, an anticipation of the heliocentric theory, even if it be right to say with Burnet that "the identification of the central fire with the

sun was a detail in comparison with setting the earth to revolve in an orbit.

Guthrie continues:

> The center of the whole system the Pythagoreans believed to be occupied by a "fire" which we do not see because the side of the earth on which we live is turned away from it. The same system included, along with the sun, moon and other known planets, a "counter-earth" invisible to us for the same reason. The relation of the sun, as a heat and light-giving body, to the central fire is not explained by Aristotle in his extant works, but according to later sources it was a case of reflexion like that of the moon's light from the sun. (*HGP*, vol. 1, 282–83)

Aristotle himself states:

> Concerning the position of the earth, there is some divergence of opinion. Most of those who hold that the whole universe is finite say that it lies at the center, but this is contradicted by the Italian school called Pythagoreans. These affirm that the center is occupied by fire, and that the earth is one of the stars, and creates night and day as it travels in a circle about the center. In addition, they invent another earth, lying opposite our own, which they call by the name of "counter-earth," not seeking accounts and explanations in conformity with the appearances, but trying by violence to bring the appearances in line with accounts and opinions of their own.[25]

Aristotle gives us the most succinct outline of the system. It boils down to the fact that the natural philosophers and scientists believed that the Earth was at the center of a finite universe, while the Pythagoreans had placed the earth as a planet orbiting the central fire. Guthrie notes that the reason we could not see the central fire was "because the side of the earth on which we live is turned away from it." On the other hand he credits the eminent philosopher John Burnet as stating that the identification of the central fire was with the Sun. We note there are three concepts mentioned here. The first is the Pythagorean belief in the heliocentric theory of

---

25 Aristotle, *De Caelo*, 293 a 1.

cosmology; the second concerns the "central fire" and the third involves the "counter-earth."

Speculation about the counter-earth has persisted all the way down to the twenty-first century. Therefore, it is useful to obtain the perspective of Pythagoras on this mystery. As Schuré states:

> The idea of ethereal stars, invisible to us, but forming a part of our solar system and serving as a place of sojourn for happy souls, is often spoken of in the Mysteries and in esoteric tradition. Pythagoras calls it a counterpart of earth, *the antichton* lighted by the central Fire, that is, by divine Light. At the end of his *Phaedo*, Plato describes this spiritual earth at length, although in a disguised manner. (Schuré 336)

Here Schuré is telling us that the counter-earth is not a place on the other side of the earth that we cannot see. It is a non-sensible, ethereal "place" where souls sojourn, which implies they are only there for a time, perhaps until a new transmigration takes place. Pythagoras says this spiritual place, which *we* might equate with a temporary "heaven," is a counterpart to earth and that it is lighted by the central Fire, or the divine Light.

Similar speculation has been rife about the nature and position in the heavens of the mysterious "central fire." As we have seen, John Burnet identified the central fire with the Sun, and Guthrie states that although Aristotle did not explain the relationship of the central fire to the Sun, later sources placed that relation as parallel to the relation of the Sun casting reflective light upon the Moon, meaning that the Sun received its own light from the central fire, or what Pythagoras calls the divine Light. It is worth remembering that this divine Light is also said to light the counter-earth where the souls are sojourning.

There is much to ponder in Schuré's explanation of Pythagorean philosophy, and these issues will be further discussed in the commentary.

Commentary: Two-Principle Theory

The fragments of Philolaus are pivotal regarding the question of whether two material principles are the origin of the cosmos. He was known as an influential Pythagorean teacher in Thebes, was taught by Lysis, a direct disciple of Pythagoras, and included by Schuré as one who carried the principles of his Master to later generations.

These are solid Pythagorean credentials, and yet, according to Kahn, Philolaus would have been exposed to both Ionian natural philosophy and Eleatic ontology (by which we mean Parmenides). "He merged the Unlimited, the starting point of Milesian cosmology, with Limit, equated to Parmenidean Being, by means of the concept of *harmonia*, "bringing diverse and dischordant elements into agreement with one another" (Kahn 25). And Huffman titles his book *Philolaus of Croton: Pythagorean and Pre-Socratic*.

If we consider Philolaus's two principles using the terms Unlimited and Limit from the Pre-Socratic perspective, we surmise that they are meant to apply to our sensible world as originating, material principles. But then Philolaus mystifies us because in Fragment 6, he states that of the things known to us, "it was impossible for any of them to have come into being if there was not already the Being (*esto*) of those things from which the world order is composed: both the limiting and the unlimited." Here, I read Philolaus as implying that the two principles, the limiting and the limited, are *derived from* the ultimate principle, Being. That would be considered a Pythagorean statement, except that Philolaus muddies the waters by substituting the terms Limiting and the Unlimited for Monad and creative Dyad.

Fragment 8a (Syrianus), considered one of the spurious or doubtful fragments, only adds to the confusion: "As a whole these men did not begin from opposites, but recognized what is beyond the two orders of opposites. Witness Philolaus who says that *god established limit and unlimited*. He indicated the whole order that is most related to the one by the [term] limit, and the order opposite to this by the [term] unlimited, and still ranked the cause that is unitary and transcends all things before these two principles." Spurious or not, this is a true Pythagorean cosmological statement.

If, on the other hand, we assume that later in his life Philolaus swerved away from his Pythagorean doctrines and added to them or supplanted them with the more scientific Pre-Socratic inquiries, then his use of the terms Limit and Unlimited is more suspect. As a true Pythagorean it would be impossible for him to hold to the position that the Monad is the starting point of existence while at the same time arguing that the sensible world had two material or quasi-material *originating* sources. To be simplistic, we have a uni-verse. If indeed Philolaus was—or became a Pre-Socratic—we would expect him to use the terms *Limit* and *Unlimited* in that scientific sense, in that they are indeed two *originating, material* principles.

Does this mean that Philolaus was wrong when he ascribed the Limit and Unlimited as the two principles governing our sensible world? Surprisingly, Shure would say that, *in context*, Philolaus is correct, because in fact two principles *do* govern the *manifested* world. What must be taken into account for Pythagoras, however, is that *beyond* those two principles lies the source of them, the unchangeable, eternal and unitary Monad.

The question then becomes: was Philolaus a Pythagorean or Pre-Socratic, or both?

Some of Philolaus's fragments appear to be Pythagorean in allegiance, a few are non-committal and the balance are clearly Pre-Socratic, and this renders Philolaus's allegiance as ambiguous. Since Philolaus was the last link back to Pythagoras, it is essential to understand his interpretation of Unlimited and Limit because if it is Pre-Socratic, it would indicate a breach with Pythagoras. How we view Philolaus may determine whether we accept a transcendental or materialist world view, and incidentally, how we view certain aspects of ancient philosophy.

So far Philolaus turns out to be an ambiguous figure. Some of the Neo-Pythagoreans claim him for the transcendental side of the argument, while a great many of the scientifically-based modern scholars have chosen to view him as one of those who espoused two material principles, the Limit and Unlimited, as originating principles.

What is the explanation? One possibility is that he was forbidden from mentioning some aspects of Pythagorean doctrine because of an oath of silence. And yet crucial fragments reveal he did mention the One beyond limit and unlimited. Another possibility is that indeed he later became a Pre-Socratic, and bought into the scientific and material doctrine that Limit and Unlimited were *originating, material* principles. For me that would mean he had rejected the teachings of Pythagoras. Last, and perhaps more likely, in my opinion, is that later investigators misconstrued his references to Limit and Unlimited as presupposing a Pre-Socratic hypothesis, when in fact he may just as well have subsumed them into the Monad. How we interpret his fragments puts us on the horns of a dilemma; does he reflect a *transcendental* or a *scientific* view of the origin of the cosmos?

Analysis of Two-Principle Theory

Owing to the inconclusive evidence regarding Philolaus's position between Pythagoras and the Pre-Socratics, it is necessary to re-examine that whole hypothesis in greater detail. This scenario is outlined by Kahn (23–29), and we shall follow him closely because what emerges is confusing.

Philolaus has been partly aligned with the Pre-Socratics by Huffman and by Kahn, and the Pre-Socratics sought material answers to the origin of the cosmos—specifically in the four elements: fire, air, water, and earth. The only reference in the fragments of Philolaus to fire is the "central fire."

> There are many ones in the cosmos and the cosmos itself is one (Fr 17). But the *first one* is the central fire. And "the primitive **One**" is not thought of as an abstract entity, but a fiery unit with a *definite position* in the center of the sphere. (Kahn 29)

Note that this does not describe the *element* of fire. So the first observation is that any reference to the four elements of the Pre-Socratics is conspicuously absent. Second, why is it that Pre-Socratics seem to accept the primitive **One** as a first principle, and then argue for the two-principle hypothesis? The crux of the issue is outlined by Kahn:

> The Unlimited (*apeiron*) is of course the starting point from which the world develops in Milesian cosmology. The contrasting notion of the limit (*peras*) is emphasized by Parmenides (Fr. 8.30, 42) as a mark

of the perfection of Being. Thus Philolaus's two principles combine Ionian natural philosophy with Eleatic ontology, and they are *joined together* by means of the concept of harmonia, or consonance.

Since Parmenides refused to recognize the world of becoming, it is possible that Kahn saw Philolaus as the first one to attempt to bridge the chasm between Being and becoming in bringing the two principles, Limit and Unlimited, into consonance. The problem here is that Limit and Unlimited would generally have a *Pre-Socratic* designation and be considered *material* principles. But Kahn is ascribing a material designation to Unlimited, the starting point, the *active* participant of Milesian cosmology, whereas Parmenidean Being, equated with the *receptive* participant, Limit, would traditionally be assigned a *transcendental* designation.

If we allow that the Unlimited is material, and that the contrasting, receptive principle, Limit, equates to transcendental Parmenidean Being, we end up with an unworkable hypothesis, because Parmenides, a rigid metaphysician, rejected the world of becoming or change. For him, all that existed was Being, or "what is." There was no second principle. To him, even the term *Unlimited*, as an originating, *material* principle, would have been completely meaningless. And matter, the Unlimited, would certainly not have taken precedence over Being in any purely transcendental Parmenidean cosmos.

In view of this problem, we must examine the Parmenidean fragment referenced by Kahn where Limit is defined as "emphasizing the mark of the perfection of Being." The fragment is found in *A PreSocratics Reader* (p. 56) edited by Patricia Curd. In the introduction to *Parmenides of Elea*, she states:

> The poem proceeds (in the crucial fragment B8) to explore the features of genuine being: What-is must be whole, complete, unchanging, and one. It can neither come to be nor pass away, nor undergo any qualitative change. Only what-is in this way can be grasped by thought and genuinely known. (Curd 56)

Fragment 8, as said, is dealing with the question of the nature of Being, or what-is. The fragment is approximately two pages long, and it emphasizes that what-is is eternal, unchanging, One. There are only three lines in Fragment 8 that include the world "limit" and two of these are the lines that Kahn references. For example, in line 30, I presume he means to draw attention to the phrase "for mighty Necessity holds it (what-is) in bonds of a limit which holds it in on all sides" but that line can be countered by line 25 that states that what-is is *unchanging* in the limits of great bonds." And line 40 states, "But since the limit is ultimate, it (namely, what-is) is *complete* from all directions."

As Curd points out, Parmenides "apparently rejected the world of sensory experience as unreal," and from the Parmenidean view any mention of limit is ancillary to what-is because what-is *does not undergo any qualitative change*. It cannot, therefore, be a *second receptive principle* to the first principle, the Unlimited, with its material designation. Why? Because Being is "whole, complete, unchanging and one." Therefore, Parmenides would not even entertain the notion that there were two principles, let alone that the one taking precedence was *material*.

In addition, when Kahn states that the Unlimited is the starting point for Milesian cosmology, the inference is overwhelming that the Unlimited is a single principle, and that cosmology flows from that single principle, first into its opposing principle, the Limit, and then further afield. But Kahn's whole argument rests upon the fact that Philolaus is positing *two principles*, the Unlimited and Limit, as originating principles.

Last, In Kahn's case, he specifically connects Milesian natural philosophy with Parmenidean Being, and asserts that these opposing principles were brought into consonance by a cosmic harmonia that was specifically Pythagorean in nature. This would also appear to be an unworkable hypothesis, because the purpose and function of the Pythagorean harmonia that supposedly joined together *Kahn's* two opposing, originating principles of Limit and Unlimited would, in my view, be at variance with the description and cosmic function of the Pythagorean harmonia in *Pythagorean* cosmology.

When Philolaus's fragment declared that the cosmos was fitted together from unlimited and limited things, Kahn assumed that he was referring to Milesian cosmology. But *was* he? Was the use of Unlimited and Limit a specifically PreSocratic designation? The eminent philosopher F. M. Cornford can throw some light on this question. In his book, *Plato and Parmenides*,[1] whose first chapter consists of an analysis of "the earliest Pythagorean cosmology," he states:

---

1   Cornford, *Plato and Parmenides*, 3.

> From first to last, the fundamental distinction between the two main traditions, Ionian and Italian, is that whereas the Ionian sought the nature of things in some kind of matter, the Italian laid stress on the principle of limit or form, which first appears as geometrical shape and number. (Cornford 3)

What this tells me is that the earliest Pythagoreans were *themselves* using the term "limit" and that it was not a term solely assigned to the Pre-Socratics. Therefore, when *Philolaus* was using the terms Unlimited and Limit he *could* have been using them in a Pythagorean sense rather than a Pre Socratic one. And, when the earliest Pythagoreans were using the term "limit" it was not as matter, but as *form*, a form whose structure depended on *geometrical shape and number.*

Another statement from Cornford is illuminating: "A system of the Italian type, seeking the reality of things in form rather than matter, will not take for its starting point an unlimited and 'indiscriminate mass'" (Cornford 5). These two statements highlight the difference between the Pythagorean and Milesian schools.

The materialists have no proper starting point for their philosophical doctrine other than the very vague term the Unlimited, which does not to this researcher appear to be rooted in matter at all, but is, rather, an abstraction. On the other hand, the Pythagoreans, certain of the divine origin of the cosmos, posit the eternal and unchanging Monad as the starting point, and rely on strict mathematical principles of geometry and number to elucidate how the cosmos was generated.

One other point worth bearing in mind is that Guthrie, in examining the *apeiron*, says that for the ancient Greeks, it would have been described as "unorganized chaos." No true metaphysician could accept that the entire structure, order and beauty of the cosmos are, in the end, attributed to "unorganized chaos" since, for them, God created the world, and its structure, order and beauty are evidence of divine handiwork. This view is confirmed by Cornford, above.

And, we must insert into the conversation, even if only momentarily, the fact that these Pre-Socratic and Pythagorean hypotheses are greatly complicated by theories about how number might influence the outcome of this debate on the origin of the cosmos. I have purposely separated the theories of number from the two-principle argument, so that each may be

Commentary: Two-Principle Theory

examined on its own, but I will deal with the crucial question of number under its own heading.

From our analysis it would appear that the Pre-Socratics were not really certain whether the cosmos originated from One principle, a seed, the *apeiron*, the central fire... or from two opposing principles, Unlimited and Limit, where Unlimited appears to take precedence over Limit because it is the starting point of Milesian cosmology and because the contrasting, or second, principle, Being, breathes in the Unlimited.

In the case of Philolaus, the designation of *Limit* and *Unlimited* in a Pythagorean sense shows that he *could* be aligned with Pythagorean cosmology, with the transcendental Monad as starting point and two principles governing the material world. Even if that proved not to be the case, and there *are* other philosophical problems with the fragments from a Pythagorean point of view, I would still conclude that Kahn's hypothesis that Philolaus merged Milesian cosmology with Parmenidean Being appears to be unfounded and unworkable.

Further investigation of the fragments of Philolaus is required if we are to solve that vexing question of whether he was a Pythagorean or a Pre-Socratic. These fragments are conveniently gathered together in Carl A. Huffman's book, *Philolaus of Croton: Pythagorean and Pre-Socratic*, in which he has analyzed them in depth. In reviewing those fragments myself, I concluded that there are some that can be assigned a Pythagorean correlation, and others that appear not to have any Pythagorean source. The most promising fragments in favor of Pythagoras are the testimonia, mainly on number, especially numbers A7a, A29, A22, A10, A11, A29, and A24. Testimonia A12 and A13 are possibly Pythagorean. Of the fragments themselves, some of the most important ones appear to have a Pre-Socratic source, including Fragments 1, 2, 3, and 5. Fragments 4, 6, 6a, 13, and 25 *might* be construed as Pythagorean. Fragments 7, 16, 17, 21, and 24 are non-committal. Fragments 8, 8a, 9, 10, 11, 14, 18, 19, 20, 22, 23, and 26 are judged to be Pythagorean. As we can see, the fragments have champions on both sides of the debate. In the case of Philolaus, I pointed out that the terms *Limit* and *Unlimited* were common knowledge to early Pythagoreans and should not necessarily exclude him from aligning with the Pythagoreans.

However, he uses some terms that a Pythagorean would not have used. For example, a Pythagorean would not say, as Philolaus does in Fragment

5, that as well as odd and even, there is also a number "Odd–Even." And I do not think a Pythagorean would be explaining the cosmos by saying that the unlimiteds and limiters were "fitted together." These and other terms scattered throughout the fragments cause one to have doubts as to the Pythagorean allegiance of Philolaus.

Such doubt is problematic when one bears in mind that Philolaus had the great privilege of being taught by Lysis, a direct disciple of Pythagoras. And one would therefore imagine that Philolaus, of all people, would have been privy to the most accurate knowledge handed down from the Master. In reviewing the fragments of Philolaus, and after much soul-searching on this issue, I find that it would be more accurate a designation to place him with the Pre-Socratics. Obviously, Pythagorean principles are found in the fragments, but one gets the sense that Philolaus moved toward the Pre-Socratics, although he complicated even that endeavor by applying a Pythagorean harmonia to a Pre-Socratic definition of Limit and Unlimited.

But to return to Huffman, I would like to offer a slightly different take on his explication of limiters and Unlimited in part 2, page 37 of his book. I start from Guthrie commenting on Aristotle's understanding of the Unlimited, the *apeiron*:

> The first unit consisted of a seed, the seed of the world...and...the unit is to be understood as both a number and the nucleus of the physical world.... How the unit-seed was sown in the Unlimited we know no more than Aristotle. Once there, it grew by drawing in the Unlimited outside it and assimilating it, that is conforming it to limit and giving it numerical structure. The physical side of this process [which mathematically considered is the generation of the number series] resembles breathing, the Unlimited being called pneuma as well as *kenon* [emptiness, void]. (Guthrie *HGP,* vol. I, 278)

Guthrie has already explained that the *apeiron* was considered a particularly tenuous form of matter. He has now added that Aristotle has no idea of the *origin,* the *apeiron,* this "seed" of the cosmos, or how it appeared in the Unlimited. Going back to Kahn's description of the *apeiron* as the starting point of Milesian cosmology, we find that curious ambiguity and ambivalence in the ancient philosophers about the One, the Primitive One, which is often equated with the central fire, but where cosmology is interpreted as involving *two* originating, opposing principles, the Unlimited and Limit.

Speculating on this, let's assume that the Unlimited is everything that exists "beyond" the cosmos, seen either as outside it, or above it, or just beyond it. In my view, those things that Huffman calls unlimiteds—time, the void, and sound would be defined differently—i.e., as precisely the things that *distinguish* the emerging cosmos from the Unlimited. Thus time structures our world and allows us to reduce the Unlimited to discrete, knowable moments. Time is therefore a fundamental limit on the Unlimited. Similarly, void, if equated with space, it is what makes it possible for us to define the discrete objects in the three-dimensional world. Thus space is seen as another, primary and fundamental limit on the Unlimited. Third, sound, interestingly enough, is described in the New Testament as the first principle to manifest the cosmos. "In the beginning was the Word, and the Word was with God, and the Word was God" (John 1:1). A similar designation for sound is found in Hinduism, where the sacred word, Om, is considered the source of the cosmos and contains all other syllables and words within it.

But in the case before us, sound is something that emerges out of the silence of the Unlimited. Sound, *as the harmonia*, is what orders the vague continuum of the Unlimited into distinct melodies and harmonies. Mathematics is the ordering principle of music, and the foundation of music is made up of numerical intervals that, if placed in the correct ratios, produce harmonious sounds amenable to the sense of hearing. In essence, we can view time, the void and sound as fundamental ordering principles, each of which determines its specific kind of limit on the Unlimited, and therefore contributes to the emerging cosmic structure.

Huffman says that limiters and limited are a natural pair. Perhaps they form an *original* pair that was "fitted together" and perhaps all the other "fittings together" depend on that original pair. On the other hand, perhaps the Unlimited is the starting point for Milesian cosmology and is, after all, designated as the One or the Primitive One. If there was originally a single principle, was it the central fire or the *apeiron*, the "seed" sown into the Unlimited? From what source would a *second* principle be generated? Another seed thrown into the Limit? Or, might it be engendered by the *apeiron* itself? Perhaps the "seed" is symbolic of an embryo in a mother's womb, who is assimilating many kinds of energies, including food and breath from the mother. This would indicate that the "seed" was being nourished into existence by the Unlimited, what has no real form or discrete designation, and about which one cannot really speak. The notion of the "seed" as a material principle is a mystery.

What we do know about the Limit and Unlimited as a natural pair is that they are opposing in nature and require a concept of harmonia, an ordering principle whose being is defined as harmony. Without the principle of harmonia, those opposing principles might *not* be "fitted together" and a world might *not* emerge. One other problem surfaces here, indicated in Fragment 17, which states, "The first thing fitted together, the one in the center of the sphere, is called the hearth." How does one resolve that the opposing principles, limiters and limiteds, are the *originating* principles that need to be joined by the harmonia, when at the same time it is said that the first thing fitted together is the hearth in the center of the sphere?

Leaving these questions aside, questions for which materialists owe an explanation, let us follow Huffman as he turns back to the Pre-Socratics in order to discover the *origin* of Limit and Unlimited. He states:

> Anaximander is famous for positing the unlimited as the starting point from which the cosmos arose. It is not completely clear what Anaximander meant by unlimited, but it appears to be *a limitless expanse of indeterminate nature*... out of which emerge the basic elements which constitute our world. He seems to have laid particular emphasis on the opposites, such as hot and cold and dry and wet, as emerging from the unlimited, and pictures the world as arising in part out of the balanced conflict of opposites, although it is doubtful that he had a clearly defined set of elements. The opposition between limited and unlimited could be seen in the contrast between the unlimited and the distinct things which emerge from it. (Huffman 50)

I have often pondered when reading the Pre-Socratics that it is hard to tell whether they inhabit a transcendental world or the material world they are trying to define. And, in a way, Anaximander is a perfect expression of that ancient ambiguity of how things came-to-be.

I would like to paint for you a similar picture, which includes most of the elements mentioned in Anaximander, but it represents the cosmology of Pythagoras. Before the cosmos came into being, the transcendental Monad existed, eternal, changeless and one. For the sake of argument let's equate the Monad with the "limitless expanse of indeterminate nature." The starting point of the cosmos occurs when the Monad, or "limitless expanse of indeterminate nature" projects itself into its feminine and temporal side, the creative Dyad, who creates the world. This act of initial projection creates the duality of eternal and temporal, male and female, light and dark, and the rest of the primary dualities. The union or relation between these two faculties or principles creates a third faculty that equates with the harmonia, with its musical intervals and numerical ratios, and it is the ordering principle of the harmonia that *actualizes* the manifestation of the material cosmos. Thus the manifold relations that obtain among these three divine principles help to bring about the four elements as well as all the discrete objects in the material world.

Although this is a vast simplification, Anaximander and Pythagoras start with the Form-less or the "limitless expanse of indeterminate nature," from which emerge the opposites, and from them, eventually, the four elements and then the discrete objects of the material world. As Anaximander says, the opposition between Limit and Unlimited can be seen in the contrast between the Unlimited and the *distinct things* that emerge from it. And I think Pythagoras would agree. The way Anaximander and Pythagoras conceive of cosmology is somewhat similar. Of course, they differ in that Pythagoras ascribes a transcendental origin to the Monad, and Anaximander probably ascribes a material origin to Unlimited. Given the vagueness of the term, that, however, is not certain.

Aristotle—Commentary

Let us start by noting that for almost all modern scholars investigating ancient philosophy, including Guthrie, Ross, Kahn, Huffman, and a host of others—Aristotle is clearly the primary authority. Second, Aristotle was the first Greek thinker who systematized scientific knowledge—of *all* known disciplines. His learning was prodigious, and he can rightly be called the first scientist in the modern, western interpretation of the term. As a biographical note, it is important to bear in mind that Aristotle spent twenty years under Plato's tutelage at the Academy, and then totally jettisoned Plato's metaphysical doctrines in favor of his own science. As we know, opposition of Plato's Ideal Forms finds its most vigorous opponent in Aristotle!

It will not come as a surprise, then, to know that Aristotle rejected similar doctrines found in the Pythagoreans. In fact, it is instructive to be reminded of Aristotle's *interpretation* of Pythagorean doctrine. He states:

> They hold that the elements of number are the even and the odd, and that of these the latter is limited and the former unlimited; and that the One proceeds from both of these (for it is both even and odd) and number from the One; and that the whole heaven, as has been said, is numbers. (*Meta.* 986a 17; McKeon 698)

Aristotle shows by his inclusion of the terms Unlimited and Limited that he is accepting the two-principle theory ascribed by scientists to Philolaus, but we note he has introduced *number*—and conflated odd with Unlimited and even with Limit. We also see he has completely misunderstood or misrepresented the Pythagorean doctrine of originating principles, because the Pythagorean cosmos starts with the eternal and unchanging, transcendental Monad, the *One*, and the relation between the *two* faculties, Monad and creative Dyad, produces a *third* faculty that completes the Divine Triad. In Aristotle's *interpretation* of the Pythagorean cosmos, it originates with *two* opposing *material* principles, the Unlimited and Limit, and the relation or union between them generates a "*One*" that is both even and odd ("the One proceeds from both of these") and asserts that from the "One" come numbers. In this passage Aristotle reveals that he has not only misconstrued the Pythagorean doctrine of how the cosmos came to be, but has actually turned the Pythagorean doctrine upside down, in such a way that it lacks truth and coherence. Since Aristotle's place in western philosophy and science is paramount, it is impossible to gauge how many generations of scholars have accepted his misrepresentation of Pythagorean doctrines of the origin of the cosmos.

Aristotle also appears baffled by the question of being and unity (*Meta.* 1001a 4–12): "Plato and the Pythagoreans maintain that unity and being are not attributes but that those terms correspond to natures, the essence of each being unity itself and being itself." This creates a headache for Aristotle because the notion of essences, being each individual and yet united, makes of unity a plurality, something Aristotle vigorously rejects. The very notion of essences being identical and a unity is seen by Aristotle as inconceivable, something simply not possible within the framework of his four causes.

In our modern era we have only to point to that influential historian W. K. C. Guthrie, as well as W. D. Ross, Charles Kahn and Carl Huffman, as following Aristotle on these matters. One also includes Walter Burkert, who rejected that a religious leader such as Pythagoras had the ability to bring forth a scientific body of doctrines even though Pythagoras was known to have introduced mathematics into Greece, was credited with the Pythagorean theorem, discovered the basic musical intervals that are the foundation of western music, and had formulated a heliocentric theory of cosmology that was validated by Copernicus and Kepler two thousand years later. Guthrie himself accepted the fact that Aristotle's interpretations could not always be relied on, but makes certain allowances for him, as do most other philosophers who hold to the scientific interpretation of things.

Aristotle rejects all metaphysical hypotheses. And his judgment about the Pythagoreans is colored by the fact that nothing can be accepted that does not correspond to his four causes. This view is confirmed by Philip (50-51) as follows:

> Here Aristotle is forcing Pythagorean doctrine into the pattern of his own four causes. In labeling as material cause everything that constituted, or contributed, to the constitution of their universe, he is guilty of over simplification. When he interprets their equation of things or concepts with numbers as an anticipation of definition of essence, he is being arbitrary. But what is important for our present purpose is what he has to say of their material cause. He says that Limited (15–16) [*peperasmenon*—what has been limited] and Unlimited, a pair that has no other "matter" constituting it, is the Pythagorean material cause. But immediately thereafter (18) the pair

is referred to as the One and the Unlimited. So "that which has been limited" is the One.

I concur with Philip in his analysis of Aristotle. His insistence on squeezing metaphysical statements into his own four causes creates a situation where he not only misses the metaphysical meaning, but can lead him to misinterpret or even distort them to the point where all of his metaphysical pronouncements become questionable. In addition, we see in Aristotle the same ambiguity and ambivalence as to whether there were two Pre-Socratic, originating, material principles, or a One that had been limited.

I have already noted that Aristotle appears to have turned the Pythagorean doctrine of originating principles upside down. It is therefore instructive to hear what Guthrie says about Aristotle's understanding of the Unlimited, the *apeiron*. He (Aristotle) says that the "first unit consisted of a seed, the seed of the world...and...the unit is to be understood as both a number and the nucleus of the physical world..." Guthrie continues:

> How the unit-seed was sown in the Unlimited we know no more than Aristotle. Once there, it grew by drawing in the Unlimited outside it and assimilating it, that is, conforming it to limit and giving it numerical structure. The physical side of this process (which mathematically considered is the generation of the number series) resembles breathing, the Unlimited being called *pneuma* as well as *ad kenon* [emptiness, void]. (Guthrie, HOP, vol. 1, 278).

What Guthrie is saying is that Aristotle has no idea of the origin of the "seed" of the *apeiron*, or how it was sown into the Unlimited. In other words, his material analysis of originating principles was based on vague speculation and lacked scientific proof. In addition the statement that "the unit is to be understood as both a number and the nucleus of the physical world" contradicts Aristotle's own judgment that number did not begin with the emergence of the two material principles, Unlimited and Limit, but with the "One" that was the product of their union.

There are quite a number of other references in Aristotle to Pythagorean number and his interpretation of how number relates to the origin of the cosmos. Aristotle's biggest blunder was insisting that for the Pythagoreans the numbers *were* or *were in* all sensible objects in the cosmos, and therefore were to be considered immanent. However, I am deliberately leaving that crucial topic for the section on Number.

For the sake of this analysis, I conclude that Aristotle is squarely on the side of the two-principle, material, and scientific origin of the cosmos, however that may be interpreted. He apparently turned Pythagorean cosmological doctrine upside down, rejected the notion that metaphysical principles could be causes of generation, did not understand the Pythagorean positions on being, unity, and essences, and completely missed the mark when he claimed that for Pythagoreans number—and their cosmos—was strictly immanent, even though he was irritated and baffled by their metaphysical statements to the contrary.

In conclusion, Aristotle's understanding of Pythagorean cosmology is woefully off the mark and, unlike Pythagoras's own doctrine, does not appear to resolve into a coherent system. To be fair, however, Aristotle was operating with a handicap because Pythagorean cosmology was couched in veils of myth, symbol and numbers and because, as Porphyry declares: "the first principles were difficult to comprehend and explain."

Plato Commentary

We will not belabor review of Plato because in the *Republic* he established that, for him, the Good was the single, eternal, unchanging, transcendental principle governing the cosmos. The dialogues up to and including the *Republic* reveal a moral imperative and a metaphysical intention. Even W. D. Ross in his book *Plato's Theory of Ideas* argues that, although Plato's project starts with immanent instantiations of the virtues, his dialogues up to the *Republic* move steadily toward a transcendental interpretation of existence.

I suggested in Part I of this book that in the *Republic*, the Good is Plato's way of speaking about God, whether we refer to God as Being, Nous, the Absolute, or the creator. I pointed out that in the *Republic* Plato distinguishes between the *Good Itself* from the Form of the Good, the latter being what we can discuss using reason. The *Good Itself*, being the transcendental formless principle that *manifest*s the Form of the Good, can only be *experienced* in the moment of divine initiation, because, in that moment, the subject-object relation falls away into the unity of the soul with God.

Only secondarily, and late in his work, namely in the *Timaeus*, does Plato deal with the question of cosmology. And, we may surmise, he may have been reluctant to involve himself in such issues, since he would have known he would be drawn into the great debate about whether transcendental or material principles generate the cosmos. When Plato does tackle the issue of cosmology in the *Timaeus*, many of his statements appear baffling or incomprehensible. It is worth bearing in mind, however, that Plato is advocating *three* principles in the creation of the world (see 168–170). The first of these is God, eternal, transcendental, unitary, and good, who made the world in his own image. The second principle is the corporeal world that is the temporal pattern of the eternal one. Plato here says that God created the soul and diffused her throughout the corporeal universe, stating that, whereas *she* was invisible, the *body* of heaven is *visible*.

Later on in the dialogue Plato tells us that a third principle contributes to creation of the world, the "nurse of all generation." This third principle Plato calls the "mother" but states clearly that she is *formless...wherefore that which is to receive all forms should have no form*" (*Timaeus* 50-e). Note that Plato is advocating for three transcendental principles as originating the cosmos. It is also of interest that Plato mentions those mysterious "triangles" that contribute to the creation of the material world and specifically the four elements. Here we detect a Pythagorean correlation to the Divine Triad that actualizes creation of the cosmos.

When broaching the baffling and incomprehensible doctrines set out in the *Timaeus*, it is worth bearing in mind Schuré's comment that "what our philosophers generally accept as the physics of Pythagoras and Plato is nothing but a figurative description of their secret philosophy" (Schuré 322). Nevertheless, Plato has established that *three* principles govern our cosmos and not the two principles advocated by the scientists and Pre-Socratics.

Commentary: Two-Principle Theory

PYTHAGORAS—COMMENTARY

Pythagoras has forever lived in the shadows of history. Part of the reason for this is the terrible persecution that the Pythagoreans experienced in Southern Italy after the house they were staying in was burnt to the ground, killing the Master and almost all of his students. The other reason is that Pythagoras was a universal genius, at least two thousand years ahead of his time, who was not understood by anyone, least of all his fellow philosophers and scientists. It is true that his works were esoteric and veiled from the public by symbols, by myth, and by numbers, but in my view he stands, along with Leonardo da Vinci, as the greatest universal genius the world has ever seen.

Let us be clear from the outset that Pythagoras posited the eternal, unchanging Monad as the source of our cosmos. He held that the Monad, by self-reflection, manifested the creative Dyad, she who was responsible for creating, and was at the same time the *embodiment* of the temporal, mundane universe. From their union was manifested the "Son," the third divine principle of the Divine Triad from which all creation emerged—from the dimensionless point of the Monad all the way through to the many sensible objects of our world.

There is no question that all of Pythagoras's doctrines trace their source to the transcendental and eternal Monad. And it is equally clear, as we shall see later, that to pigeonhole Pythagoras as one who adopted an immanent position on cosmology is completely without foundation or evidence. This misunderstanding, no doubt, can be traced back to Aristotle's misrepresentations of Pythagoras's doctrines due to his insistence on a scientific explanation of the cosmos, and to his complete misunderstanding of the role of number in Pythagoras. Aristotle, along with Pythagoras's own contemporaries, quite failed to understand the universal genius in his scientific and mathematical discoveries, especially as they applied to cosmology.

Let us, therefore, take a closer look at some of the achievements of Pythagoras, because his scientific and mathematical contributions to world culture are astonishing. He was credited with bringing mathematics to Greece; his name is on the Pythagorean theorem; he was the first to proclaim—twenty-five hundred years ago—that mathematics was the language that explained the *cosmos*, a word, incidentally, which he introduced into Greece. The Pythagoreans are mentioned, even by Aristotle, as *advocating a heliocentric model of cosmology*, a theory judged to be strange at a time when the earth was considered the center of our solar system. The heliocentric theory was finally validated, scientifically, in the sixteenth century by Copernicus and Kepler, who publicly acknowledged their debt to Pythagoras and Philolaus. That theory revolutionized western science and is a watershed moment in western civilization.

In fact, the scholar Jocelyn Godwin states in his article "*Pythagoras and the Pythagoreans*"[2] that Kepler had the "conviction that the keys to understanding the cosmos lay in geometry and harmony. He had read in Pliny and Censorinus that Pythagoras measured the planetary distances according to musical intervals, and even if Kepler had more accurate figures, he trusted the principle."

Kepler's laws of planetary motion opened the path for the discoveries of Isaac Newton (1643–1727), who revisited the story of the hammers and came to a radical conclusion. As had been noticed, the results of Pythagoras's reported experiment were false, for to produce tones in the ratio 12:9:8:6, the weights hung on equal strings would have to be proportioned as the *squares* of those numbers.

But in applying this principle to the heavens, it revealed the law of gravitation—"that the weights of the Planets toward the Sun were reciprocally as the squares of their distances from the Sun." Newton humbly concluded that he had only rediscovered a law that the Pythagoreans had known and concealed in the story of the hammers and the idea of the harmony of the spheres. In the field of optics, Newton made his own quasi-Pythagorean discovery. Through experimentation with sunlight shining through prisms, he found that the colors of the spectrum are related in the same proportions as the tones of the diatonic scale.

Pythagoras is also officially acknowledged as discovering the numerical ratios and musical intervals that became the foundations of western music, and he mystified all by advocating a symbolic correlation between the mathematics of music and the foundational structure of cosmology. From that mathematical cosmology he developed the controversial theory that each planet in our solar system had a vibratory rate that could be

---

2   Magee, ed., *The Cambridge Handbook to Mysticism and Western Esotericism*.

translated into a musical note, and that as the planets came into alignment with one another in various geometrical configurations, the music of the spheres could be heard by one with attuned inner senses.

Pythagoras developed the mysterious Tetrad to symbolize how the cosmos projected itself out from the eternal and changeless Monad, through deeper and deeper dimensions of materiality, until it fully sank into the corporeal world. The deceptively simple diagram of the Tetrad—those ten dots in the shape of a triangle—was to be the subject of endless speculation and so many contradictory theories down through the ages. Many mistook those dots for mere numerals, and one claim was that the dots represented atoms and that the space around them represented the void! There was a multitude of such explanations, all of them incorrect. It was left to the disciples of Pythagoras to reveal that the simple diagram of the Tetrad encapsulated the four major stages of cosmogenesis, each stage of which involved eons of time. Moreover, Pythagoras was well aware of its significance twenty-five hundred years ago.

It was Pythagoras who recognized that mathematics is not only inherent in the structure of the universe, but is also the language of explanation. The latter was not understood until the twentieth century, and perhaps it is best exemplified by the theorem $E=mc^2$, which was announced to the world by the great physicist Albert Einstein. Einstein's theory was another watershed moment in the history of civilization, and though it might have confirmed the exoteric view of Pythagorean mathematical theory, we have not yet collectively understood mathematics in the way Pythagoras did—as a living expression of divine faculties in the world and in man.

In view of these many accomplishments and contributions to world science and culture it is, therefore, somewhat tragic that the misrepresentation and misinterpretation of Pythagoras by Aristotle—blinkered by his four causes and his acrid rejection of metaphysical doctrine—should have been the cause of so much misunderstanding of the genius of Pythagoras through the ages infecting even our own times. To be fair, Aristotle was, and is, preaching to those in attunement with his own scientific and philosophical theories, many of whom still share his disdain of metaphysics.

To what can Pythagoras's genius and his prodigious feats be attributed? It was rooted in his journey to Egypt, where he was guided to study the *science of God,* in the mystery school with the high priests of Memphis. There he learned of the sacred mathematics that was to inform his later work, and there, in Egypt, he labored for twenty-two years to achieve his cherished goal—the mystical initiation that would unify his soul with the One, with the Monad. It is fair to say that when he finally achieved that lofty goal, all of his prodigious works flowed out of that fountain of higher knowledge. And what are the specific manifestations of that higher knowledge?

In the first place, it gave Pythagoras his advanced understanding of cosmology as divine law. It showed him that the Monad, the Absolute, was not a static, lifeless, scientific principle, but a living transcendental *presence* in the creation. He understood that the eternal and unchangeable Monad projected himself into his feminine and temporal counterpart, the creative Dyad who was responsible for creating the corporeal universe. He understood that their union, or relation, was a harmonia with a mathematical structure, such that it became the vehicle not only for the manifestation of the third divine principle, but eventually of the entire manifested universe.

These vast cosmological processes were encapsulated by Pythagoras in the Tetrad in a most unique way because, on the one hand point, line, plane and solid showed the motion of the undifferentiated One into ever deepening levels of dimensionality, and on the other hand it symbolized this differentiation in the four main stages of cosmogenesis, processes that took eons of time to complete. Pythagoras symbolized the mathematical relationship between the cosmic forces in yet another way, and that was through the agency of music, whose intervals Pythagoras discovered to be as strictly mathematical as the cosmic structure itself.

Thus, the greatest discovery of Pythagoras was to reveal that the cosmos has a mathematical structure and explanation, but one that is not merely scientific, lifeless or abstract, but alive with divine energies. This discovery, that the cosmos was explained by mathematics, was completely misunderstood by Aristotle to mean that the objects in the world *consisted* of number, and that therefore number, for Pythagoras, was immanent.

Another great discovery of Pythagoras was that of the heliocentric theory of cosmology that governs our solar system. As Guthrie says, "the most remarkable feature of the Pythagorean cosmology recorded by Aristotle is that it displaced the earth from the centre of the universe and made it into a planet circling the center like the others." Guthrie himself dismissed the idea that Pythagoras had discovered the heliocentric theory over two thousand years ago despite the fact that Copernicus and Kepler had publicly acknowledged their debt to Pythagoras and Philolaus in the sixteenth century.

Two important ancillary hypotheses are entwined with the heliocentric theory, first the notion of the counter-earth, and second the question of the central fire. The counter-earth has been explained in a way that no scientist expected. It was not a sensible body requiring scientific description! Pythagoras described it as an ethereal counterpart to earth where souls sojourned for a time, from which I infer that in time the inhabitants moved on, perhaps to another transmigration.

The other notion, that of the central fire, has definite consequences for ancient cosmology. Pythagoras would have rejected Guthrie's idea that the center of the cosmos was a fire that "we do not see, because the side of the earth on which we live is turned away from it."

Was that considered to be a permanent state of affairs? If so, there would be little hope of ever resolving that issue. In fact, this sounds to me like an example of a Pythagorean statement couched in symbolic terms that was misunderstood by material investigators as scientific fact.

The central fire is perhaps the single most important ancient hypothesis regarding the origination of our cosmos. Even Aristotle records that the Pythagoreans "affirm that the centre is occupied by fire." According to Huffman, the view taken by Philolaus (Fr. 1) is that the world order and everything in the cosmos was "fitted together" by limiters and unlimiteds, and Huffman states that they are plural. The other statement made by Philoaus (Fr. 17) is that the *first* "fitting together" was of the central fire or the "hearth" in the center of the sphere.

The question here is: Which of these concepts is *originating?* If the Unlimited and Limit are two opposing forces that need to be brought into consonance by a harmonia, isn't it necessary for that procedure to be completed before limiters and unlimiteds then set about "fitting together" the central fire in the center of the sphere. Here again the ambiguity surfaces regarding the references to originating principles that are commonly found in scientific and material interpretations of the cosmos. The limiters and unlimited infer two material originating principles, and yet the central fire, so often described as the One, or the Primitive One, is obviously a singular principle. Lurking around the idea that the central fire was "fitted together" inside the sphere is the unspoken notion that the sphere *preceded* the "fitting together" of the central fire at its center. Isn't the sphere also fitted together? And did *its* fitting together precede that of the central fire? These questions have never been resolved, and it leaves the whole question of ancient material descriptions of cosmology under a cloud of confusion. The placement of the earth at the center of the cosmos, the unknown origin of the central fire, the unknown nature of the two opposing originating material principles, the abstruse and vague terms used to describe them, the unknown nature and source of the *apeiron*, the seed, the start of Milesian cosmology, all confirm my doubts.

One problem that cannot be evaded is that if the scientists and natural philosophers place the earth at the center of the cosmos, then the universal fire is *not* at its center, and may be relegated to a place somewhere beyond earth, and possibly even seen as circling it. Since the central fire was primordial, placing the earth at the center of the cosmos presents a problem because the earth and the central fire cannot both be at the center, and the earth is not fire.

To reiterate, even Aristotle accepted that the Pythagoreans displaced the earth from the center and made it into a planet circling the center like the others. The heliocentric theory, despite it possibly being veiled in symbols, confirms that the central fire, even if it is the sun, is the place of authority and focus. Even on a mundane level, without the light and warmth of the sun there would be no life on this planet, and no philosophers to debate its importance.

I would like to present a Pythagorean hypothesis of cosmology. It begins with the eternal Monad, which at the moment of manifestation is described as follows: "At first it is only a brilliant dot, then it opens like a flower, the incandescent center spreading out like a rose of light with a thousand petals" (Schuré 315). This is a far cry from Guthrie's description of the *apeiron* as "unorganized chaos." Note that the transcendental "dot" could well be mistaken for the material "seed" of the universe. That cosmic seed, the dot, contains everything within itself, and there can be nothing in the cosmos that is not inherently a part of it.

If we accept the central fire and the sphere as originating the cosmic processes, which seems reasonable, we would, at the same time, reject the notion that the central fire was "fitted together" in the center of the sphere. However, Pythagoras would say that, after the transcendental Monad, *the sphere is the first manifested "object" of the cosmos*. The sphere *is* the cosmos. What has been projected outward from that dimensionless point is a sphere, the perfect geometric figure—whether interpreted from an ideal or a mundane point of view. The sphere would thus appear to be the first confirmation that mathematics is inherent in the cosmological structure.

Then, to adopt Huffman's terminology, it is possible to argue that the Monad is limited by time (temporality), by space (which allows us to distinguish discrete objects from the "limitless expanse of indeterminate nature"), and by sound, where the harmonia expresses the structure (and therefore a limit) of the emerging universe. For Pythagoras, the cosmos is not "fitted together" as an automaker fits parts together to make a car. Rather, it is projected outward from a transcendental center, and all manifestation results from that ongoing cosmological process toward corporeality.

In the last analysis, my position is that the hypothesis regarding the central fire only makes sense if you place the Sun at the center of the cosmos and adopt the heliocentric theory of Pythagoras. This is true even if, with Burnet, you consider the central fire to be another name for the Sun. As we know today, the Earth *does* orbit the Sun, along with the other planets—as Pythagoras indicated. And on this hypothesis, the inconsistencies of the central fire and that of the "originating" principles of limit and unlimited, and the question of the *apeiron* being seen as "unorganized chaos" are resolved.

However, there is another level to this argument. In the *Republic* Socrates states that as the visible Sun is to the sensible world, so the Good (namely, the *invisible* Sun in the intelligible world) is the cause of all knowledge and truth as far as known. In fact, just as Socrates distinguished the Form of the Good (known by rational discourse) from the Good Itself (which is Formless and only known by mystical experience), so, by inference, the central fire, the invisible Sun is what references the source of the universe, God, or the Pythagorean Monad. Thus, the central fire is not the Sun (the visible, sensible sign) but is the *intelligible* Sun—namely, the *Cosmic Fire, the Monad*. Indeed, it is the central fire, as the Monad, that *creates the universe*. "At first (manifestation) it is only a brilliant dot, then it opens like a flower, the incandescent center spreading out like a rose of light with a thousand petals (Schuré 315).

The Sun has ever been a sign and a referent of the Cosmic Fire, but not always accepted or understood. As Schuré states it:

> From the beginning of civilization, the worship of man was directed to the sun as the source of light, warmth and life. But when the thought of the wise men rose from the phenomenon to cause, they perceived behind this sensitive fire and visible light a non-material fire and an intelligible light. They identified the first with the male principle, with creative spirit, the intellectual essence of the universe, and the second with its female principle, its formative soul, its plastic substance.... It flows in the Vedic hymns under the form of Agni, the universal fire which penetrates everything. It unfolds in the religion of Zoroaster.... In the crypts of Egypt the initiates look for this same Sun under the name Osiris, and in Greece, he is Apollo. He is the Word of the One God who is eternally manifest in the world. (Schuré 288–295)

By revealing the central fire as the Cosmic Light, or the Monad, Pythagoras shows himself to be part of a spiritual/religious tradition that traces its roots back into the mists of antiquity. And in deriving the heliocentric hypothesis to correctly render the Earth's relation *orbiting* the *symbol* of the central fire, namely the Sun, Pythagoras shows himself, once again, to be two thousand years ahead of his time.

One last surprising—and unexpected—finding in the cosmology of Pythagoras is the central importance that he assigned to the threefold law. We might have been debating the pros and cons of the two-principle material theory vs. the unitary transcendental theory, but as Pythagoras makes clear:

> The real world is threefold. Man is composed of three elements, distinct yet blended into one another: body, soul and spirit. The universe likewise is divided into three concentric spheres: the natural world, the human world, and the divine world. The Triad of the threefold law, therefore, is the essential law of things and the actual key to life.... For this law is found at all stages of the ladder of life, from the constitution of the organic cell (all the way through)...the constitution of man, universe and God.

In the end Pythagoras was, surprisingly, more closely aligned with Christianity, Buddhism, and Hinduism when he advocated that the "three-fold law" governed existence. For the Christians it was God the Father, God the Son, and God the Holy Ghost (a suppressed form of the Mother); in Buddhism it was the One, the Two, and the relation between them that makes Three. For the Hindus, it was Brahman, the Absolute, who has three faces: Brahma, the creator; Vishnu, the sustainer; and Shiva, the destroyer. In the case of Pythagoras it was the Monad, the creative Dyad, and the divine third faculty, the Son, who represented God in Three Persons in the culture of Greece. In the end Pythagoras may surprise the scientists by turning out to be one of the greatest exponents of Monism the western world has ever known.

Conclusions: Two-Principle Theory

The question asked at the beginning of this section was: Did Pythagoras posit two ultimate, *material* principles? The reason for this particular question is now clear. It separates those who maintain the two-principle, scientific and material theory from others who hold to the unitary, transcendental doctrine. We have also asked this question to reveal where Philolaus's allegiances lay. Was it with the Pythagoreans, as might have been expected, or with the Pre-Socratics.

We have no trouble aligning Aristotle to the two-principle theory because he is a scientist who rejects the notion that the material cosmos could have a transcendental source. He also rejects Plato's ideal, intelligible objects, the Forms, and rejects anything Pythagorean that hints at the transcendental. We have no trouble assigning Plato to the unitary, transcendental theory, because as even Aristotle admits, Plato separated out sensible objects from intelligible, transcendental ones.

The conclusions regarding Philolaus and Pythagoras may be more surprising. Those who may initially have believed Philolaus to be a Pythagorean have been exposed to evidence in the fragments, not made fully available until 1993 by Huffman, that might challenge their initial suppositions. In reviewing these fragments for myself, I came to the conclusion that Philolaus started out as a Pythagorean but later on swerved his allegiances to Pre-Socratic lines of inquiry. Therefore, I have moved him from the transcendental camp and into alignment with the Pre-Socratics and others who accepted the scientific version of the two-principle theory of cosmology.

However, unlike Kahn, I do not see Philolaus as a Pythagorean *and* a Pre-Socratic, and unlike Huffman I do not agree that Philolaus had no debt to Pythagoras. In my view Pythagorean and Pre-Socratic doctrines are incompatible. The fact that Philolaus tore the Pythagorean harmonia out of its transcendental structure and attempted to apply it to Milesian cosmology and Parmenidean Being does not give him Pythagorean credentials on this issue, because the function of the real Pythagorean harmonia—to *actualize* the material cosmos—has been jettisoned in favor of "fitting together" the opposing principles of Unlimited and Limit. At best, I hold that Philolaus was earlier a Pythagorean, and later, a Pre-Socratic.

The case of Pythagoras may be the one that is most surprising, especially to the scientists. From the time of Aristotle onward, the philosophers, historians and scientists have been led to understand that Pythagoras posited everything *was* numbers. And, in conveniently rejecting obvious transcendental doctrine that he either did not understand, or totally misinterpreted, Aristotle has influenced countless generations of scholars to pigeonhole Pythagoras as a philosopher whose main doctrine was immanence. But, those investigators failed to appreciate the fact that he spent twenty-two years studying sacred mathematics with the priests in the temple of Memphis, and that all of Pythagoras's prodigious knowledge and works flowed out of the *experience* of the transcendental source of our cosmos. Therefore, in my view, Pythagoras should be moved squarely into the transcendental camp.

One last point. We have been reviewing the opposition between a unitary theory and a two-principle theory of cosmology. However, it is worth bearing in mind that Pythagoras essentially advocates for a *threefold law* to life, one that applies throughout the cosmos, but in different ways, to the natural world, the human world, and the divine world. And although he may have been obscure and arcane in the *Timaeus*, Plato follows Pythagoras in advocating for that same threefold law, which since time immemorial has represented God in three Persons.

Number as It relates to Monad vs. Unlimited/Limit

In the previous section we dealt with the question of whether one or two principles are the ultimate, originating principles of the cosmos. The One is the Pythagorean Monad, an eternal, transcendent, and unitary principle, and the Unlimited/Limit are considered to be two material principles governing the cosmos.

Therein lies the importance of this debate. It deals with the age-old controversy as to whether the cosmos has a transcendent or a material source. Contributing substantially to the debate are: a) Philolaus's fragments on number; and b) Aristotle's interpretation of them.

Although these two positions were analyzed in the previous section, it was also stated that the question of number would be deliberately postponed from that debate in order to tackle each strand of the argument on its own. Now that we have laid out the positions on the side of the Monad and Unlimited/Limit, the inclusion of number is crucial because number inheres in the very structure of the argument regarding originating principles.

How are we to define the *relation* of Unlimited and Limit? Are we going to subsume them *upward* into the single transcendent principle, the Monad, or are we going to claim that Unlimited and Limit are ultimate, *material* principles? And will we therefore posit that their relation *downward* generates an offspring, what Aristotle calls a "*One*"? There are champions for each side.

Let us simply lay out the positions on this issue by Philolaus, Aristotle, Plato and Pythagoras, understanding that the scientists will not be persuaded by the metaphysicians, and vice versa.

Philolaus

Philolaus has so far been ambiguous. Huffman suggests that he was not a professional mathematician, but was convinced that mathematics played a crucial role in interpreting the physical world. Fragment 5 is important. It states: "Number, indeed, has two proper kinds, odd and even, and a third from both mixed together, the even-odd" (Huffman 178).

This single fragment appears to take the view (supported by Aristotle) that the Unlimited and Limit are two material originating principles and that odd and even generate the "even-odd" or the Aristotelian "One." Fragment 4 states that all things are known to have number.

However, Kahn had explained that Philolaus's two originating principles, the Unlimited and Limit, combined Ionian natural philosophy with Eleatic ontology and that they were joined together by means of the concept of *harmonia*, or consonance... but that Philolaus gave it "an unprecedented, specifically *Pythagorean* development in terms of numerical ratios and musical scales" (Kahn 24).

The first consonance, the scale, one octave long, is called precisely by this name, *harmonia*; it corresponds to the ratio 2:1. The other two consonances, the fifth (3:2) and the fourth (4:3), are also specified by Philolaus in Fragment 6a. Now if we add these four integers together, their sum is the number that according to Aristotle (*Meta.* A5, 986 a8) the Pythagoreans regard as perfect: 1+2+3+4=10 (Kahn 25).

Philolaus once again lives up to his reputation for ambiguity, because the harmonia that supposedly connects Milesian natural philosophy and Eleatic ontology is the *Pythagorean* harmonia. I took the position in the prior section that it was impossible for a rigid metaphysician such as Parmenides to accept Being as the second principle, the receptive principle, which breathes in the Unlimited, a Pre-Socratic term for the start of Milesian cosmology, because the Unlimited is *material* in origin and Being is *transcendental*. For a metaphysician, matter *cannot* precede Being.

It is also impossible to apply the *Pythagorean* harmonia to bring Limit and Unlimited into consonance for the same reason—namely, that the Pythagorean harmonia has a *transcendental* source and function. The Pythagorean harmonia would, in Philolaus's theory, be applied to the Unlimited, a material principle, and Second to Being, a transcendental principle. Since the Pythagorean harmonia has its own mathematical and musical structure, it cannot be torn from its transcendental structure and applied to a hybrid consonance between two opposing, Pre-Socratic schools of thought. In my view, the entire theory is unworkable.

Let us bear in mind that the purpose of Philolaus's harmonia is to bring into consonance two otherwise opposing principles, the Unlimited and Limit. On the other hand, the Pythagorean harmonia has a quite different purpose and *function* from that of Philolaus. This question can only be decided when Pythagoras's harmonia is described from a *Pythagorean* point of view, and when its structure is applied to its function. This will be done in the section on Pythagoras. In the meantime, Philolaus's position outlined in Fragment 5 (where he says that number has two proper kinds, odd and even, and a third from both mixed together, the even-odd) would appear to contradict his explanation of the Pythagorean *harmonia* detailed by Kahn (24), again because the Pythagorean harmonia is transcendental in origin. Once again, the ambiguity surfaces as to whether he is a Pythagorean, or, later in life, he adopted other Pre-Socratic doctrines. Unless we take the harmonia *of Philolaus as advocating the same purpose and function as Pythagoras's harmonia* with its musical and metaphysical interpretation of the cosmos, we will have to conclude that Philolaus is not a Pythagorean in determining the role of the harmonia as it applies to the Monad -vs- Unlimited/Limit argument.

Aristotle on Number

The main areas where Aristotle shows an interest in Pythagorean number are: 1) his *interpretation* of Pythagorean originating principles of the cosmos; 2) his interpretation of how Pythagoreans differ from Plato regarding number; 3) how Pythagoreans and Plato derive generation from eternal things; and 4) his judgment that Pythagoreans mistook numbers for magnitudes.

Before embarking on our investigation it is instructive to recall from Huffman that Aristotle had "considerable information" on and had written a treatise "devoted exclusively to the Pythagoreans." Huffman also makes the point that it was Philolaus who was the primary source for Aristotle's information on the Pythagoreans. In addition, since Aristotle had spent twenty years studying at Plato's Academy, he was well aware of the ideal and mundane application of number. Nevertheless, Aristotle's well-known interpretation of how the Pythagoreans construe number is as follows:

> They hold that the elements of number are the even and the odd, and that of these the latter is limited, and the former unlimited; and that the One proceeds from both of these (for it is both even and odd) and number from the One; and that the whole heaven, as has been said, is numbers. (*Meta.* 1, ch. 5, 986a 17–20)

Even if he derived most of his knowledge about the Pythagoreans from Philolaus, Aristotle must still be held responsible for his own misrepresentations and judgments against them.

There are four crucial judgments made by Aristotle in this one statement, each of which are in direct contradiction to the cosmology of Pythagoras.

> First, he calls the even and odd the elements of number. And he conflates the notion of these *elements* of number with the originating material principles of the cosmos, the Unlimited and Limit. As he states it, *the even is unlimited and the odd is limited*.
> Second, from the harmonizing of these opposing principles of Even and Odd (Limited and Unlimited), Aristotle claims there proceeds a "One" that combines both—i.e., is "Odd–Even."
> Third, Aristotle asserts that (for the Pythagoreans) number *proceeds from* the "One."
> Fourth, he adds that the "whole of heaven *is* number."

First, Aristotle's *interpretation* of Pythagorean cosmology starts with the two opposing principles, Unlimited and Limit, and conflates them with the elements of number, the Even and the Odd. Why Aristotle arrived at such a conflation is a mystery because there is no evidence in the fragments of Philolaus to support such a claim. As Huffman tells us, for Philolaus the *Unlimited and Limit* were the originating principles.

In making this conflation, however, Aristotle has equated Unlimited with Even and Limit with Odd. While he asserts that Even and Odd are elements of number, he omits giving these originating principles "Even–Odd" any specific values or designations. For me, lurking in the background is the notion that Aristotle consciously or unconsciously has already *inferred* numbers in describing the Even and Odd (Unlimited/

Number as It relates to Monad vs. Unlimited/Limit

Limit) but has not *specified* them or perhaps even *recognized* them as such. (This position is complicated by Aristotle's suggestion that "the first unit consisted of a seed, the seed of the world...(and)...that the unit is to be understood as both a number and the nucleus of the physical world" (Guthrie *HGP*, vol. 1, 278). Parenthetically, if you posit that Even and Odd are solely *elements* of number—i.e., preceding any specific number—I wonder if you have turned the elements of number into *intelligible* objects because they are not recognized until an object in the natural world instantiates them. Even for Plato, the form of Courage must have an instantiation in the sensible world.

Second, Aristotle makes the statement that the "One" proceeds from both of these—i.e., *proceeds from* Even (Unlimited) and Odd (Limit). Notice that Aristotle's "One" is not the *harmonia* mentioned by Philolaus, which brings the two opposing forces into consonance through the use of mathematical, and musical, relationship. For Aristotle, it is a *product* of their union. The "One" thereby contains both principles (Unlimited and Limit), but it also contains the elements of numbers Even and Odd. If we pursue our notion that Aristotle *infers* that the elements of number have specific values, we come to the conclusion that Even = 1, and Odd = 2, because the *apeiron,* the Unlimited, is specified, by some, as the first principle, the start of Milesian cosmology.

What proceeds from them should be a *third* principle, not a "One" that Aristotle judges to *contains all things, including all numbers.* Note that Aristotle's "One" *is not an originating principle,* but is derived from the union of Even and Odd (Unlimited and Limit), two opposing principles that have no apparent source. It would seem impossible that from unknown, opposing forces (even if Aristotle terms them as Unlimited and Limit—designations that are abstruse and vague) he can justify his assertion that the product of their union contains a "One" that contains Unlimited and Limit, Even and Odd *and all things including number.* Aristotle's "One," then, appears to be a hybrid, a distortion of the cosmology of Pythagoras.

If you claim the opposing forces of Even and Odd (Unlimited/Limit) did create the *"One,"* that is to infer that numbers were already inherent in those opposing forces, not just as abstract elements of Even and Odd, but as specific values of 1 and 2. Why? Because in the first place even Philolaus has referred to the *two opposing principles,* the Unlimited and

Limit, as the originating (material) principles of the cosmos. Second, the "One" *contains* Even and Odd, and they had to have a source. That source would be the *two* opposing principles of Unlimited and Limit. And if you claim these opposing forces did not contain number, then number cannot exist because number cannot appear, willy-nilly, in the "One" without reference to a source.

Even if Aristotle has not already inferred numbers 1 and 2 in describing Even and Odd (Unlimited and Limit), he cannot assert that that number *proceeds from* the "One." Since Aristotle's "One" is a *product* of the union of Even and Odd (Unlimited and Limit), it is impossible for number to originate with the "One" and at the same time have its source in Unlimited and Limit, the two originating principles of Philolaus.

Third, Aristotle's assumption that "number [proceeds from] the 'One,'" implies that since the "One" contains all within it, all numbers are derived from it. Again this turns the cosmology of Pythagoras upside down since even for Philolaus, numbers—namely, musical intervals—*constitute* the Pythagorean *harmonia* that brings the opposing principles of Unlimited and Limit into consonance. In addition, because number is fundamental for the Pythagorean understanding of the cosmos, number must proceed from *original* principles, not their "offspring," namely not from Aristotle's "One."

Fourth, Aristotle says that for Pythagoreans "the whole heaven, as has been said, *is* number." We know that Aristotle has claimed that number proceeds from the "One," but here Aristotle is making his famous charge against the Pythagoreans, namely that they construed the cosmos and the "whole heaven" *as* number.

As Huffman points out (54-57), Aristotle makes these charges in a number of places. He states that for Pythagoreans "all things *are* numbers" or they "*make*" or construct the world order "*out of*" numbers, or things "*resemble*" numbers or "*imitate*" numbers. I join Huffman and others who suggest that in making these charges Aristotle was not reflecting Pythagorean beliefs, but *his own (incorrect) interpretation* and judgment of them. As Huffman points out, the fragments of Philolaus do not state that all things are numbers, but "rather that all things that are known are known *through number*" (Huffman 56). As is quite clear today, Aristotle's judgments about number constitute a major misreading of Pythagorean

Number as It relates to Monad vs. Unlimited/Limit

mathematics, one that will skew most, if not all, of Aristotle's charges against Plato and the Pythagoreans. For example, Aristotle compares Pythagorean number with that in Plato:

> [It is Plato's] view that Numbers exist apart from sensible things, while *they* (the Pythagoreans) say that *things themselves* are Numbers, and do not place the objects of mathematics *between* Forms and sensible things. (*Meta.* 987 b 24–30)

Compare this to the following comment by Aristotle:

> In this respect [in denying that numbers have an existence separate from things], the Pythagoreans are in no way at fault, but when they construct physical bodies out of number—things which possess lightness and weight out of elements which possess neither—they appear to be talking about some other universe and other bodies, not those that we perceive. (Guthrie *HGP,* vol. 1, 235)

In the first comment Aristotle is interpreting the Pythagoreans to say that "things themselves" are numbers where Aristotle means sensible things, immanent things. (Note the ambiguity. It could have an ideal interpretation.) In the second comment Aristotle is baffled because on the one hand the Pythagoreans seem to deny numbers have an existence apart from material objects, but on the other hand he claims they construct physical bodies *out of number,* meaning they construct physical things that have lightness and weight out of elements, number, which have neither. In this particular case he is accusing the Pythagoreans of being confused when it comes to number. This is the reason why Aristotle is baffled. He can never understand the real principles upon which the Pythagoreans operate, and he is further hampered by his insistence in reducing all generation to his four causes. The Pythagoreans, in Aristotle's view, simply refuse to submit to his scientific will.

Two other statements will serve to highlight Aristotle's bafflement at the Pythagoreans:

> The Pythagoreans...denial that number has separate existence removes many impossibilities but the statement that bodies are composed of numbers and that this refers to mathematical number, is incredible. It is false to say that there are indivisible magnitudes, and

even if there were, units do not have magnitude. And how could a magnitude consist of indivisibles? But *arithmetical number is monadic* (consists of incorporeal units). They on the other hand identify real things with number. At any rate they apply their speculations to bodies as if they consisted of numbers of this kind. (*HGP*, vol. 1, 235)

Compare that comment to the following:

The Pythagoreans also [as well as Speusippus] recognize a single type of number, but not as apart from sensible things [which was the view of the Platonists in general] which they regard as being composed of it. They (the Pythagoreans) in fact construct the whole universe out of numbers, not however truly monadic numbers (i.e., incorporeal unextended numbers), for they suppose the units to possess magnitude. (*Meta* 1080 b 16).

Guthrie explains: "The notion of incorporeal reality was not yet grasped by the Pythagoreans or any of their contemporaries" (Guthrie *HGP*, vol. 1, 234).

In the first comment Aristotle is in conflict with the notion that for the Pythagoreans bodies are composed of number, and that number refers to mathematical number (i.e., incorporeal and unextended), a situation he says is incredible, and in the second comment he contradicts himself by saying that the Pythagoreans composed the whole universe out of number, but *not out of monadic numbers* (incorporeal, unextended) but units with magnitude.

Guthrie adds qualifying commentary of his own as follows: "Obviously number, whether thought of arithmetically, geometrically, or as manifested in musical intervals, is a formal component: hence Aristotle's chief complaint against the Pythagoreans is that they confused formal and material causes. More specifically they imagined that physical bodies could be constructed out of what were in fact abstractions, or as he put it still more concretely, things with weight out of what has no weight" (Guthrie *HGP*, vol. 1, 236-237).

Aristotle seems unaware of the confusion or contradictions in his own thinking. When analyzing the issue of being and unity, he aligns the Pythagoreans and Plato together on the side of transcendence. But when dealing with the question of number, he aligns Plato with transcendence (and rejects the Forms) and aligns the Pythagoreans as holding that numbers are immanent—are *in* or *constitute* sensibles in the corporeal world.

This problem is further highlighted:

> Regarding the question of essence they [the Pythagoreans] began to make statements and definitions, but treated the matter too simply. For they defined both superficially, and thought that the first subject of which a given definition was predicable was the substance of the thing defined, as if one supposed that "double" and "2" were the same, because 2 is the first thing of which "double" is predicable. But surely, to be double and to be 2 are not the same; if they are, one thing will be many—a consequence which they actually drew. (*Meta.* 987 a20-25; McKeon 700)

Despite his insistence that for the Pythagoreans number was immanent, Aristotle can still assert the following: "It is indeed impossible to erect a theory ascribing coming-to-be (genesis) to eternal things. Yet without a doubt the Pythagoreans do so."

Aristotle also wonders how the Pythagoreans understand the thesis that number and its modifications are the causes of things that come to be in the universe... *when there exists no number other than that out of which the universe was framed.*

As Guthrie observes, Aristotle expressed great bafflement and irritation at the notion of the Pythagoreans ascribing magnitude to numbers, but W. D. Ross quotes that the Pythagoreans did not reduce reality to an abstraction, but failed to recognize the abstract nature of numbers (*HGP*, vol. 1, 240-242). In my view this conclusion by Ross does not hold weight if we bear in mind that Pythagoras had studied sacred mathematics for twenty-two years in the temples of Egypt, and therefore, he, more than most human beings, understood *the ideal* and transcendental nature of number.

Be that as it may, an illuminating fact from Guthrie regarding number is that the ancient Greeks commonly ascribed to number both mundane *and* ideal designations. How is it that Aristotle did not take that fact into consideration when making his judgments against the Pythagoreans? Could it be that he simply *rejected* number as ideal in the same way he had rejected Plato's Forms? Given the facts, that seems a reasonable assumption.

Number in Plato

Since the references to number in Plato are few, and in some instances arcane, I will not dwell on his particular contribution, except to highlight that he referred to the Odd and Even as the Forms of number, and some have said that Plato places mathematicals in between the Forms and the sensible world. Given that Plato emulates a great deal of Pythagorean doctrine, my view is that Plato would have seen Number as a transcendental Form and, following Pythagoras, as part of the mathematical structure of the cosmos.

In speaking of the relation between God (eternal) and the corporeal cosmos (temporal), Plato states that it is the principle of *proportion* that effects such a union. And, Plato subscribes to the notion that three divine principles bring about the creation of the cosmos. He also states that when there are any three numbers, whether cube or square, there is a *proportion* between them that he calls the mean, and that "God placed water and air in the mean between fire and earth, and made them to have the same proportion as far as possible" (*Timaeus* 32-c).

In the *Timaeus* Plato also refers to those mysterious *triangles,* and says of them that "we assume (them) to be the original elements of fire and other bodies, but the principles which are prior to these God only knows" (*Timaeus* 53-c-e). These are obvious references to Pythagorean doctrine, but in my view, many of the baffling statements in the *Timaeus* can be put down to the fact that Plato, like Pythagoras, concealed secret or esoteric knowledge from the general public. As Schuré says, "what our philosophers generally accept as the physics of Pythagoras and Plato is nothing but a figurative description of their secret philosophy" (Schuré 322).

Number in Pythagoras's Cosmology

In his own lifetime Pythagoras was known by his contemporaries as a man of prodigious learning, a man of knowledge without a peer. In my view the best analogy would be to a universal genius such as Leonardo da Vinci, whose accomplishments in every field still astonish us because the advances the modern world has made in science, mathematics and technology all find evidence in his prophetic vision.

In the case of Pythagoras, his scientific and mathematical theories were so little understood in his own time that it was not until the twentieth century that Albert Einstein's famous equation, $E=mc^2$, showed all the world that *mathematics* was *indeed* the language that interpreted the universe. But Pythagoras's mathematics was not an abstract language. It was, as Schuré tells us, a symbolic representation of cosmic forces that were "hard to comprehend."

> His sacred mathematics or science of principles was both transcendent and more alive than the secular mathematics known to our modern scientists and philosophers. Number was not considered an abstract quantity, but an intrinsic and living virtue of the supreme One, of God, the Source of universal harmony. The science of *numbers* was that of the living forces of divine faculties in action in the world and in man, in macrocosm and microcosm. (Schuré 311)

How were numbers and the Tetrad related to the cosmology of Pythagoras? In brief, Schuré has shown that numbers were a *mode of representation,* and that what they represented were the divine faculties. And he has stated that numbers, mathematics, are an *integral aspect* of the divine, and that they represent divine principles governing the cosmos. If mathematics can explain the universe, then mathematics is *inherent* in the universe.

> The cosmos of Pythagoras has at its heart the Monad, God, the Source of all. Pythagoras called this the first One, composed of harmony, the Male Fire, which passes through everything, the Spirit which moves by itself, the Indivisible, great non-manifest, the Unique, the Eternal, the Unchangeable hidden under the many things which pass away and change.... At first it is only a brilliant dot, then it opens like a flower, the incandescent center spreading out like a rose of light with a thousand petals. (Schuré 315)

The creation of the material world required that the Monad project itself outward from its eternal repose toward matter. This was accomplished by the Monad bringing forth *from Himself* a divine faculty that would be opposite and equal to him, the creative Dyad, the Second divine faculty, she who creates the cosmos with its temporal change and material form. "Pythagoras said that the Great Monad *acts as* a creative Dyad. From the moment God is manifest, **He is Double**; indivisible Essence, divisible Substance, masculine, active, animating, and passive feminine principles."

The great mystery here is that from the moment God is manifest *he is double*. One cannot but hear the echoes of Aristotle's charge against the Pythagoreans attempting to refute that doctrine.

In addition, we hear the clamor of the natural philosophers who recognized the two principles, Unlimited and Limit, *in* manifestation, but did not recognize their transcendental origin. Perhaps this gave rise to the notion among the ancient scientists that the Unlimited and Limit, were *opposing* principles that needed to be brought into consonance by means of the *harmonia?*

Nothing could be further from the truth for Pythagoras. In his cosmology, once the Monad projects Himself out toward matter, *He acts as* a creative Dyad. In other words, God is in disguise—hidden behind the many things that pass away and change, God exists *as* the creative Dyad, *as* the manifested world. The Monad has limited himself—by time, by space, by matter, and by change.

But the great truth remains. The Monad and creative Dyad are one, and their divine faculties are *complementary* and not opposing in nature. We notice here that what, for Pythagoras, are *complementary* divine faculties, are interpreted by the scientists as mere principles that lack life, and are opposing in nature.

And, when Schuré describes the Monad as at first a brilliant dot (315), one wonders whether there is not an echo in the natural scientists' description of the *apeiron,* the Unlimited, as a "seed" flung into the cosmos. If this were the case, as seems reasonable, the difference would be that the scientists could not give an explanation for its source, whereas for Pythagoras it refers to the Monad at the moment of manifestation.

Before we discuss the Pythagorean *harmonia*, let us emphasize that "number was considered to be an intrinsic and living virtue of the Supreme One, of God, the *Source of universal harmony.*" What this phrase indicates is that harmony is a *faculty of the Monad*, and thus is inherent in the universe at its very source. What it also suggests is that the *purpose* of the harmonia in Pythagoras's cosmology is entirely different from that of the scientists and natural philosophers. The latter viewed the *harmonia* as the principle needed to bring into consonance the two opposing material principles. This joining together of opposing principles was the *necessary* function of their harmonia, a function without which the two principles would have no possibility of consonance. And if those opposing principles failed to be harmonized, perhaps here would be no "fitting together" of other aspects of the cosmos, since all else depended on the harmonizing of the originating, material principles, Unlimited and Limit.

Such is not the case with the cosmology of Pythagoras, where the second divine faculty, the creative Dyad, *is brought forth* from the transcendental, unitary Monad. Thus the two divine faculties are *complementary* from the outset. They do not oppose one another despite the fact that the Monad retains its eternal and unchanging status, and the creative Dyad becomes identified with the creation of the temporal and material cosmos. In fact, the Monad *acts as* the creative Dyad. In other words, the Monad, who has surrendered creation of the cosmos to his feminine counterpart, *is at the same time that very female aspect of Himself.*

For this reason, the Monad and the creative Dyad have no *need* of a harmonia to bring them into *consonance*. They are *eternally* in consonance. In addition, the Monad is described as the source of *universal harmony*. What this indicates is that harmony is also *intrinsic* to the divine nature of the Monad. We would, therefore, challenge Aristotle's interpretation of Pythagorean cosmology when he judges that the union of the opposing forces of Unlimited and Limit generated a "One" that was both Unlimited and Limited, Even and Odd. From a metaphysical standpoint that is an impossibility.

For Pythagoras the *harmonia* represents the union, or the relation, between the Monad and creative Dyad that completes the Divine Triad, and its purpose is not to harmonize opposing principles, *but to actualize the creation of the material world*. This cosmic process is best described in Kenneth Sylvan Guthrie's book, *The Pythagorean Sourcebook and Library* (22). In the introduction, David R. Fideler summarizes it as follows:

With the Dyad arises the duality of subject and object, the knower and the known. With the advent of the Triad, however, the gulf of dualism is bridged, for it is through the third term that a Relation or Harmonia ("joining together") is obtained between the two extremes. While Two represents the first *possibility* of logos, the relation of one thing to another, the Triad achieves that relation in *actuality*....

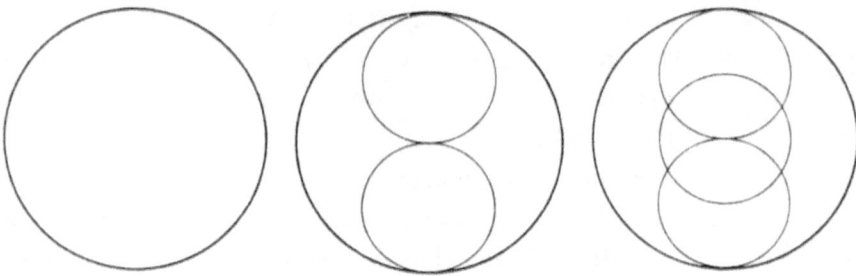

The Triad not only binds together the Two, but also, in the process centrally reflects the nature of the One in a "microcosmic" and balanced fashion...the emergence of Duality out of Unity, and the subsequent unification of duality, which in turn results in a dynamic, differentiated image of the One in three parts—a continuum of beginning, middle and end, or of two extremes bound together with a mean term. This process, in fact, is the archaic and archetypal paradigm of cosmogenesis, the pattern of creation which results in the world (*PSL* 22).

The only places where I would slightly differ from Fideler is that I would not describe the harmonia as a mere third term that is joining together two extremes. And I would not refer to the third term as bridging the "gulf of dualism" as though dualism is a "real" actuality, whereas for Pythagoras, it would be an *illusory* duality. Why? Because the Monad *acts as* the creative Dyad and, though concealed, is ever present in the world.

What this process of differentiation shows is that the harmonia is, in fact, *the vehicle* by which the Monad and creative Dyad *actualize* the world of matter (Schuré 315). That is accomplished by the permutations of relations among these three divine faculties, for they bring into actuality the sensible, corporeal world with its multitude of objects. Let us confirm our analysis by recalling words from Christmas Humphreys in his book, *Buddhism*:

Number as It relates to Monad vs. Unlimited/Limit

In the beginning is the One, and only the One *is*. From the One comes Two, the innumerable Pairs of Opposites. But there is no such thing as two, for no two things can be conceived without their relationship, and this makes Three, the basic Trinity of all manifestation. From the three (or its six permutations and integrating seventh) come the manifold things of "usual life," which the Chinese call the Ten Thousand Things.

Thus, the most abstruse of all possible philosophical concepts, namely the mysterious processes of cosmogenesis, have been rendered in a most succinct form, one that may not be challenged regarding its clarity, even if scientists and natural philosophers disagree with its intelligible nature and source.

What Humphreys is confirming is that a *threefold law* governs the gradual manifestation of the material world. This same divine threefold law may be found in Christianity—as Father, Son, and Holy Ghost (a suppressed form of the Mother)—and in Hinduism, where the actual functions of the three divine "persons" are spelled out. Brahman, the Absolute, has three aspects: Brahma, the Creator; Vishnu, the Preserver or Sustainer; and Shiva, the destroyer.

Parenthetically, one cannot help but be intrigued by Humphreys' statement that from the "six permutations and integrating seventh" come the manifold things of the sensible world, because it calls forth an echo of Pythagoras's *harmonia*, the mathematical and *musical* nature of which, at the very least is a symbolic representation of these cosmic processes under review.

We shall return to this issue shortly, but for the present we want to understand the cosmic processes just described in terms of Pythagoras's mysterious Tetrad. What do those dots, arranged in the form of a triangle in four rows, actually *mean*? I have dealt with that issue in the previous section (p. 177) where point, line, plane and solid represent the cosmic movement from non-dimensionality into different degrees of differentiation. Number is involved here, but on a symbolic basis.

This outline is confirmed by Speusippus, Plato's nephew and successor, who wrote that the number ten: "contains in itself, besides all the basic ratios [this seems to refer to the ratios of the "concordant" musical notes] the 'formulae' of the line, surface and solid; for one is a point, two a line, three a triangle and four a pyramid and all these are primary and fundamental to the other figures in each class." (Guthrie *HGP*, vol. 1, 260)

According to Guthrie senior, Aristotle claims that the doctrine formulated above by Speusippus goes back to writings by Philolaus. It shows in the simplest of terms how different dimensions of materiality are expressed in relation to one another. However, these deceptively easy arithmetic/geometric dots that even Meno could understand are, in fact, a symbolic representation of cosmic processes that involve vast eons of time as the Monad makes its incomprehensible journey into matter (see p. 178).

In conclusion, let us be quite clear that number is integral in Pythagoras's cosmology. The Monad is One, and the creative Dyad, his feminine and temporal counterpart, is the Number Two. The Monad and the Creative Dyad are not opposing principles, but rather complementary, divine faculties. And they are not "fitted together" *by a scientific harmonia* even if it depends on number in some fashion. The union or relation of the divine complementary faculties results in a third divine faculty who completes the Divine Triad (Number Three). The third faculty *consists of* a harmonia, whose mathematical and musical source is not only intrinsic to the internal, transcendent structure of the cosmos, but that also provides the vehicle for the divine faculties to *actualize* the manifestation of the material universe. For Pythagoras, mathematics originates with the Monad, as does the concept of harmony. Indeed, we cannot conclude this analysis without a brief discussion of the Pythagorean *harmonia* and its musical significance.

Pythagorean Harmonia

Let us start from the premise that for Pythagoras the Monad was "the Source of universal harmony," and that the harmonia itself, with its mathematical ratios and musical intervals, was intrinsic to the structure of the emerging cosmos. Whether the apocryphal story is true about Pythagoras hearing the musical intervals as he passed by a blacksmith at work in his forge does not obscure the fact that Pythagoras is officially recognized as discovering the intervals that are the foundation of western music. As a result, we cannot summarily dismiss his musical hypothesis as being fanciful and untrue, as most modern scientists and philosophers do, especially when we take into consideration his other scientific achievements. As Fideler describes it in *The Pythagoras Sourcebook*: "In the realm of music, it will be seen that the Tetraktys also contains the symphonic ratios which underlie the mathematical harmony of the musical scale: 1:2, the octave; 2:3, the perfect fifth; and 3:4, the perfect fourth" (*PS* p. 29).

Interested readers can consult this informative work on how these intervals relate to the issue of the continuum on the monochord. However, I wish to focus here on how the intervals were arrived at mathematically. Fideler continues:

> To arrive at whole number solutions, we will use the octave of 6:12.
>
> 1) The first step is one of *arithmetic mediation*. To find the arithmetic mean we take the two extremes, add them together, and divide by two. The result is a vibration of 9, which in relation to 6, is in the ratio of 2:3. This is the *perfect fifth*, the most powerful musical relationship.
>
> 2) The second form of mediation is *harmonic*. It is arrived at by multiplying together the two extremes, doubling the sum, and dividing the result by the sum of the two extremes (i.e., 2AB/A+B). The harmonic mean linking together 6 and 12 then is 8. This proportion, 6:8 or 3:4, is the perfect fourth, which is actually the inverse of the perfect fifth.
>
> 3) Through only two operations we have arrived at the foundation of the musical scale, the so-called "musical" or "harmonic" proportion 6:8 :: 9:12, the discovery of which was attributed to Pythagoras" (*PSL*, 25–26; page 27 details how each of the tones in our regular octave are formed).

The genius of Pythagoras saw that if mathematics was the language that explained music, it also explained the entire cosmos, and vice versa. And not necessarily in that order. "For the Pythagoreans the Tetraktys symbolized the perfection of Number and the elements which compose it. In one sense it would be proper to say that the Tetraktys symbolizes, like the musical scale, a differentiated image of Unity.... In the realm of space the Tetraktys represent the continuity linking the dimensionless point with the manifestation of the first body; ...it represents the vertical hierarchy of relation between

Unity and emerging Multiplicity. In the realm of music the Tetraktys also contains the symphonic ratios which underlie the mathematical harmony of the musical scale: 1:2, the octave; 2:3, the perfect fifth; 3:4, the perfect fourth. (*PSL,* 29)

Whereas I have shown the fourfold manifestation from point, line, plane, and solid (which itself is a symbolic representation of the Tetraktys) and then shown that same relation in terms of the movement of undifferentiated Unity into multiplicity via the Monad, creative Dyad, Divine Triad, and the creation of the material world, that same Tetrakys is reflected once again in the perfection of the musical scale, the octave and the musical intervals that are an intrinsic part of it. If mathematics can *explain* the cosmos, then mathematics is *inherent in the very structure* of the cosmos, as well as in the foundation of music.

Was Number Immanent for Pythagoras?

The question of how we are to pinpoint the origination of the number series rests, from the side of science, with Aristotle, and then upon the commentators throughout the centuries who have used those judgments as a basis for their own conclusions. Guthrie is not alone when he says he placed his trust in Aristotle when it came to all matters scientific. Philolaus also plays a role in this drama, but the main joust is between Aristotle himself and the Pythagoreans, or, to be more precise, with Pythagoras. It represents, once again, the ongoing battle between a transcendental view of number and cosmology as opposed to a scientific and material one.

Philolaus opens this debate when he makes his claim in Fragment 5 that "number, indeed, is of two proper kinds odd and even, and a third from both mixed together, the Even–Odd" (Huffman 178). This assertion appears to have contributed to Aristotle's confident misinterpretation of the Pythagoreans as follows: "…they hold that the elements of number are the even and the odd and that of these the latter is limited and the former unlimited; and that the One proceeds from both of these (for it is both even and odd) and number from the One; and that the whole heaven, as has been said, is number" (*Meta* I, 5 986a 17).

From this statement, and others on number and cosmology that we have reviewed, Aristotle came to his famous conclusion that for Pythagoreans, the numbers were *in*, or *constituted* the sensibles, and therefore they conceived of number as immanent. This conclusion, that the numbers *were* the sensibles, has finally been disproven by advances in physics in the twentieth century that have confirmed that mathematics is indeed the language that *explains* the cosmos. Aristotle's judgment of the Pythagoreans is shown to be a complete misunderstanding and misrepresentation of their cosmology. As usual, Aristotle is blinded by his insistence on viewing all theories through the prism of his four causes, and this scientific mindset vexed him considerably when it was turned on metaphysical matters, because it did not give him the results he wished to obtain.

Aristotle's misinterpretation of Pythagorean cosmology only serves to highlight his own view, if only by turning Pythagorean ideas upside down. Aristotle clearly accepted the natural philosophers's description of the *apeiron* as the starting point of cosmology, although we have mentioned the inconsistency of there being two originating material principles, the Unlimited and the Limit, and at the same time the notion of the originating cosmic principle also described as the One, or the Primitive One. That ambiguity in Aristotle's position is referred to in Guthrie (HGP, vol. I, 278), where he, Aristotle, suggests that (for the Pythagoreans) "the first unit consisted of a seed, the seed of the world...[and] the unit is to be understood as both a number and the nucleus of the physical world."

Nevertheless those two principles, Unlimited and Limit, are the ones Aristotle accepts as original, except that he conflates them with the elements of number such that Unlimited equates with even and Limit equates with odd. This appears to be a quite arbitrary change because Huffman tells us there is no evidence that Philolaus made such a conflation. For Philolaus, the originating principles were Unlimited and Limit.

In addition, Aristotle has determined that the relation between Unlimited and Limit—two opposing, material principles generate a "One" that contains all things, including numbers, and claims that numbers proceed from the "One." Notice that there is no mention of the harmonia that Philolaus claims brings the two opposing principles into harmony, or consonance. We must infer that for Aristotle, there was a union or relation between Unlimited and Limit, two material principles, and that it produced the "One." As we know, Aristotle asserted that the "One" contained all things; that numbers proceeded from the One; and the whole heavens *was* number.

Although the original statement about number by Philolaus clearly influenced him, Aristotle arbitrarily changed its structure and meaning in significant ways such that it no longer conveyed the same exact intent. For example, the omission of the harmonia is significant because it no longer reflects Philolaus's position in how Unlimited and Limit were brought into consonance. And when Philolaus tells us that the odd and even generated the "Odd–Even," he meant it to be correlated to number, not necessarily to Limit and Unlimited. We merely remind ourselves of these facts.

For a metaphysician such as Pythagoras, the view of Aristotle would have been considered nothing short of preposterous. He would have chided Aristotle for assuming the existence of two opposing material principles, described in the most abstruse, vague and non-materialistic terms, as the originating principles of our cosmos—without stating their source, and without giving good scientific evidence for his claim.

In addition, Aristotle assumes that the relation between Unlimited and Limit produce a "One" that contains all things, including number, and that the number series supposedly begins with the "One." For a metaphysician, such a view is rejected entirely on the grounds that number *cannot* begin from a principle that is not originating, it cannot proceed from opposing principles that do not already embody number in some way, nor where the principle, the "One," is a *product* of the two originating principles and not the originating principle itself. For a metaphysician, that position is untenable because it flies in the face of common sense logic, and because some of the natural philosophers believed that the universe had its origins in the One, or the Primitive One, but it was for them an *originating* principle and not the "One" of Aristotle that was the product of *two other* originating principles. Since he accepted the materiality of the originating principles, Unlimited and Limit, perhaps the term *immanent* more rightly should be assigned to Aristotle than to Pythagoras.

For Pythagoras, the metaphysical understanding of the origin of the cosmos is with the eternal and changeless Monad, a single universal principle, or, as he describes it, "divine faculty."

The Monad projects itself out into matter, and the first thing manifested is the creative Dyad, his feminine and temporal side, who creates the universe. Their union produces the third divine faculty, which completes the Divine Triad, and makes possible the actualization of the world of matter. The endless permutations of their relationships eventually manifest the corporeal world.

The progression is logical—one, two, three and four—and the cosmic processes and the differentiation that express these principles correlate with one another.

For Pythagoras, the view of the cosmos was not one of blind speculation, but of *personal experience* of the transcendental nature and origin of the Monad. It is worth remembering that Pythagoras only turned to number, ideal number, to represent other transcendental principles and processes *that were hard for others to comprehend.*

Thus, despite Aristotle's misrepresentations and misjudgments, Pythagoras reveals himself to be a transcendentalist of the first order. One must bear in mind, however, that when the Monad has brought forth the creative Dyad, *two faculties now exist*, and two principles do, in fact, govern the *material* world. But beyond those two principles lies the eternal and changeless Monad that governs *everything*. That is the first point.

The second point rests on the discussion of when and how the number series originates. For Pythagoras, and for Christmas Humphreys, in his book *Buddhism,* the answer is clear. The originating cosmic principle is described as a Unity, but the moment the Monad manifests the creative Dyad, it becomes Two. Even if the Greeks gave no designation for zero, the above case would still hold, because the Monad contains everything within it, even the number One. And once Unity (when the One is in unmanifest form) manifests itself, the number One becomes apparent, and most clearly, because its counterpart, the creative Dyad, is Two. Therefore I submit that for Pythagoras the number series is generated in correlation with the cosmic mathematical processes that are the expression of the unfolding cosmos. And if we want some proof of Pythagoras's mathematical hypothesis, we only have to recall that the first manifestation, from the "seed" of the universe (equated with the "dot") is the sphere, a perfect geometrical form, which, as Guthrie reminds us, is made of a particularly tenuous form of matter. And, since our subject is number, we cannot forget that despite the fact that two principles appear to govern the material world, Pythagoras calls our attention to the threefold law as being the key to life.

In review, it would appear that Aristotle has turned the cosmology of Pythagoras on its head. Where Pythagoras posits one originating, transcendental principle, Aristotle posits two opposing forces with no apparent source. Where Pythagoras's Monad and creative Dyad are *corresponding* faculties, Aristotle's are opposing. Where in Pythagoras the harmonia is the vehicle for actualizing the corporeal world, in Aristotle it creates a "One" that despite being material seems to have all the powers of a transcendent principle, since it includes everything in it, and from it all numbers flow. The conclusion is that Aristotle's materialist theory lacks truth and coherence. For the metaphysicians, the hypothesis of Pythagoras is compelling and coherent.

The origination of the number series then, for Pythagoras, begins with the transcendental Monad. It is simple, clear, and coherent. The matter is vastly more complicated and entangled for the scientists and natural philosophers. The argument is laid out in Kahn's book (p. 27), and a good place to start is with Fragment 4 of Philolaus: "All things which are known have number." Kahn continues: "Hence the process by which the cosmos came into existence seems to have been conceived as analogous to a generation of the numbers. The first thing harmoniously fitted together, the one in the center of the sphere, is called Hestia, the hearth" (Fr. 7).

> My account [says Kahn] follows Aristotle in assuming that the Pythagoreans generate the heavens by the same process that generates the natural numbers, so that [for Philolaus] "the one in the center of the sphere" is both the central fire, or Hearth, and also the first integer.

Thus Aristotle reports that the Pythagoreans "construct the whole heaven out of numbers, but not out of monads, for they assume the monads have magnitude" (*Meta* 1080b 18). My translation of Aristotle (McKeon) includes an extra sentence that reads: "But how the first I (One) was constructed as to have magnitude they [the Pythagoreans] seem unable to say" (McKeon 898).

Kahn then tells us that "this interpretation (by Aristotle) has been challenged by Huffman, who claims that Philolaus did not confuse things with numbers but that it was Aristotle (in his rather uncharitable interpretation) who attributed this confusion to the Pythagoreans. On Huffman's reading of fragment 5, things "signify" or "point" to [*semainei*] the forms of number. Hence the central fire points to the number one but is not identical with it. It is, Huffman claims, impossible to imagine that he [Philolaus] confused the arithmetical unit with the central fire. For if he did, his arithmetical unit is more than a bare monad with position; it is also fiery and orbited by ten bodies" (Huffman 205).

My interpretation of this situation from the point of Pythagoras is as follows: Kahn states that for Philolaus, the one in the center of the sphere is both the central fire and also the first integer. Aristotle complicates the argument by stating that the Pythagoreans create the heavens out of number, but not out of monads, because for the Pythagoreans the monads have magnitude. Huffman rebuts by saying that Aristotle has uncharitably judged Philolaus as confusing monads and magnitude and that for him, Huffman, things "signify" or "point to" the forms of number. He concludes that "the central fire points to the number one but is not identical with it." Except for Aristotle, who always seems to be wrong on metaphysical questions, we might infer that both Philolaus and Huffman are correct—from their own points of view. In order to contextualize their positions, it is necessary to present the hypothesis of Pythagoras.

The central fire, in its sensible sign, represents the Sun, which, indeed, is fiery and has ten bodies orbiting it. This means that Philolaus sees the number one as correlating with the Sun. Huffman declares that the central fire *points to* the number one but is not identical with it. I presume when Huffman makes mention of the central fire, he too is correlating it to the Sun.

For Pythagoras the central fire is not only a reference to the sensible Sun, but the Sun is a reference to the *intelligible* Sun, the Cosmic Fire that originates both the cosmos and the corresponding number series. The Cosmic Fire, or divine Light is, of course, the Monad. Pythagoras's cosmology was so advanced and beyond the understanding of his contemporaries that he used signs and symbols to make the part that *could* be made available to his contemporaries understood more easily. At the same time, as an initiate, it was his duty to keep the sacred and esoteric knowledge concealed. For him, in the last analysis, the Divine Monad was the originator of the cosmos, and to answer Aristotle's question, Pythagoras derived the first Number One from the Monad itself. The fact that some of the natural philosophers made the inference that the "central fire" was perhaps a reference for the Sun merely concealed the transcendental truth from the public, namely that the *Divine Monad* originated the cosmos and might be defined as the *intelligible* light, and the Sun was the *visible* referent of the Monad because, in its sensible form, it, too, was fire and light.

When Huffman asserts that the central fire points to the number one, but is not identical with it, he is correct, but not for the reason he supposes. The central fire points to the number one, but the number one is not identical with the Sun, but rather with the *intelligible Sun*, the Monad. And when Kahn asserts that for Philolaus the one in the center of the sphere is both the central fire and also the first integer, he has half of the meaning. The part that eludes him was that the Sun was the visible referent of the Monad, and that the first integer correlated with the Monad, in such a way that the number series and the unfolding of cosmology were identical.

Let's conclude by revisiting the question posed at the beginning of this section: Was number immanent for Pythagoras? This question was prompted due to Aristotle's insistence that, for the Pythagoreans, number was *in* things and therefore number was immanent. As I hope I have shown, for Pythagoras number had its source in transcendence, even though it had a mundane application in the sensible world. Aristotle's theory is, in my view, disproved. To tie up the loose ends, in respect of their approach to number and its origination, we can identify Philolaus and Aristotle on the side of the scientists and natural philosophers, while Pythagoras and Plato are aligned on the side of transcendence. This may not have been what the scientists expected.

Pythagoras Today

Why are we *still* asking the question as to whether number was immanent for Pythagoras and the Pythagoreans? The reason is quite simple. It is due to a misunderstanding of Pythagorean mathematics that has persisted from his own lifetime two thousand five hundred years ago to the present era. Part of the reason is because no texts of Pythagoras are extant that could provide evidence of his doctrines, and the other part is that Pythagoras veiled the esoteric kernel of his message in veils and symbols that were unintelligible except to initiates.

The first person linked back to Pythagoras who wrote anything down was Philolaus, but the historical record he left behind is ambiguous. And since some of the crucial fragments dealing with the originating principles of the cosmos, including number, are written in what appears to be Pre-Socratic terminology, it does appear that later on Philolaus aligned himself more with Pre-Socratic doctrines than those of Pythagoras. If there is one fragment that, for me, pinpoints Philolaus as a Pre-Socratic, it is Fragment 6, which states:

> Concerning nature and harmony things are as follows: The Being (*esto*) of things, which is eternal, and Nature itself (*physis*) admits divine but not human knowledge (gnosis) except that of the things-that-are (*ta onta*) and that are known by us, it was impossible for any of them to have come into being if there was not already the being (*esto*) of those things from which the world order is composed; both the limiting and the unlimited. (Kahn 25)

Here Philolaus declares that the Being of things, which is eternal, and Nature itself admit of divine knowledge, but not human knowledge. This may be a statement that a Pre-Socratic could accept. But for a true Pythagorean, such an assertion could never be accepted, the reason being that the school of Pythagoras in Croton was a *mystical* school, one where the mysteries of the Being of things and Nature herself were the precise studies undertaken to achieve the goal of union of the soul with God. The very *purpose* of Pythagoras's school was to show students *how* to attain *knowledge and the experience* of God! If Philolaus did not believe such divine knowledge was possible, whether of Being or of Nature, then it is my judgment that he was no longer a true Pythagorean.

There are two other reasons why Philolaus is suspect as being a Pre-Socratic. First, if Philolaus had understood and imbibed the teaching of Pythagoras as follows:

> Number was not considered an abstract quantity, but an intrinsic and living virtue of the supreme One, of God, the Source of universal harmony. The *science of numbers* was that of the living forces of *divine faculties* in action in the world and in man, in macrocosm and microcosm. (Schuré 311)

Philolaus would never have been swayed by Pre-Socratic doctrines that sought to apotheosize *material* principles as the origin of our world, because his Pythagorean studies would have revealed to him that *divine* faculties lay behind the creation of the entire cosmos, including "originating" material principles.

Second, if Philolaus had understood the *Pythagorean* harmonia, and the significance of the mathematical ratios and musical intervals as they applied to the *cosmos*, he would never have tried to impose it on a hybrid joining together of the Eleatic ontology of Parmenidean Being (eternal, static) and Ionian natural philosophy (the search for material origins of the cosmos), because he would have understood that the purpose of the *Pre-Socratic* harmonia was to join together two opposing material principles, whereas the *Pythagorean harmonia* represented mathematical cosmological law and cosmogenesis in action. The Pythagorean *harmonia* provided the vehicle for divine and eternal faculties of the Monad and Creative Dyad to differentiate into ever-denser dimensions of matter. In addition, Philolaus would have known from his own experience that material principles are *not* originating, but depend for their very existence upon the differentiation of those divine faculties. In short, Philolaus would have understood that the supreme Monad, God, was the transcendental Source of the cosmos.

For all of the above reasons, it is my conclusion that Philolaus was not, in the end, a true Pythagorean; that his fragments are at best ambiguous; and that his Pre-Socratic leanings make assessment unreliable and his allegiance unproven. Nevertheless, the fragments of Philolaus are important historically, because they purport to be the first written documents publicly outlining Pythagorean doctrines. And *how* they would be interpreted would sway investigators down through the ages either to the transcendental or to the material origin of the cosmos.

Aristotle, whom Huffman tells us derived most of his knowledge about the Pythagoreans from Philolaus, was a scientist who insisted on interpreting knowledge of all disciplines by his own four causes. He mocked the Pythagorean doctrine of divine origins by declaring: "It is indeed impossible to erect a theory ascribing coming-to-be (genesis) to eternal things. Yet without a doubt the Pythagoreans do so."

We may ponder the enormity of Aristotle's blunderings when it comes to metaphysical matters, but the truth is that his towering stature and reputation swept over the western world like a great wave that swamped everything in its path. As a result, he has influenced philosophers and historians in age after age to accept his pronouncements on metaphysics even if, like Guthrie, they are quite aware of Aristotle's failings and unreliability.

The Neoplatonists of the second and third centuries CE—Plotinus, Porphyry and Iamblichus—all of whom were considered sages and perhaps initiates in their own time, revived an interest and reverence for Pythagoras and wrote books on his life that are still valuable sources for scholars. The pupil of Plotinus, Porphyry, wrote *Porphyry's Life of Pythagoras*, and Iamblichus, the pupil of Porphyry, wrote *Iamblichus: The Pythagorean Life*. Porphyry tells us that his Master, Plotinus, had experienced the transcendental state of mystical union on at least four occasions, and that he, Porphyry, was also granted the mystical union once in his life, when he was sixty-eight years old. These transcendental experiences put them in a better position than most other commentators to confirm the truth of Pythagoras's teachings. Guthrie, however, dismisses them as overly naive, and as too willing to ascribe all Pythagorean doctrine to Pythagoras himself.

There are other examples of misunderstanding by eminent scholars from the twentieth century. In the Preface to the German edition of Walter

Burkert's book, *Lore and Science in Ancient Pythagoreanism*, he states of Pythagoras: "From the very beginning, his influence was mainly felt in an atmosphere of miracle, secrecy, and revelation. In that twilight period between old and new, when Greeks, in a historically unique achievement, were discovering the rational interpretation of the world and quantitative natural science, Pythagoras represents not the origin of the new, but the survival or revival of ancient, pre-scientific lore, based on superhuman authority and expressed in ritual obligation."

One has respect for the sheer detail of Burkert's scholarship, but, like most scholars within the discipline of philosophy, they have not given serious attention to the neighboring discipline of religion, and particularly the mysteries. To ignore the twenty-two years that Pythagoras spent in the Egyptian temples studying sacred mathematics, and the twelve years he spent as a prisoner in Babylon, where he studied all forms of religion—monism, dualism, trinitarianism, etc.—is to miss the kernel of Pythagoras's teachings, which were meant for the initiated because they contained the principles of nature and such principles could only be entrusted to those who had achieved moral purity. To mistake those savage feasts of blood and mania of the Bacchantes for the advanced state of initiation achieved by Pythagoras, the preliminary slopes of which demanded control of *all* the faculties, only underscores the fact that many scholars fail to grasp the big picture in cases where philosophy and religion merge, and this is even more the case with the mysteries, whose higher, esoteric knowledge required an oath of secrecy to guard it, and that guaranteed experience that transcended mere rational exposition.

Such misunderstanding causes Burkert to judge, quite incorrectly, that Pythagoras belongs to an earlier era where superstition and a reliance on pre-scientific lore were the norms of the day. Burkert continues: "That which was later regarded as the philosophy of Pythagoras had its roots in the school of Plato.... As the old and the new interpenetrated and influenced each other, the picture of Pythagoras became distorted until, with the victory of rational science, he came to seem its true founder."

A judgment such as this made by Burkert is quite astonishing when one remembers that Pythagoras is credited—by ancient commentators—with bringing mathematics to Greece, with the Pythagorean theorem, the heliocentric theory of cosmology (even Aristotle mentions this), and was credited with discovering the intervals and ratios that provided the foundation of western music. The scientific achievements speak for themselves. From an objective point of view, such discoveries can only be judged as included along with those of the Greeks who were discovering the "rational interpretation of the world and quantitative natural science."

W. K. C. Guthrie, *the* historian of philosophy, evidently concurs with Burkert when he writes that "the modern mind experiences difficulty in reconciling adherence to a comparatively primitive set of religious and superstitious beliefs with the rational pursuit of mathematical science and cosmic speculation" (*HGP*, vol. 1., 181).

Furthermore, in discussing the question of Pythagorean number, Guthrie quotes the scholar, W. D. Ross, "that the Pythagoreans did not reduce reality to an abstraction, but failed to recognize the abstract nature of numbers" (*HGP*, vol. 1., 240–242). When we consider that Ross was the author of the influential book, *Plato's Theory of Ideas*, it is jarring to see him making statements that are not only subjective, but imperious and pejorative in nature.

Again, on the question of Pythagorean number, Guthrie is guilty of the same imperiousness. He quotes Aristotle from *Metaphysics* (1080b 16)—on monads and magnitude, and Guthrie comments that Aristotle means by this that the monads were not incorporeal or unextended; *and that the notion of incorporeal reality was not yet grasped by the Pythagoreans or any of their contemporaries.*

My response to these assertions by Ross and Guthrie, who are representative of so many other modern philosophers and historians, is complete astonishment at their scientific hubris and entrenched Aristotelian mindset. Quite aside from the fact that Pythagoras had studied sacred mathematics for twenty-two years in the Egyptian temples, and that there was scarcely a human being in world history who knew more about incorporeal reality than Pythagoras, were there not transcendental metaphysical expressions of Being in the ancient world, for example in Parmenides? And apart from any scientific interpretations of reality, did not the ancient Greeks, the ancient Egyptians and every other ancient civilization have their *gods* to remind them of their transcendental and *incorporeal* source?

When we look back to Aristotle and his pivotal position in western civilization, we can see a slow but definite trend toward a more scientizing approach to philosophy. It is ironic, then, that the Copernican Revolution, which ushered in the "new" heliocentric theory of cosmology—should have had its sources in Pythagoras (and apparently Philolaus?). As we know, that theory revolutionized how we perceive ourselves in relation to our solar system by displacing the Earth from the center and replacing it with the Sun. It is, therefore, interesting to note that when Guthrie discussed the Pythagorean heliocentric theory, he completely dismissed it as anticipating the "scientific" heliocentric theory validated by Copernicus and Kepler, even when they had publicly acknowledged their debt to Pythagoras and Philolaus in the sixteenth century.

From the Age of Enlightenment in the seventeenth century, that trend toward scientizing most academic disciplines, including philosophy, has only become more pronounced. And yet, that scientizing trend also brought about remarkable developments in mathematics and in physics. In the twentieth century, with Albert Einstein's theories of general and special relativity, and his most famous equation $E=mc^2$ scientists, philosophers at long last came to understand that mathematics *is indeed* the language that explains our cosmos. And the modern physicists and mathematicians did not make the same mistake as Aristotle in assuming that sensible things were *made out* of numbers. They understood that mathematics was a language of *symbolic representation,* as Einstein's equation makes clear.

We may nod our heads and agree that Pythagoras was right after all in stating that all things *were known* through number. But do we really understand Pythagoras, even now? In order to do that we would need to understand the *purpose* of Pythagorean mathematics, and the best place to begin that brief investigation is with Plato.

Plato makes quite clear in the *Republic* what *role* number plays, especially for a guardian, in pursuit of divine initiation. First, the student was to engage in the *Pythagorean* course of study—arithmetic, geometry, astronomy and music. However, Socrates emphasizes that the disciplines should be studied *in contrary fashion* to what was commonly taught. He states: "Numbers should compel one toward pure thought" (*Republic* 526-a-b) with a view to truth itself. "Geometry is the knowledge of the eternally existent" and it should not therefore be satisfied with the visible diagrams, but should "facilitate the apprehension of the idea of the

Good" (*Republic* 526-c). Likewise in the case of astronomy, it should not be used for vulgar utilitarian purposes, but understood correctly, it "turns the soul's gaze upward and leads it away from things here to those higher things" (*Republic* 529). Socrates also makes his famous statement that astronomy and music are in some way "kindred sciences," as the Pythagoreans affirm and we admit (*Republic* 530-d).

Socrates continues that these studies should be pursued in such a way that their affinities and their kinship will be revealed, and of dialectic he states that such studies will be *useless* if they take their assumptions and argue down to a conclusion (i.e. to theories of the sensible world that rely on diagrams whose assumptions have not been examined), and fruitful only if it leads upward to the unhypothesized first principle, which he later correlates with the Good. In short, the various disciplines of mathematics are to help the disciple detach his consciousness from the objects of sense in order to allow it to soar higher into the unity of the intelligible world—and finally into the transcendent experience of the Good.

Perhaps, then, in the *Republic* Plato gives us a glimpse into how mathematics was studied under Pythagoras himself. It was to lead the soul upward toward transcendence.

What does Schuré have to tell us about number and a mathematical interpretation of the universe? Briefly, he says that for Pythagoras mathematics was a sacred science, one that was "both transcendent and more alive than secular mathematics known to our modern scientists and philosophers.... The science of numbers was that of the living forces of divine faculties in action, in the world and in man" (311). Here, Schuré is confirming that when Pythagoras refers to number, he sees number as a living force; he sees it as a divine faculty; he says it is more alive and transcendent than secular mathematics.

This is a mathematics that few, if any, twenty-first-century mathematician could comprehend. And the reason that they don't understand Pythagorean mathematics is because those physicists, mathematicians and philosophers are still working with theoretical diagrams and tying them back to conclusions in the sensible world. Without question, such theories further the horizons of science. But they do not get to the ultimate questions. Mathematics is a divine faculty, but employing mathematics—the same *rigorous* mathematics adopted by the scientists—as a springboard to higher knowledge and eventual union of the soul with the Good is stated by Socrates in Plato's *Republic* as the ultimate goal of all knowledge.

And that is the function of mathematics for Pythagoras. It can and does explain the world, but it also has a higher purpose of which the twenty-first century theorists know almost nothing. That is why they do not understand Pythagoras. They do not understand his mathematics, and they do not understand his world. As Schuré tells us: "Pythagoras explained the universe as a living being, animated by a great Soul, and permeated with a great Intelligence."

It is unfortunate, therefore, that those who did not understand the cosmic vision and mystical experience in such a statement should have mocked Pythagoras by dismissing him as one being involved in primitive religion and superstitious rites. What those scholars did not know was that "the science of numbers was known under various names in the temples of Egypt and Asia. Since it provided the key to all doctrine, it was carefully concealed from the uninitiated" (Schuré 310–311).

Furtheremore, those scholars were and are unaware that "his astronomy was entirely symbolic.... Therefore, what our philosophers generally accept as the physics of Pythagoras and Plato is nothing but a figurative description of their secret philosophy" (Schuré 322).

We don't need to accept the views of Schuré at face value. Porphyry, the Neoplatonist, says: "Since the Pythagoreans were unable to express clearly in speech the first forms and first principles, because these are *difficult to comprehend and explain, they turned to numbers for the sake of clear teaching....* "

Comparison of Plato and Pythagoras

Most modern investigators agree that there has been a definite Pythagorean influence upon Plato's philosophy.. The question is: how *much* influence? Let us try to determine the answer to that question by comparing their lives and works.

Pythagorean/Platonic Schools

Both Pythagoras and Plato ran schools that disseminated their philosophical and spiritual teachings. In the case of Pythagoras, his school was in Croton, Southern Italy, and it is described as a spiritual/religious community. Strict training over a period of many years was required, and purification of the soul was a pre-requisite to receiving higher, esoteric, secret knowledge. The disciple began his or her journey by honoring moral and ethical precepts, and a vow of silence was required lasting for the first five years.

The students were divided into two broad groups: the *acousmatikoi*, those attuned to the moral side of the teachings, and the *mathematikoi*, those who could grasp the mathematical and scientific aspect of his work. The mathematical teachings were in addition to the moral and ethical teachings and were not in place of them.

What was Pythagoras's ultimate purpose with his school? It was to teach what he had himself learned in Egypt and Babylon—namely, higher esoteric knowledge, leading to union of the soul with God. Pythagoras also used his school to further a social experiment. He extended his teachings into many of the cities of Southern Italy, and originated a lay form of initiation for many of its residents. An enormously charismatic figure, in time Pythagoras won over a large part of southern Italy to his higher ideals of justice and truth. As Schuré tells us, the Pythagorean institute was a small model city under the direction of a great initiate.

Plato also had a school, the Academy in Athens. He attracted the great minds of his time to the Academy, and for twenty years Aristotle himself was a student. The purpose of the teachings was "care for the soul" and the early dialogues, dealing with definitions of the virtues, courage, piety, friendship, amd justice can be considered Plato's expression of moral and ethical teachings, precisely those virtues that prepared the soul for higher knowledge.

Perhaps the goal of the Academy had its highest expression in the ideals of the *Republic,* where Plato sets out to show how justice can govern the individual soul (the microcosm) in the same way as justice can govern the external city (the macrocosm). Parenthetically, I wonder whether Plato did not model his ideal city of the *Republic* upon the actual social experiment of Pythagoras in Southern Italy. I believe that view is shared by C. J. Vogel in her book *Pythagoras and Early Pythagoreanism.*

In Plato's Academy, as in the *Republic,* worthy students were seeking higher knowledge, namely the keys to the unity of existence by way of the forms, dialectic, and ultimately the mystic experience of union with the Good, with God. As Plato tells us, the most advanced students were the guardians who were chosen, even before their birth, to rule their cities with truth and justice. Thus, from a very early age they lived a cloistered, virtuous life, and as the years of study bore fruit, the worthy disciples were gradually allowed exposure to higher knowledge. It began with the doctrine of recollection, as found in the *Meno*; it was expanded in the *Phaedo* to an understanding of the immortality of the soul, and in the *Phaedrus* to the doctrines of transmigration and the laws of karma. These doctrines, it must be emphasized, were not known in Greece during Plato's lifetime. They were considered esoteric and arcane.

When these studies had been mastered, the neophyte was then exposed to the main academic curriculum, which—as Plato plainly states—was Pythagorean in origin and consisted of mathematics, geometry, astronomy, and music, studies intended to draw the soul away from the world of sensible objects and toward the higher, intelligible world of eternal truths. The goal of the guardians was to achieve the mystical identification of their soul with the Good, or God, so that they could return to their communities and become just and wise rulers of their people. The ultimate purpose in the *Republic,* then, is for the creation of a small model city under the direction of an initiate. And the purpose of their schools, both under Pythagoras and Plato, is "care for the soul." Here we have the first confluence between the philosophical purposes of Pythagoras and Plato.

Education of Pythagorean Initiates and Platonic Guardians

Any knowledge of higher esoteric studies undertaken by Pythagorean students in the Institute is a closed book, because of the oath of silence that was the price of the knowledge acquired. What tangential fragments have come down are due to ancient historical commentators, such as Philolaus, Aristotle, and Diogenes Laertius, or Neoplatonists such as Porphyry, Plotinus, and Iamblichus. But we do know from Plato that the curriculum of the guardians in the *Republic* emulated that of Pythagoras, and therefore included arithmetic, geometry, astronomy, and music. Suffice it to say that Plato included these specific disciplines to train the soul of the seeker toward the intelligible realm of the transcendental Forms. These Forms could only be truly contemplated when detached from sensory impressions, and the whole endeavor had two purposes: 1) to help the seeker reach and maintain a connection to the intelligible realm of eternal laws and the Good, and 2) to prepare the seeker for the experience of divine initiation or identification of the soul with the Good. This event was so momentous that it required the jettisoning of all former stages, or supports, in favor of a final mystic experience in which the relation of subject and object—and the world of duality it represents—was completely swept away, and the seeker came to recognize, through experience and not from theory or received wisdom, that one's soul was not only a spark of God, but was also *identical* with God. *This* was the truth that could not be spoken.

There are some, such as C. J. de Vogel in her book *Pythagoras and Early Pythagoreanism*, who see a difference in the aims of the Pythagorean and Platonic quadrivium of disciplines. As she states it,

> To Pythagoras the study of mathematics was not a *preparation* for the contemplation of a divine Reality, *it was the contemplation itself. It presupposed* rather than effected a cleansing of the soul.... It was a direct contact with a divine Reality: Divinity immanent in

the cosmos. It was different for Plato. He adopts the Pythagorean notion that number is the principle of order in the cosmos and in life... but it points at a purely intelligible Number which is a Form—no immanent principle of order within objects but a transcendental example. This is the basic difference between the Pythagorean doctrine of number and Plato's Theory of Forms. Plato's philosophy is a metaphysic of the transcendent, the Pythagorean philosophy is a metaphysic of immanent order. (de Vogel 197)

This would be an adequate explanation—*if* we did not know from Plotinus, Porphyry, Schuré and other sources that, for Pythagoras, beyond the dualistic principles of Unlimited-Limit lies the great unitary Monad, transcendental, eternal, indivisible and uncreated. When we take the Monad into consideration, the picture changes radically.

For example, de Vogel says that for the Pythagoreans the study of mathematics was not a *preparation* for the contemplation of a divine Reality, *it was the contemplation itself.* But to contemplate in this way neglects to take into consideration the *aim* of such contemplation—namely, the identification of the soul with the Divine. Unless the divine initiation has been actually *attained*, the contemplation occurs within the subject–object relationship, and remains just that—contemplation. If the initiation *has* been successful, the subject–object relation has been overcome, and all things, whether intelligible *or sensible*, are then seen as part of the great unity of the One, of the Monad, of God. In that case contemplation of the heavens is no longer "mere" contemplation; it is *direct experience of the divine Reality.*

When a seeker becomes an initiate and contemplates the heavens *or* the sensible things of this world, he is no longer trapped in immanent explanations of the cosmos. Therefore it is a misunderstanding to suppose that Pythagoras's philosophy is a metaphysic of immanent order. Such a view can only be held if you accept the Unlimited and Limit as the two *ultimate, material* principles of the cosmos and number as immanent—as Aristotle tries to claim. As Schuré reminds us once again, for Pythagoras the Monad and creative Dyad (two principles) do operate *as* a duality as soon as there is manifestation, but beyond and behind those two principles lies the transcendental Monad that is the source of all, and that *precedes all manifestation.* It is the very existence of the Monad that makes possible the experience of divine initiation. Therefore, Pythagoras clearly had a metaphysic of the transcendental order as well as of immanent order.

This is the second confluence between Plato and Pythagoras.

Immortality of the Soul/Reincarnation/Karma

Pythagoras and Plato shared a strong belief in the concept of the immortality of the soul and the nexus of doctrines that accompany it—namely, belief in the transmigration of the soul (reincarnation) and the law of karma. In the case of Pythagoras, those beliefs are traced back to the poet-musician-initiate Orpheus who, according to Schuré, lived approximately five centuries before Homer. Their common beliefs fall under the heading of the Orphic-Pythagorean tradition, and since these doctrines are not the rubric of commonly held Greek beliefs, investigators tend to project pejorative terms upon them, such as that they are "primitive" or are due to "superstition" or sympathetic magic. Guthrie confirms, however, that the consonance of Orphic and Pythagorean beliefs is held on incontrovertible evidence.

In fact, Guthrie *embodies* the pejorative opinions about Pythagoras when he writes that "the modern mind experiences difficulty in reconciling adherence to a comparatively primitive set of religious and superstitious beliefs with the rational pursuit of mathematical science and cosmic speculation" (*HGP*, vol. 1, 181). On the other hand, Schuré reminds us that before he was born, the parents of Pythagoras went to the temple of Apollo at Delphi and consulted the Oracle about their son. The Pythoness promised them "a son who will be useful to all men for all time." Thus, there is every reason to hold Pythagoras in the same esteem as that maintained by the divine oracle at Delphi.

Schuré tells us that "Pythagoras explained the universe as a living being, animated by a great Soul, and permeated with a great Intelligence" (Schuré 321). He believed in the immortality of the soul and taught that *the very purpose* of life was for the salvation of the soul—namely, union of the soul with God. Pythagoras rejected the idea of animal sacrifice at a time when it was the general custom in Greece; in his school he banned the killing of animals, and also held what was felt by others at the time to be a "peculiar" belief—namely, belief in the kinship of all life.

When we truly understand kinship of all life in the context of Pythagoras's beliefs and doctrines, his affirmation of it is not as peculiar as Guthrie makes it sound, nor is it the mere expression of superstition or sympathetic magic. For Pythagoras, it would have been the highest expression of his understanding that everything in the cosmos owes its existence to the transcendental, unitary Monad. As if to confirm such a view, Guthrie tells us that as well known a Pre-Socratic as "Empedocles (held that) *everything* had a share of consciousness" (Fr. 110.10). It may well be, then, that the concept of the kinship of all life may turn out to be the *highest* cosmic understanding, one that results in a compassionate attitude toward all living beings, such as is exemplified today by the Dalai Lama, head of Tibetan Buddhism. Superstition and sympathetic magic might conceivably be identified with some of the Bacchic cults engaging in orgiastic frenzy and blood sacrifice, but the divine initiation Pythagoras had attained in Egypt was one that gave him enlightenment and an understanding of the unity of all life within the Monad. Kinship of all life would have been integral to that understanding.

As to transmigration, or reincarnation, Guthrie (*HGP*, vol. 1, 199) confirms that assimilation of the soul to the divine was held by Pythagoras as "the legitimate and essential aim of human life." It was understood by Pythagoras that such assimilation required a series of lifetimes, in each of which one had the free will to act in ways that would either further, or hinder, the soul's journey. It is known from various ancient sources that Pythagoras actually had the ability to recall his own prior lifetimes and that he revealed some of them to his disciples. Porphyry[1] lists them as follows: 1) Euphorbus, a Greek hero; 2) Aithalides, a son of the god Hermes, said to be one of the Argonauts; 3) Hermotimus; 4) Pyhrrus, a fisherman from Delos; and 5) his current life as Pythagoras, by which he showed, says Porphyry, "that the soul is immortal, and in those who have been purified it attains to memory of its ancient life."

The doctrine of transmigration of the soul places it in a vast cosmic plan, one that sees beyond the current life, and it states that one's actions here and now, for good or ill, will determine one's fate in future lives. The

---

1 Hadas and Smith, *Heroes and Gods*, p. 122

law of necessity, or karma, is the objective law that judges human actions in the light of divine justice, and acknowledges that the soul has a divine source and destination.

These three concepts—immortality of the soul, reincarnation/transmigration, and the law of karma—are inextricably bound up not only with each other, but also to Eastern sources. Guthrie is inconsistent here because whereas in his analysis of the "unit" and the "opposites" he admits that attempts have been made to connect these ideas to Persia, India, and even China, he appears to make no such similar connections in terms of immortality of the soul, transmigration, or the laws of necessity/karma that are *quintessentially* Eastern doctrines.

The fact remains that many scholars possessed a condescending attitude whose main thrust was to cast as "primitive" or "uncivilized" beliefs they did not even trouble to fully investigate. This situation is to be regretted, because those Eastern beliefs in the immortality of the soul, transmigration/reincarnation, and the law of karma are the essential teachings of great Eastern religions that came into being long before Christianity, and are still followed today by untold millions of people in the East.

As far as Plato is concerned, his teachings about the immortality of the soul, her divine source and destination, are scattered throughout some of his most important dialogues. After he has set the stage in the early dialogues—*Laches, Charmides, Euthyphro*, and so on—for the acquisition of the virtues, Plato moves on to those dialogues that reveal higher cosmic principles. Chief among these is the understanding of the immortality of the soul, beginning in the *Meno* with an explanation of the doctrine of recollection. He continues in perhaps the most soaring of all his dialogues, the *Phaedo*, which is a veritable paean of praise for immortality of the soul and its right to divine transcendence. Plato focuses on the law of karma in the *Phaedrus*, reveals the soul's ineffable mystic union in the *Symposium*, and provides a rational exposition of it in the *Republic*, where he starts out by explaining that the ideal city-state is in fact a representation, a mirror, of the human soul, thereby inferring that every single one of us contains *within u*s the ideal city—the state of the soul in its higher aspect—and that it is only waiting for us to recognize and honor it.

In this dialogue Plato shows us that the soul is a microcosm of the greater macrocosm, and he explains that the soul has a tripartite nature.

Here we can find echoes of the description of the three divine faculties found in Pythagoras. It is not described in exactly the same way in Pythagoras, but it preserves the essential threefold nature of it.

In the *Phaedrus* Plato reveals how each person originally inhabited the divine world but comes to earth and inhabits a series of bodies, the purpose of which is the perfection of one's soul in order to attain to a true understanding of one's divine nature, source, and destination.

Plato and Pythagoras thus share the doctrines of the immortality of the soul, transmigration, and the law of karma as part of a cosmic framework. Plato does not state in the dialogues that his source is Pythagoras, but few today doubt that is the case. This is the third great confluence between them.

Monad vs. Unlimited/Limit

Although he was accused by Aristotle of adhering to the two-principle theory (unlimited and limit), Pythagoras ultimately posited a single divine principle, the Monad, as the source of our universe. Pythagoras understood, and experienced, the cosmic principles (including number and the planets) as *expressions* of the divine faculties of the Monad. Schuré tells us that for Pythagoras the Monad was the Divine Masculine and the creative Dyad was the Divine Feminine, and that their union brought about an offspring that, from a purely mathematical view, we could call Number Three, but for Pythagoras was the third faculty of a Divine Triad, whose various relationships eventually differentiated the dimensions of the corporeal world.

It is here that ambiguity and confusion have set in because, for the scientists, the Unlimited (*apeiron*) and Limit (*peras*) are taken to be ultimate and original material principles, and therefore are considered to be immanent. I concede that this subtle distinction between a unitary, unmanifest, divine Monad and the duality that arises when the creative Dyad—his generative and reproductive aspect—begins manifestation is difficult to untangle, and could well give rise to Aristotle's interpretation. On the other hand, the sacred and esoteric mathematics studied by Pythagoras in Egypt, as well as the transcendental state attained in his Egyptian initiation, would certainly have allowed *him* to make the distinction. The fact that the *Monad* and *creative Dyad* operate in the sensible world does not take away from their divine nature, and nor does it contradict the essential truth that there is a single, uncreated, indivisible source of the universe—the unitary, transcendental Monad.

As for Plato, despite his references to Unlimited and Limit in the *Philebus*, we understand from the *Republic* that the Good (God) is the cause of all truth and knowledge, and the source of *everything* in the universe. In the *Timaeus* Plato asserts that three divine forces created the world. First, Timaeus says there is God, uncreated, indivisible, always the same, who created the Soul and diffused it throughout the universe, which is a pattern of the eternal world. These two principles, the Good (God) and the World Soul, *may* correlate with the Pythagorean Monad and the Creative Dyad. The third principle, "nurse" to all generations, may be correlated to the *harmonia* of Pythagoras, that third aspect of the Divine Triad that makes possible the differentiation of the corporeal world.

I conclude that, like Pythagoras, Plato accepts that dual principles apply to the sensible world, but he differentiates the sensible world from the intelligible world. However, like Pythagoras, Plato subsumes *all* manifestation back into the unitary transcendent principle—in his case, the Good. And, despite the continual focus on the two-principle theory in our investigations, ultimately Plato and Pythagoras both hold to a *triad* of divine principles being responsible for the creation of the world, a position that puts them in alignment with Christianity, Hinduism and Buddhism. This is the fourth confluence between Pythagoras and Plato.

Number: Pythagoras and Plato

Aristotle insisted that for the Pythagoreans number was immanent, and my response is to note that those early reports of immanent number were a gross misunderstanding of his mathematical doctrine. It was inconceivable for Pythagoras—as a full initiate, steeped in transcendent experience and esoteric knowledge—not to have been *fully aware* of ideal number, and to have understood its agency in serving as a symbol for those first principles that were too difficult for others to comprehend. The secret knowledge sought by his disciples involved an oath of silence as a price for that knowledge. The reason for that silence was that Pythagoras's views of

God—like those of Socrates after him—were so advanced and so different from those accepted by the state that they would have been considered cause for persecution, a persecution that, tragically, in both cases, caused their death. Such was the price each had to pay for being a significant evolutionary force in western civilization.

As for Plato, the transcendent nature of number was included as a Form, as were the elements of number, Even and Odd. And Plato held that geometric diagrams—of rectangles and triangles in the *Meno*, and indeed the whole diagram of the heavens itself—were what we might term "immanent tools" by which, if you managed to go beyond the mere representations of the diagrams and examined their assumptions, you would be led back to the unhypothesized principle, the Good. When a neophyte had finally experienced the mystical union with God, then and only then was the transcendent source of existence revealed, including number as the explanation of *all* things. At that point the understanding dawned that transcendence and immanence were two sides of the same coin.

When I compare Pythagoras and Plato then, I assume *both* of them have a metaphysic of the transcendent. Pythagoras's metaphysic of the transcendent is secret and concealed, whereas Plato's transcendent Forms and the Good are made public for all to investigate. Pythagoras is described as having a metaphysic of the immanent, which is publicly known. But Plato also has a metaphysic of the immanent (not publicly known), because the virtues of courage, piety, and justice of the early dialogues *cannot be known* unless there are immanent instantiations of them. It is true that Pythagoras *appears to focus on* the metaphysic of the immanent, but as we have seen it was the *transcendent* doctrines that were taught to the initiates of his school. Plato may *appear* to focus exclusively on the Forms, but immanence is always in the background. It is "participation" in the virtues that provides the first link in that process of recollection that leads ultimately to the apprehension of divine Reality. To one who had attained that divine Reality, immanence and transcendence are merely two sides of the same cosmic coin.

I maintain that Pythagoras and Plato both held that there was a single transcendental source of the universe, the Monad, or the Good, but that both advocated that where there was duality, number had an immanent instantiation. This is the fifth confluence of their doctrines.

Cosmology in Pythagoras and Plato

Although Aristotle is quoted as claiming that Pythagoras accepted the two-principle system (Unlimited and Limit), I would argue along with Plato that those two material principles have not been traced back to the unhypothesized first principle, the Monad. Pythagoras's cosmology *depends upon and starts from* that transcendental, undifferentiated Monad, which is in a state of *formless* unity *only* when it rests within itself—before manifestation. Under cosmic law, the Monad (the Divine Masculine) unfolds *part of itself* into its opposite—into the Eternal Feminine, the creative Dyad, the generative and reproductive faculty of the Monad. Let us be clear that when the Monad engages in this unfolding, it is in no way *affected* by it, which means that the *unmanifest* part of the Monad remains in its state of utter and absolute transcendence and repose. The creative Dyad is also eternal, but she manifests the corporeal universe and everything in it.

The projection of the Monad into the creative Dyad gives rise to the first duality, that between eternal/temporal, but also to the several other *pairs of opposites* including male/female, subject/object, and the numbers one and two. As Schuré reminds us, it is only after this "split" has taken place—when the Monad and creative Dyad are in manifestation—that the notion of duality arises. Some have argued that the number series starts with Aristotle's "One" or that the first integer is to be distinguished from the source of the universe, but, for Pythagoras, number arises when the Monad (One) differentiates into the creative Dyad (Two). Even if you insist that the Monad is Unity, as soon as the creative Dyad is created, the Unity expresses itself as the number One, and the creative Dyad is number Two. The union or relation that takes place between the Monad and the creative Dyad gives rise to their offspring—the Third faculty (Three), comprising the Divine Triad, those three principles through which the corporeal world is created.

Pythagoras held that "the universe is divided into three concentric spheres: the natural world, the human world, and the divine world." He also states that human beings are "composed of three elements...body, soul and spirit.... The Triad or the threefold law, therefore, is the essential law of things and the actual key to life" (Schuré 316). Schuré tells us there are parallels for his view—both looking back to India (Brahma, Vishnu, Shiva) to Buddhism (One, Two, Three) and looking forward to Christianity (Father, Son, Holy Spirit) where the Godhead is expressed as three forces in One, a single Godhead with three aspects, or Persons.

Pythagoras is known by the dictum that the things of this world are known by number. For Pythagoras number was a divine faculty of the Monad and was the living expression of it. Schuré adds: "Pythagoras pursued the teaching of Numbers still further. In each of them he defined a principle, a law, an active force of the universe." Here we see that Pythagoras's cosmology is inseparable from its *divine* mathematical expression. Schuré goes on to say that the basic principles are contained in the first four numbers, since in adding or multiplying them, one finds all the others" (Schuré 319).

Pythagoras represented his cosmology in the diagram of the Tetrad, that deceptively simple image that contains four rows of dots that add up to ten, but whose dots form the shape of a triangle, a Triad (Schuré 319). I have suggested that—with the one dot at the top, symbolizing the Monad; the two dots symbolizing Monad and Creative Dyad; the three dots the harmonia and the relationship between Monad and Creative Dyad, the Divine Triad; and the four dots representing the creation of the corporeal world—the Tetrad reveals that divine faculties govern all of manifestation.

And, what of Plato's cosmology? Guthrie admits that there are definite Pythagorean influences in Plato's *Timaeus,* but he falls short of the claim of A. E. Taylor that Plato's cosmology is in fact the work of a fifth-century BCE Pythagorean. Before and since Taylor there have been many interpretations of that mystifying cosmology unfolded in the *Timaeus*. Let me, therefore, take a different starting point. I refer back to Schuré who tells us (297) the Pythagorean school of esoteric philosophy is to be considered the "mother" of the Platonic School and that Pythagoras wrote his doctrine in secret signs and symbolic form. Therefore, if Plato is considered the "disciple" or "descendant" of Pythagoras, then we must resign ourselves to the fact that what is mystifying to us in the *Timaeus* is because it is similarly couched in secret signs and symbolic form.

If we take the *Republic* as a point of reference, we know that for Plato the highest and single principle was the Good (*Republic* 508-e). As I have pointed out elsewhere, when Plato speaks of the Good as the cause of knowledge and truth, it is, in fact, the *Form* of the Good that he means. But the Form of the Good is not the *Good Itself*. I have argued, based on Plato's own statements, that the Good Itself is *formless*. This first principle—the *Good Itself* as formless, eternal, unified and unmanifest—therefore corresponds to the Pythagorean Monad.

In the voice of Timaeus, Plato tells us that *God created the universe* and God is distinguished between what *always is* and has no becoming, from what *has* becoming (*Timaeus 27*). This is the first duality. Building on that distinction he says that the universe had an Artificer, a Maker, who was "past finding out," but that he had used *eternal patterns of the unchangeable* when he created it. Some researchers have made much of the fact that God had to use eternal patterns, insinuating that God was in fact *subject* to those patterns, but I have made the point throughout this book that the transcendental Monad incorporates *everything* within it, including the eternal patterns or Ideal Forms, a concept that Plato expresses when he says the Good is the cause of all truth and knowledge.

There is a slight ambiguity in Plato's explanation because he speaks of the Artificer as creating the world, whereas for Pythagoras it would be the creative Dyad, his Feminine counterpart, who creates the world. If we correlate the Artificer with the creative Dyad, perhaps the Artificer is another name for her. Yet Plato's World Soul appears to approximate the creative Dyad of Pythagoras as the second divine faculty, and she precedes creation of the corporeal world since she is diffused throughout it. A similar ambiguity inheres in the third divine faculty involved in creating the cosmos, the "nurse of all generation," because on the one hand Plato has described her as always the same, uncreated and indestructible, imperceptible to the senses and known only to the intelligence, but on the other hand "there is another nature of *the same name* with it, *and like to it, perceived by sense*, created, always in motion" (*Timaeus* 49-d; 52-a). There is a suggestion here that the nurse has two expressions, one of them eternal and uncreated, known only through intelligence, and the other, which is created and known through sense.

Perhaps this is what Schuré meant when he said that even the exoteric aspects of Plato's philosophy were couched in symbols to conceal their real meaning. Since later on Plato talks about those famous "triangles" that he assumed "to be the original elements of fire and other bodies," he does adhere to some form of threefold law in the manifestation of the universe, but the idea is abstrusely explicated, and it is hard to make sense of it. However, he confirms that threefold law in the *Republic*, where he speaks of the tripartite nature of the soul. In fact, Schuré says that the threefold nature of man and universe is concealed in Plato's exoteric writings, but completely misunderstood by later philosophers (318). "Plato replaced the doctrine of the three worlds of Pythagoras with three *concepts* which, in the absence of organized initiation, remained for two thousand years as three roads leading to the supreme goal. These three concepts were: The True, the Beautiful and the Good... three rays from the same Source which, when united constitute this Source Itself, that is, God" (Schuré 390).

The cosmologies of Plato and Pythagoras concur in essence, and this represents the sixth confluence between them.

The Tetrad

I have included a very brief section on the Tetrad because it rounds out our knowledge of Pythagoras's philosophy, and because it is a quintessential aspect of his metaphysics. Many interpretations have been put forth about the Tetrad—some of them arithmetical, others that attempt to re-create the musical consonances as a cosmological corollary. Others still are pure conjecture, and there are those that fly in the face of all logic. My own interpretation of the Tetrad is general, and certainly not new. First, going back to the vision Pythagoras saw, it was of a temple with columns, base, and architrave, surmounted by a triangular pediment, and Pythagoras saw it as a *symbol* of the threefold nature of reality. The columns, base, and architrave make the shape of a four-sided figure, most likely a rectangle (since most temples were rectangular) but possibly a square. The number four is usually seen as representing *matter* and concrete things. Therefore, here it represents the sensible world and all things in the sensible world. The material temple is surmounted by a triangular pediment, representing the three divine faculties, which eternally nourish the world of matter with their divine influx of forces, interpenetrating matter on every level of manifestation.

Another way of stating this is that Tetrad is a symbolic representation of the unfolding cosmos. Here the single dot at the top represents the Monad in its purely unified and transcendental state of absolute rest. The two dots below represents cosmological processes that take eons of time as the Monad moves from its initial formless aspect into the beginning of form as the Creative Dyad who represents the corporeal body of the universe. The duality of eternal and temporal, as well as the other dualities of light–dark, male–female, one–two, and so on are part of that cosmogenesis. The three dots represent the Divine Triad, the three divine faculties necessary to bring about the generation of the universe. And finally, the four dots represent the world we recognize, the material world with all its sensible things, and time and space as its boundaries. The Tetrad thus symbolizes these cosmological processes—which take place over vast eons of time—that Pythagoras could not explain to others because they were too difficult to understand, and as a result he used number to symbolize them. Pythagoras demonstrates once again that there is only One transcendent, divine Monad in that role since he places a single dot at the apex of his Tetrad.

As to a brief description of actual Pythagorean cosmology, Schuré states: "If one relies upon the divisions of heaven which we find in the esoteric fragments of the Pythagoreans, this astronomy would be similar to the astronomy of Ptolemy—a motionless earth with the sun, planets and the entire firmament revolving around it. But the very nature of this astronomy indicates that it is entirely symbolic. At the center of his universe Pythagoras places Fire, of which the sun is but a reflection. And in all esotericism of the East, Fire is the sign of Spirit, of divine universal consciousness. Therefore, what our philosophers generally accept as the physics of Pythagoras and Plato is nothing but a figurative description of their secret philosophy" (Schuré 322).

Conclusions about Pythagoras/Plato

I have undertaken this brief comparison between Plato and Pythagoras to show the similarities—indeed, the direct parallels—to be found in their philosophical doctrines. Such a comparison would not have been possible without taking into consideration those secret doctrines that were the direct result of Pythagoras's initiation in Egypt, as well as his studies with the Babylonians and the descendants of Zoroaster, the Persian Magi. It is the recognition and acceptance of Ideal Number in Pythagoras's transcendental teachings that allows us to see beyond the "immanent metaphysic" assigned to him, and creates the bridge to Plato's Ideal Forms as eternal patterns that provide the structure for our temporal world.

It is Pythagoras's initiation that gives us grounds for understanding that his system was not dualistic but that the two-principles of "Unlimited–Limit" were ultimately manifestations of the uncreated, eternal, unified, transcendental source of all—the Monad. The other doctrines, immortality of the soul, transmigration, and laws of karma that structure the soul's earthbound journey, are held in complete consonance by Plato and Pythagoras. In fact, if allowances are made for time and place and differing historical conditions, the evidence would appear to support the hypothesis that their philosophies are in essence *identical*. In fact, as Schuré points out, "First he [Plato] owed the science and substance of his ideas to his initiation into the Mysteries," and second, that having "purchased one of the master's [Pythagoras'] manuscripts at a high price...and having dipped into the esoteric traditions of Pythagoras at its very source, he borrowed the main ideas and framework of his system from that philosopher" (Schuré 387–388). It turns out, then, that A. E. Taylor was correct that Plato's philosophy was to be attributed to a fifth-century (actually, sixth-century) BCE Pythagorean. He just didn't quite surmise that it was Pythagoras himself!

There are those defenders of Plato who will throw up their hands at the suggestion that Plato borrowed his ideas and philosophical framework from Pythagoras, as though such a claim would detract from his unsurpassed reputation. But they might take heart from the other denouement—namely that Plato had himself been initiated into the Mysteries! What the initiate understood and experienced was that there was One truth in the universe and that it led like a thread through all historical time periods, and each of the world's religions contained some part of that one truth. The highest manifestation, however, was in the true expression of the Mysteries themselves, and those great Teachers—Pythagoras and Plato—not only unveil the same universal truth for the appropriate historical time and place, but also stand as the very initiators of great cultural movements of consciousness that propel evolution forward. In the case of Plato, whatever his debt to Pythagoras, he emerged as the pivotal western philosopher who placed in writing those dialogues dedicated to reason that are also revealed as the path to initiation. In addition, despite Socrates's martyrdom for the new idea of the Good, of God, Plato made the *mysteries public*, with a few notable exceptions, such as the myth of Er, or those passages in the *Timaeus* which divulged secret information in symbolic form. And Plato stands not only for the new ideals of reason in the fifth and fourth centuries BCE, but has remained the pre-eminent philosopher of the western tradition for the last two thousand years! What has been overlooked for most of that time is that the philosophical systems initiated by Plato—and Pythagoras before him—ultimately owed their existence and their truth to the Mystery tradition, in which both are still considered Great Initiates.

PART THREE

Tracing the Source of those "Foreign" Doctrines

Firm links have been established between Plato and Pythagoras, but where do we go from here? In brief, we are seeking to discover the original source of those doctrines that found their way into *The Collected Dialogues of Plato* described as "foreign." To be specific, the doctrines of immortality of the soul; the transmigration of the soul into a series of bodies (reincarnation) and the law of cause and effect, or karma—doctrines that were almost unknown in Plato's Greece and have a distinctly Eastern flavor.

We have already taken the first step in this journey of discovery by finding those same doctrines in Pythagoras. Our next destination will be Egypt, since Pythagoras spent twenty-two years in the mystery school in Memphis. However, no study of these foreign doctrines is complete without first linking them to the legendary Greek musician Orpheus, whose beliefs in the immortality of the soul, transmigration/reincarnation, and the law of cause and effect (karma) were so similar to those of Pythagoras that they are often referred to as the Orphic-Pythagorean tradition. This is interesting when we consider that Guthrie dates the written works of Orpheus to the sixth century BCE, which would make him somewhat of a contemporary of Pythagoras.

There are some contra-indications of that view, found in Guthrie himself, who states that in the sixth century BCE, Orpheus was known by the Greek poets Ibycus and Pindar as *already being of ancient renown*. The Greek dramatists Aeschylus and Euripides are also known to have honored him. Guthrie suggests that there is some question of his historicity, but that the eminent Greek scholar Jane Harrison is convinced that he was a flesh and blood person, even though he lived "in the dawn of history." Guthrie is noncommittal, has lingering doubts. Again, he is more likely to follow Aristotle in believing that Orpheus was not a historical person, that writings attributed to him were instead by one Onomakritos, and that "Orphism always was a *literature*, first and foremost."[1] Schuré says Orpheus lived 400 years before Homer, which would place him around 1300 BCE.

The Orpheus myth runs as follows: He was the son of Apollo, or of the Thracian river God Oiagros and the Muse Calliope, and Apollo gave him a lyre, a stringed instrument that he taught Orpheus to play. Orpheus became renowned for his inspired gift of music, and his magical ability to charm not only people, but the birds, fishes, and wild beasts, was legendary. One legend, now disputed, is that Orpheus accompanied the Argonauts in their quest for the golden fleece, and that after his return he fell in love with Eurydice, who, while fleeing from the advances of Aristaues (another son of Apollo) fell and was fatally bitten by a snake.

Orpheus was so devastated by her loss that on the advice of the nymphs and gods, he was even willing to travel to the underworld to try to get her back again. It is part of the legend that no one had ever journeyed to the underworld before and returned alive. Nonetheless, Orpheus struck a bargain with Hades, the lord of the underworld, in which he would be allowed to take Eurydice back to the upper world—provided he did not look back at her as they ascended upward. However, in the ascent, somehow distracted by Eurydice, Orpheus looked back at her, broke his word, and she was taken from him a second time. In his grief Orpheus swore to avoid all other women and to give his sole worship to the Sun, to Apollo. His followers, the Maenads, were so offended by his turning away from them that in the frenzy and passion of their Bacchic madness they tore him to pieces and flung his head into the river—where, the legend ran, Orpheus continued singing his mournful songs.

This legend became the source of myth and religious ritual. It should be noted, however, that from the very beginning Orpheus was associated with Apollo, who gave him his lyre. It is said that the dramatist Euripides was the first to connect Orpheus with the chthonic god Dionysus. This resulted in a split between Apollo, the god of reason, symmetry, light, and Dionysus, the god of ecstasy, wine, and chthonic energies. Orpheus eventually became connected by various commentators to each of these opposing gods.

---

1 Guthrie, *Orpheus and Greek Religion*, 10 (hereafter *Orpheus*).

Tracing the Source of those "Foreign" Doctrines

What is more important is that Orpheus is known to have made a major contribution to the culture of the time. In fact, he was known as a pioneer of civilization, having taught humanity the arts of medicine, agriculture, possibly writing, but most important, as being the creator and founder of the mystery religions. In this respect he is said to have used music as a way to soothe the passions; he was a seer and a mystic; was versed in "magical" arts such as astrology, and he established the cults of Apollo *and* Dionysus, which included rites of purification and initiation—both private and public.

Various interpretations are given as to why Orpheus failed in his quest to bring Eurydice back to the upper world of earth, but what is lost is the fact that Orpheus is known as the first person who ever entered the underworld of Hades—and returned to tell the tale. When one considers that at the time of Pythagoras, the final test for initiation was that the disciple should experience his own death *and resurrection*, one can see the parallel in the myth of Orpheus's descent into the underworld. One then begins to understand the significance of his renown as the founder and creator of the mystery religions.

Orpheus's tale might have remained in the realm of myth were it not for the fact that celebrated Greek dramatists such as Aeschylus, Euripides and Aristophanes, almost a thousand years after the time of Orpheus, credit him as the teacher of religious initiations as well as abstinence from murder. As Guthrie himself states: "Plato mentions the poet several times and quotes from his writings...in *Cratylus* (402-b), the *Philebus* (66-c); the *Republic* (2. 364-e), where the itinerant priests are spoken of as producing 'a mass of books of Orpheus and Musaios,' and in the *Laws* (8. 829-d), where the Hymns of Orpheus are mentioned (*Orpheus* 12). Other sources also mention the *Apology, Protagoras, Ion,* and *Symposium*. The number of such references in Plato's work is quite extraordinary when we consider that Orpheus may have lived nearly a thousand years earlier, and that Plato mentions Pythagoras, a much closer contemporary, only once or twice. That is something to ponder.

Be that as it may, it was common knowledge that the Pythagoreans and Orphics were seen as sharing similar doctrines, and there were well-known references to works of Pythagoras that supposedly bore Orpheus's name. One probable explanation of this is that even today, it is a common practice in Eastern religions, before the Teacher, or guru, dies he passes on his power and authority to a successor, and for the duration of the successor's lifetime, he, or in modern times, she, will always refer to the teachings as being the possession of and having the authority of the Master who died. If Pythagoras was aware of this cultural practice—as his travels in Egypt, Babylon, Chaldea, and his exposure to the Persian religion may well have done—it would not be not surprising if he honored his own Greek ancestor, creator of the mystery religion, in dedicating some of those Pythagorean works to Orpheus, especially if Orpheus was, like him, a Great Initiate.

The Teachings of Orpheus and Pythagoras

What *were* the doctrines Pythagoras and Orpheus had in common? The guide here is again Guthrie, whose book *Orpheus and Greek Religion* is perhaps the most substantive investigation of Orpheus in modern times. Guthrie opens by saying that whereas Plato believed in Orpheus the man, and had quoted from him in a number of his dialogues, Aristotle not only doubted the existence of Orpheus himself, but also of his poems, suggesting they were written by someone else, Onomakritos. This is not surprising in the scientifically oriented Aristotle, but as Guthrie attests, many, if not most, ancient writers knew of Orpheus, including Aeschylus, Euripides, and Aristophanes. And since they were playwrights, it is reasonable to suggest that through their works the general public was also well aware of Orpheus, as his renown was legendary.

However, what is crucial is that, while written Orphic references are dated to the sixth century BCE, a poet as eminent as Ibycus tells us that the tales of Orpheus were already considered *ancient* in the sixth century BCE. No mention is made of Orpheus in Homer or Hesiod, both of whom date back approximately to the ninth century BCE, which is somewhat surprising if, as some ancient authors suggest, Orpheus should be dated to around the time of Homer. The celebrated port, Pindar, credits him with being on the journey of the Argonauts (a claim now disputed), and his name was recorded by Pherecydes and Hellicanus, the latter declaring him the *ancestor* of both Homer and Hesiod. In fact, Guthrie himself states: "His date was generally supposed *in antiquity* to lie in the heroic age, *several generations before Homer*... and (sometimes) we find him represented by some of the Greek historians to be *Homer's direct ancestor"* (*Orpheus* 26). Schuré dates Orpheus to 400 years before Homer, and that takes us back to 1300 BCE, and, if this is correct, he is generally aligned with Kern and confirms that Orpheus was ancient indeed!

All the more curious, then, is that while Guthrie is aware of at least some of these claims of Orpheus's antiquity, he seems to dismiss them all and date Orpheus to the Orphic writings in the sixth century BCE, thereby contradicting Ibycus who himself lived in the sixth century BCE and expressly spoke of Orpheus's ancient origin. Guthrie concedes that the plastic art of the seventh century BCE—vases, coins, and so on—reveal Easternizing influences, and there are many recorded instances of such influences in the eighth century BCE, facts that Jane Harrison interprets as revealing that the Greek civilization, being in its infancy, was indeed, in the eighth and seventh centuries BCE, influenced by Eastern motifs (*Orpheus* 89). (More archeological and linguistic research would need to be done on whether artifacts remain from Homer's time and beyond to determine whether they can be connected to Orpheus, though that appears unlikely.) Guthrie's one-sided judgments need to be taken into account when evaluating Orpheus, because to some extent we are dependent on Guthrie's own painstaking investigation of the subject for our knowledge about him.

For example, Guthrie makes the claim (*Orpheus* 10) that Orphism "was always a literature first and foremost." This statement has an odd ring, implying that a literature simply appears, spontaneously complete, without a charismatic individual as the *source* of such poetry. Such a view flies in the face of logic, and appears to contradict the view of the eminent Greek historian, Jane Harrison, who unequivocally affirmed the existence of Orpheus, the man.

Turning to the Orphic doctrines themselves, Guthrie first tackles the mythologically based Orphic view of the origin of the world. It is peopled by generations of warring gods, and its genealogy is tangled and somewhat inconclusive. Our purpose is not to follow that complicated argument to its detailed conclusion, but to see if there are parallels to Pythagorean doctrines, which, if Schuré's chronology is correct, now span a period of seven hundred years! (Parenthetically, where Guthrie begins with the cosmology, it would seem intuitively more meaningful to compare the *religious* practices and doctrines, because in 1300 BCE we would assume cosmology to be in a very primitive state of development, and the Orphic mythological explanation may be expected to differ significantly from the transcendental but *scientific* explanations given by Pythagoras.

Guthrie tells us that the Orphic religion first appeared in the sixth century BCE in Southern Italy, where there were sects practicing a form of mystery religion that had much in common with Pythagorean doctrines. Instead of believing in the antiquity of Orpheus, Guthrie claims these sects wanted to give "the appearance of centuries-old antiquity" (*Orpheus* 46). As to the Orphic theogony, Guthrie relies on the three versions as found in the scholar Gruppe: one of these was attributed to Eudemos (a student of Aristotle), a second from Hieronymous and Hellikanos, and third the Rhapsodic that is considered the "usual or customary" one that, parenthetically, Guthrie discusses hardly at all. This is surprising since Guthrie tells us that Kern's work has been directed toward proving that the bulk of the Rhapsodic Theogony is an actual work of the sixth century (*Orpheus* 77).

Gruppe sees in these different versions agreement with one central doctrine, ascribed to Musaios, pupil of Orpheus, as follows: "Everything comes to be out of One and is resolved into One." Gruppe continues that "at one time Phanes, at another, Zeus, contained the seeds of all being within his own body, and from this state of mixture in the One has emerged the whole of our manifold world, and all nature, animate and inanimate" (*Orpheus* 75). Gruppe then puts his own interpretation on this statement, saying that everything first existed together in a *confused mass*, and that the process of creation was one of separation and division, with the corollary that at the end of the process, our era will return to the *primitive confusion*. Gruppe uncritically accepts his own interpretation, adding that such beliefs could be traced to the sixth and fifth centuries BCE and the physical systems of the Milesians, or to Neopythagorean, Gnostic, Neoplatonic interpretations in the Christian era that tell us that the sensible world is brought into being from the intelligible world, but that *such ideas are entirely absent from the early cosmologies*.

Instead of pursuing Musaios's statements further, which would be more likely to be authentic because they are from a pupil of Orpheus himself, Gruppe plunges into his own interpretation that "in the beginning everything existed together as a 'confused mass,' that the process of creation was one of separation and division, and that the end of our era will be a return to primitive confusion" (*Orpheus* 75).

We must dispute several aspects of this last statement quite vigorously. In the fifth century BCE, *Plato* was espousing just such a cosmology—namely, that God created the world, and that the sensible world emanated from a transcendental source. It is also clear that in the sixth century BCE, Pythagoras held the identical view, that the cause of the universe is the unitary transcendent Monad. And third, Christmas Humphries states in his book on Buddhism that creation starts with the One (*Buddhism* 16).

When Gruppe jumps to the conclusion that the One is equated to a "confused mass" he is clearly placing it within Milesian material descriptions of the universe, whereas we would suggest that if Orpheus was, like Pythagoras, a great initiate, as Schuré claims, then he is almost certain to ascribe the origin of the universe to be a *transcendental* One—which would be equivalent to the Pythagorean Monad and Plato's Good. This is clearly attested by Musaios, a pupil of Orpheus, when he stated: "Everything comes to be out of One and is resolved into One." But for a metaphysician, an initiate, that One is not a "confused mass"—it is, in its pure state, transcendental and unmanifest, although it (like Phanes) contains all things within it, including the structure and beauty, as well as the moral order of the universe. Perhaps ideas of "confusion" and "original chaos" enter human minds when they are using material and scientific principles to describe the origin of the universe. No such chaos lies within the metaphysical, transcendental view. The transcendental principle, the Monad, even in its unmanifest state, has supreme intelligence and divine order. When the One moves into manifestation, it differentiates, divides, separates, but for the initiate these processes occur as an expression of cosmic law. Therefore we must disagree with Gruppe when he says that the end of this process of creation will return to the "primitive confusion." For an initiate, nothing could be further from the truth, for the goal of human evolution is the reunion of the soul with God in the divine experience of initiation. And the transcendent God is seen as creator of the universe with all of its order, beauty and truth.

Thus, Musaios, a pupil of Orpheus, appears more likely than Gruppe to know the truth. As it is, Gruppe relies on a cosmological description by Damaskios—a pupil of Aristotle who Guthrie describes as a Neoplatonist (*Orpheus* 74). Damaskios, in turn, is using as his source a man named Eudemos, who lived in the fourth century BCE. I will elucidate that cosmology briefly, with the caveat that the view of Gruppe, and apparently affirmed by Guthrie, is one that is in consonance with the Milesians and with the scientific interpretation of the mythological story. I will try to pick out the salient points of that story and show how they can more nearly be correlated to the transcendental One espoused by Plato, Pythagoras and, I suggest, Orpheus himself.

Apparently, Eudemos claimed the first original principle to be Night, and Guthrie says Damaskios tells us nothing more about it. Of the origin of the universe of Damaskios and Athenogoras, Hieronymus and Hellikanos tell us: "There was first water and some solid matter, from which was formed a slime or mud that finally was to harden into earth" (*Orpheus* 79). Guthrie dismisses Damaskios as a Neoplatonist who was not able to accept that there are two original principles instead of an undivided One. At any rate Guthrie quotes Damaskios's next sentence as holding that "the one principle before the two is omitted by the account as being altogether unutterable." But such was not the case for Musaios. As we recall, he stated that "everything comes to be out of One and is resolved into One." I am therefore not quite as eager as Gruppe to reject the Neo-Pythagorean or Orphic accounts, since their books reveal that they had significant transcendental experiences of the One, and were therefore in a better position than most to evaluate Pythagoras's doctrines.

Damaskios's first statement confirms the Pythagorean view, namely that the One is indeed transcendental (and incidentally, formless) such that nothing can be predicated of it. Therefore it is unutterable. In other words Damaskios is affirming the Pythagorean position, not the scientific position adopted by the more material-minded Milesians.

Guthrie, commenting now on the theogony of the *Rhapsodies*, states that it begins with Time and quotes Damaskios: "The Rhapsodies omit the two earlier principles (and the one before them that has been passed over in silence) *and start with the third as* the first" (*Orpheus* 79). I would merely point out once again that Damaskios appears to affirm the Pythagorean doctrine—namely that there was a single unitary original principle, the One, the Monad, and that when the generative aspect of the Monad was activated, it gave rise to Two Principles, and their relation produced the Divine Triad. I argued earlier that whether you ascribe all existence to the unitary Monad or to the divine Triad, the cause of the universe at this level of manifestation is still divine and transcendental.

Let us synopsize the mythological story of the cosmos very briefly. Out of water and earth was born a monstrous serpent with two heads, one of a bull and the other of a lion. In between was the head of a god, Chronos (Time). Out of Chronos comes Aither, Chaos, and Erebos. Chronos fashions an egg that splits in two, and out of it springs forth Phanes the first born of the gods. Athenogoras adds that the two halves of the egg form heaven and earth (the first split into duality). Phanes bore a daughter, Night (loosely equivalent to the creative Dyad), who he took as his partner, and who assisted him with the work of creation and who became the next ruler of that universe when Phanes died.

To return to our theme, the statements of Musaios and of Damaskios both support Orpheus as holding to a single unitary Monad, of which it was impossible to speak; two principles (which we are calling the Monad and creative Dyad) and then a Third principle "as the first containing anything which may be spoken of and is commensurate with human hearing" (*Orpheus* 79).

Thus, the first confluence between Orpheus and Pythagoras is that they share the same general transcendent cosmological origin and structure. From the statements of Damaskios, our understanding is that the Orphic account would be more mythological and that of Pythagoras more scientific, has not been totally borne out. The Orphic account, according to Eudemos and Damaskios, parallels the Pythagorean account in the first Three principles. The mythological story somewhat expresses this parallel, but the tangled genealogy makes it difficult to pick out the Third Principle. There is also ambiguity because the seeming originating principles are earth and water—material principles. The cosmic analogy begins with Chronos and the fashioning of the egg that splits into heaven and earth. Orpheus, however, as the founder of the mysteries, was well aware of the transcendental origin of the universe.

What is common knowledge, however, is the Orphics and Pythagoreans both believed in the immortality of the soul, the transmigration of souls (reincarnation), and the law of cause and effect (karma). Both groups shared rituals of purification, and Orpheus and Pythagoras are both well known for 1) teaching initiation and 2) abstaining from killing animals either for food or for sacrificial offerings—doctrines that were contrary to common Greek experience at the time. Therefore, when critics attempt to dismiss Orpheus or Pythagoras as engaging in "primitive" practices, it would be well to remember that they practiced a form of compassion unknown elsewhere in the Greek world. While the sacrifice of animals was a common and accepted occurrence in the religious ceremonies of the Greek cults, both Orpheus and Pythagoras were teaching the rejection of animal sacrifice in favor of an understanding that a human being sacrificed his or her *own lower self* in the pursuit of higher knowledge. Both groups held that the fulfillment of evolution was divine initiation in which the soul would have the experience of reunion with the unitary Monad. In addition, it was the divine initiation that allowed the soul to be released from the "wheel" of rebirth.

Guthrie tells us that Plato was influenced by the Orphics in his adoption of the beliefs of immortality, reincarnation and the law of karma. Indeed, these doctrines provide the very *framework* of his discussion of the soul in the *Phaedo, Phaedrus, Symposium,* and *Republic*. However, as I have shown, despite any possible Orphic influence, Plato owes a much greater and more immediate debt to Pythagoras on these matters.

Guthrie ends his book on Orpheus with the views of Aristotle, where, in characteristic fashion, Aristotle totally rejects the notion of the soul separating from the body at death because, for him, they are joined *in* human life *in* the human being. Aristotle also rejected the cosmogonic side of Orphism and Pythagoreanism because it inferred that the world was in an evolutionary process where the most perfect stage would not be at the beginning, but rather at the end, whereas he, Aristotle, held that the best had existed from all time, and that the attempt to reach perfection was, so to speak, present before one's eyes all the time.

Aristotle might have been surprised to find his last thought echoed by Jesus some three hundred years after him when he remarked that "the kingdom of heaven is all around you and men do not see it." But what Aristotle did not seem to take into account was that once part of the Monad has limited itself—by becoming the sensible universe with its manifold creatures and objects, bounded by time and by space—the very fact of the world being sensible engenders in most people a forgetfulness of their divine nature and source. Presumably that is precisely why Aristotle so stubbornly persisted in his affirmation of the material origins of the universe, the Unlimited and Limited, and outright mocked Pythagoras's (and Plato's) claim that *eternal* principles were the cause of the sensible universe. The world surely *is* perfect from all time—but it takes purification of the soul and divine initiation to actually realize that truth in personal experience. And what that truth encompasses is *seeing the divine present in the sensible world*. Thus, there is no stigma in advocating an evolutionary movement forward toward the divine, except that it is *an inner evolutionary movement of the soul*, and not solely an external evolution of matter. (Parenthetically, how does Aristotle justify his idea of the universe being always in a state of perfection with his own notion of the teleological purpose of each and every organism?)

For some, like Darwin, that evolutionary thrust took a physical form in the evolution of the species, but for one who was initiated into the secret knowledge of the mysteries, the resulting bliss of ultimately merging with the divine was to understand, from an experiential level, that *all* of the world was divine, whether in its immanent or transcendent aspect. This, of course, *was* understood by Orpheus, Pythagoras and Plato, as their theogonies affirm.

One other matter needs attention, and that is the problem of historicity. Guthrie claims that there is no information on Orphism extant before the sixth century BCE, and because the Orphic writing can be dated to the sixth century BCE, he places Orpheus himself (if he existed!) in the sixth century BCE. This is a common practice. Scholars date historical individuals with the evidence of their achievements, usually extant texts or archaeological findings. My position on this is that a very ancient oral tradition is often neglected when we date teachings with extant texts, which in many cases might not have been written down for hundreds, even thousands of years after the death of that individual. This is the reason why it would be easy to place Orpheus at 1300 BCE rather than sixth century BCE, as I will explain.

Guthrie says Orpheus and his group lived in Southern Italy, somewhere in the vicinity of the Pythagoreans. But if the divine musician Orpheus is, as claimed, one of the pioneers of civilization, having taught humanity the arts of medicine, agriculture and writing as well as being a founder of many important religious cults including those of Dionysus and Apollo, and if he was the one who created the mystery schools, and instituted initiation, then it does not seem that these developments are consonant with cultural developments connected with either the sixth century BCE, or for the fifth or fourth centuries either. In fact, they seem to hearken back to a much earlier time. For example, the Greek mysteries are known to date to at least the eighth century BCE, and the Mycenean mysteries to several hundred years earlier. Schuré dates Orpheus to 1300 BCE so it is not surprising that almost nothing is known historically that far back.

We recall that references to Orpheus are not to be found in Homer or Hesiod, although *Herodotus* placed Homer four centuries before his own time. The anecdotal material places Homer in the ninth century BCE, a time when his own mythological explanations were a very powerful influence upon religion. But if no reference to Orpheus can be found in Homer or Hesiod, it should not be presumed that Orpheus lived *later* than either of these historian/playwrights. It fact, one can just as easily presume that Orpheus *pre-dated* Homer and Hesiod, if he lived in 1300 BCE, as is suggested by Schuré. This would perhaps place his role more accurately as one who is a *pioneer* of civilization in an earlier time period. Parenthetically, Schuré points out that after his death, the name of Orpheus was expunged from the historical record by his enemies, and that was the reason his name is lost in the mists of history.

Another matter concerns the supposed proximity of the Orphic enclave in Southern Italy to the Pythagorean school in Croton. It simply flies in the face of logic to assume that Orpheus and Pythagoras lived in *proximity during something like the same time period* when Orpheus was a pioneer of agriculture, medicine, and creation of the mystery schools, and Pythagoras was a pioneer of a later phase of culture that included cosmology, mathematics, music and science. I would suggest that these are reasons to assume that their schools were, in fact, farther apart as to time periods than history has assumed. Perhaps Shure is correct when he dates Orpheus to 1300 BCE and Pythagoras to the sixth century BCE. However,

Tracing the Source of those "Foreign" Doctrines

even if he is not correct about these dates, there is no reason to doubt the words of those poets Ibycus and Pindar who lived in the fourth century BCE and who both claimed that Orpheus was already known as an ancient and legendary musician who brought sacred teachings to those of his time.

There is one final point, the most important one. Guthrie distinguished Orphism from the worship of the Olympian gods and the cults of the Eleusian mysteries, but we have still not accounted for the existence in ancient Greece of religious doctrines that have their source in the East. I am speaking here specifically of immortality of the soul, transmigration/reincarnation, and the law of karma. These doctrines were, as I have suggested, totally foreign to Greece, with the exception of Orpheus, Pythagoras, and Plato, who attests in the *Apology*, that they were cause for persecution, prosecution, and even death—for the simple reason that these beliefs opposed and contradicted the state religion. In short, in Greece during Plato's lifetime it was considered blasphemy to claim immortality for the individual human soul.

No explanation is given for the existence in Greece of these Eastern doctrines, and very little regard was given to their source. But one important statement—admittedly by a modern interpreter—cannot be overlooked. When looking at possible sources for Orphism, Guthrie quotes Francis Cornford as saying:

> Whether or not we accept the hypothesis of direct influence from Persia on the Ionian Greeks in the sixth century, any student of Orphic and Pythagorean thought cannot fail to see that the *similarities between it and Persian religion* are so close as to warrant our regarding them as expressions of the same view of life, and using one system to interpret the other.[2]

Guthrie continues:

> When the fact we are faced with is the resemblance of the Orphic (Ageless Time) in its mythological representation to the Persian (Endless Time), a resemblance not merely to the general but extending to detail, then even the "hypothesis of direct influence" becomes difficult to escape. Yet, so it is. (*Orpheus* 89)

---

2   Cornford, *From Religion to Philosophy*, 176.

Guthrie had taken up the question of possible Persian influence on Greece in his *History of Philosopyhy* (251–56), and gives a list of ancient authors who made references to Zoroaster, founder of the Persian religion, and in particular to the case for the influence of Zoroaster on Pythagoras. Those writers included some illustrious names, including Hippolytus, Clement of Alexandria, Plutarch, Apuleius, and Porphyry the Neoplatonist. Another group had made general references to the Magi and Persia, as well as Cicero, Diogenes Laertius, Porphyry, Iamblichus and Pliny. Guthrie tells us that there was a "strong tradition" tracing back to Aristotle that Pythagoras had been directly instructed in religion by Zoroaster or the Persian Magi, but he concludes that because the details were only known from later Graeco-Roman writers, he believed such belief was no more than a "conjecture based on a real or fancied resemblance of doctrine." To dismiss so many eminent writers of their time, in one fell swoop, seems to betray a disregard for their knowledge or authority, and at the same time to close the door to the possibility of such Persian influence without adequately investigating it.

This attitude is in evidence elsewhere in *Orpheus and Greek Religion*, where, despite the claims of ancient dramatists such as Ibycus and Pindar that Orpheus was, in their time, considered to be of antiquity, Guthrie makes the judgment that because there is no earlier evidence than the sixth century BCE, that is the century to which Orpheus is to be dated. Having taken Jane Harrison's viewpoint that in the seventh and eighth centuries BCE the Hellenic mind was in a receptive state—in its "childhood"—and was thus open to influences from outside, including the East, Guthrie tells us the Greeks modified them to conform to their own standards. Greece did not care for "monstrosities" (i.e., mythological representations). While Greek art was considered to be in its period of maturity in the period covering the late sixth to the fourth centuries, the period of its "childhood" spanned the seventh century when there was a definite period of Eastern influence on Greek art, so much so that some called the Greek version a "slavish imitation" of Eastern types. Guthrie tells us that as far back as the eighth century BCE plastic forms of sphinxes and griffins could be found, but that as for Greek literature of that century, it was a blank page. One could conclude from this that an Easternizing tendency *was* found in those centuries prior to the sixth century date given for Orpheus.

One last point should be mentioned here. Guthrie is careful to place Orphism on the fringes of Greek state religion, and rightly so, for it appealed to the few rather than the masses, and as we have seen, its doctrine of the immortality of the soul was considered blasphemy. Guthrie however, continues to press the point that the Orphics depended upon ancient *sacred books* for their religious doctrines, rather than believing in the legendary but historic reality of *Orpheus the man* who was credited with *creating* those writings and, indeed, founding the entire mystery school tradition in Greece. And despite eventually extolling Orpheus as Apollonian, he continues to lump the Orphics with those other mystery cults who worshipped Orpheus in the guise of the wine drinking, orgiastic Dionysians. When we stop to consider that Orpheus was important for two reasons: 1) founding the mystery school tradition and 2) *abstaining* from killing animals either for food or for sacrifices, it would seem that Guthrie misunderstood the very purpose of the life and mission of Orpheus, namely to *transform the orgiastic and blood sacrifices* to the understanding that true worship involved the sacrifice, not of defenseless animals, but of *one's own lower self* in the search for higher knowledge and mystic union with the godhead.

This, indeed, is the interpretation of Schuré. That being the case, let us see what other contributions Schuré can make to the history and achievements of Orpheus. As noted, Schuré places Orpheus five centuries before Homer, to approximately 1300 BCE, and states that at that time Greece had been peopled for thousands of years by a branch of the white race akin to the Getes—the Scythians and primitive Celts—who had mingled with colonies from India, Egypt and Phoenicia and had established themselves in Greece. Through the mixture of these races there was formed "a flowing and harmonious language, a mixture of primitive Celtic, Zend, Sanskrit and Phoenician, and two of the gods worshipped at that time were Poseidon, the god of the water, and Ouranos, the god of the sky" (Schuré 225).

In those ancient times the female divinities were in ascendancy and were worshipped as the supreme deities. The few male cosmogonic gods were consigned to the high mountains, the people preferring the enticing procession of female divinities who represented the power of nature, whether seductive or terrible, rather than the mysterious universal god.

The female cult had degenerated, calling forth dangerous passions and blood sacrifice. Beyond Greece, Thrace was also involved in an intense and heated struggle, as the solar and lunar cults were fighting for supremacy.

According to Schuré, at that time there appeared in Thrace a young man of royal race and wondrous appeal, the son of a priestess of Apollo, whose melodious voice had a strange charm. He spoke of the gods in a new rhythm, seemed inspired, and charmed all who heard him, even the wild Bacchantes.

Suddenly this young man, called the son of Apollo, disappeared. He was said to be dead, or to have descended to hell. However, he had secretly fled to Samothrace, then to Egypt, where he asked shelter from the priests at Memphis. Having spent twenty years studying and mastering the Mysteries in Egypt (approximately the same amount of time as Pythagoras), he eventually returned to Thrace. He was now called Orpheus of Arpha, which means the *one who heals with light*.

Orpheus assumed the leadership of the majority of the Thracians, transformed and subdued the cult of Bacchus, and soon his influence penetrated into all the sanctuaries of Greece. He established the supremacy of Zeus in Thrace and that of Apollo in Delphi, where he laid the foundations for the council of the Amphyctions, which became the social unit of Greece. Finally, through the creation of the Mysteries, he formed the religious soul of his country by blending the religion of Zeus with that of Dionysus in a universal concept.

The initiates received the pure light of sublime truth through his teachings, while this same light reached the general populace in a more tempered, but no less beneficial form—under the veil of poetry and enchanting festivals. In this way Orpheus became pontiff of Thrace, high-priest of the Olympian Zeus, and the revelator of the heavenly Dionysus to the initiates" (Schuré 231).

An expanded account is thus given of Orpheus by Schuré. The parallels to Pythagoras are quite startling. He spent twenty years in the mystery school of Memphis; he was called "Orpheus of Arpha, which means the one who heals with light" (Schuré 230). He is credited with supernormal powers. A priest in the temple of Mount Kaoukaion speaks to Orpheus: "You who more than once have foretold the future, and who spoke to your disciples from a distance by appearing in a dream" (Schuré 253).

On the nature of things, Orpheus states, in his own words: "Hear the first mystery: A single Being rules in the deep sky and the abyss of earth.... He is the Breath of things, the untamed fire, eternal Male and Female" (Schuré 233). Notice here the reference to the Pythagorean Monad, the One; the description of the single Being as male *and* female; to the mystery of the breath; the breathing universe, as well as Orpheus's reference to God as the *"untamed fire"* (Pythagorean central fire, divine Consciousness).

Schuré describes the two great principles that govern the universe as Orpheus, the divine Light, the Eternal Masculine (Pythagorean Monad), who loved Eurydice, the "Eternal Feminine, the [creative Dyad], who lives and throbs *in a triple form* in nature, humanity, and Heaven [the Pythagorean Triad].... See that shining circle of constellations.... That is the body of the divine wife, who is revolving in celestial harmony to the songs of the husband. Look with the eyes of the spirit" (Schuré 228, 234). We cannot but be reminded of Pythagoras and the music of the spheres, which cannot be heard by the outer senses.

Jupiter is divine Husband *and* Wife, Man *and* Woman, Father *and* Mother. "From their sacred marriage...unceasingly come fire and water, earth and ether, night and day" (Schuré 234). (In Pythagoras and Plato the divine Monad is the creator of the world, and of the sensible world, starting with the four elements.) On the Triad, "Zeus and Dionysus, three times revelator, in hell, on earth and in heaven" (Schuré 236).

Of Orphic cosmogony: "God is One...but the gods are myriad and varied. The greatest are the souls of the stars. Suns, stars, earths and moons—each star has its own soul, and all have come out of the celestial fire of Zeus, the Primal Light" (Schuré 246).

During the divine initiation, the disciple heard a lyre sounding in a temple. "In its golden voice, its sacred rhythms the disciple heard the secret music of things. For from the leaves, waves and caverns came a formless, tender melody.... Orpheus was the animating genius of sacred Greece...his seven-stringed lyre embraces the universe. Each string corresponds to a mode of the human soul and contains the law of a science and an art" (Schuré 249, 227–228). A hint of Pythagorean sacred mathematics.

"The soul...a divine spark which guides us upon earth, is *in us*" (Schuré 243). "You know now that your soul is the daughter of Heaven.

You have beheld your origin and your end, and you are beginning to recollect" (Plato). The Orphic initiate was told by Orpheus himself: "Withdraw deep into yourself in order to lift yourself to the Principle of things, to the Great Triad" (Schuré 233). The fruit of initiation is that "you will finally leave the painful circle of births, and all of you will find yourselves as a single body, a single soul, in the light of Dionysus" (Schuré 243)—mystical union, freedom from the wheel of rebirth.

To return to the *influence* of the Orphics, we have seen that they shared with the Pythagoreans their central religious beliefs. And to those believers, in later centuries, should be added the illustrious name of Plato, and those of the Neoplatonists. What is significant is that their religious doctrines do not match the state religious doctrines or practices of the time. They seem to hear a different drum. They believe in immortality of the soul, transmigration (reincarnation), and the laws of karma, the kinship of all life, and the eventual mystic union of the soul in the godhead. Again, we conclude that these beliefs are not Greek, but emanate from "foreign" sources, from the East. We need to investigate those sources, and we will turn first to Egypt. Before doing so we might ponder a remarkable statement found in Schuré: "Pythagoras is the master of secular Greece, as Orpheus is the master of sacerdotal Greece. Pythagoras...coordinates the Orphic inspirations into a complete system (Schuré 268).

Egypt

As we recall, Pythagoras's vision as a young man compelled him to go to Egypt, the great source of those mystery school teachings that were described as *the science of God.* Tradition places the beginning of the Egyptian civilization around 3000 to 3500 BCE. Egyptian cosmology therefore has a mythological expression and must be interpreted that way.

There are several points where the Egyptian civilization touches our investigation. As Guthrie notes, it is claimed by several ancient authors that Pythagoras went to Egypt. These include Herodotus, whom he quotes as stating that the "Greeks had borrowed their most notable religious ideas and even their deities from the Egyptians," as well as the apocryphal belief that the Egyptians shared in the belief of transmigration. Guthrie rejects both of these statements (*HGP*, vol. 1, 158). In respect of transmigration,

Guthrie reports that Herodotus maintained it was a Pythagorean belief long before it was Platonic, and that "the Greek ideal of philosophia and theoria were compared and attributed by Herodotus to Solon" (640–559 BCE), the Greek lawgiver who Plato claims also went to Egypt.

Another ancient writer, Diogenes Laertius, confirms that Pythagoras went to Egypt: "While still young, so eager was he for knowledge, he left his own country and had himself initiated into all the mysteries and rites not only of Greece but also of foreign countries. Now he was in Egypt when Polykrates sent him a letter of Introduction to Amasis" (DL VIII, 2–4).

Isocrates, a rival of Plato, repeats the legend that Pythagoras owed all his wisdom to Egypt. Guthrie quotes Isocrates: "Pythagoras of Samos, who went to Egypt, and having become their pupil was the first to introduce philosophy in general to Greece." The Neoplatonist Iamblichus states in his introduction to *The Pythagorean Life* that Pythagoras had visited Pherekydes, who "shared with Pythagoras such learning as he could, then, blaming his old age and weakness, urged him to sail to Egypt and consult especially the priests at Memphis and Diospolis (Thebes) He himself, he said, had been furnished by them with what gave him his popular reputation for wisdom" (Iamblichus, 5).

Porphyry, another Neoplatonist, states in *The Life of Pythagoras*: "The attempt to connect Pythagoras's teachings if not his person with the supposed ancient *Eastern* wisdom is so widespread that Porphyry can present it as the common opinion. Connection with the mysterious East was a standard trait of the holy man." (Hadas and Smith 106). Porphyry further states: "Antiphon, in his book *On the Life of Those Who Excelled in Virtue,* describes the endurance Pythagoras showed in Egypt" (Hadas, Smith, 109) and that he had sought the tyrant Polycrates to write him a letter of introduction to Amasis, king of Egypt.

The accounts confirm not only that Pythagoras went to Egypt, but that it was a common practice for those with a deep interest in higher truths to travel there in order to learn of ancient and secret knowledge of the mysteries. As far as the history of Pythagoras is concerned, ancient writers agree that Pythagoras had a letter of introduction from the tyrant Polykrates to the Egytian Pharoah, Amasis, who in turn introduced him to the high priests of the temple of Memphis. As we know, Pythagoras spent twenty-two arduous years of study in the mystery school of Memphis, and finally attained divine initiation into the mysteries. This is the first connection with Egyptian civilization.

The second connection is when the tyrant Cambyses, headquartered in Babylon but who then became head of the mighty armies of the conquering Persian Empire, invaded and brutally subjugated Egypt while it was under the rule of the last Pharoah, Psammetichus. During this conquest, attended by many gruesome atrocities, Pythagoras himself was arrested and sent to Babylon, along with a part of the Egyptian priesthood, and was imprisoned there for twelve years.

A third and most significant link between Egypt and Greece can be found in Plato's dialogues, the *Timaeus* and the *Critias*. Before giving a brief history of that connection, let me state that whereas Plato is given credit for the clear and rational explication of his many doctrines—from the most concrete to the most ethereal metaphysical topics—I assume that where he uses myths, or gives an "incomprehensible" account of the origin of the world as in the *Timaeus*—what he is trying to convey is clear *to him* and that he is very likely restricted by the oath of silence that was the price of higher esoteric knowledge. As Schuré reveals, Plato himself had been initiated into the mysteries.

Plato startles us at the beginning of the *Timaeus* by telling us that the renowned sixth-century-BCE Greek lawgiver Solon visited Egypt and the high priests gave an account of an ancient historical connection between the Egyptian city of Sais and the Greek city of Athens. This relationship is said to have occurred *nine thousand years* before the time of Plato! The high priests tell Solon that Greece does not have records of its own past, but that the Egyptians have kept records of all happenings in the world since time immemorial. The tale of Athens and Sais runs as follows: they were considered "sister" cities, both ruled over by the same goddess—Athena in Greece, and Neith in Egypt. The Atlanteans, *a red race with a great empire*, were seeking to extend their imperial power through Egypt and into Greece itself.

According to the Egyptian high priests, in Athens at that time there lived the best and most courageous of men, and they went to do battle against the Atlanteans, where in spite of all odds, they defeated them and repelled them from Greek shores. They were honored as great heroes and liberators. Shortly after this, the tale goes, Atlantis was struck by earthquakes and tidal waves of so awesome a scope and power that the entire continent sank beneath the waves.

This story has been dismissed as fable and legend for over two thousand years. However, in the twentieth century, with the advent of modern science and sophisticated technology, many expeditions have set out to search the ocean floor for clues to Atlantis. The apocryphal Atlantis is said to have been an entire continent, stretching from Greece all the way to the eastern shores of the United States. Underwater studies around Bimini, off the coast of Florida, near the mysterious Bermuda Triangle, and around the Greek Island of Thera in the Aegean Sea have shown large stone causeways and the remnants of enormous pillars that have lain below the waves for many centuries, indeed, many *thousands* of years. Columns of ash twenty stories high, evidence of an awesome earthquake, were also recently discovered.

It is fascinating to think that these scientific expeditions in the twentieth century have, so far, transformed the perfunctory dismissals of Plato's tale into the distinct possibility that the civilization of Atlantis actually existed. More archaeological and undersea expeditions are under way in order to confirm whether the first hints of Atlantis prove Plato to have been right. And if so, what a stir *that* would create! Who would be the modern Schliemann?

Another legendary story runs that although Atlantis was very ancient it was—blink though we might in disbelief—a supposedly advanced society and in fact had technologies that western twentieth century civilization has not yet surpassed. One example is lasers and crystals, the misuse of which are purported to be the cause of Atlantis's destruction, and another is that in the King's Chamber in the Pyramid of Gizeh, a stone sarcophagus of granite, the hardest stone, has been judged by some modern engineers to have been cut by an implement that moved so fast that, again, our technologies cannot yet parallel it. In fact, the apocryphal legend is that before Atlantis sank, some of the people who were aware of its impending doom left that continent and went to Egypt and to other cultures around the world where pyramids are a signature of their culture.

It is possible that science will find further evidence that confirms Plato's account of Atlantis, which, if nothing else, will show us how far back into history the Egyptian civilization could be dated—i.e., at least nine thousand years before Plato's time. From modern times, it would mean 11,500 years ago. As it stands now, Plato—not known for excess or verbiage—*could* have given us a historical marker that would push the beginning of western civilization back approximately seven thousand years before the year 4004 BCE, the "official" date of the beginning of our world according to the Catholic Church. This Catholic doctrine was challenged by many scholars, including the French linguist Jean-François Champollion, who was the first to fully decipher the Egyptian hieroglyphs, and the Jesuit priest and paleontologist Teilhard de Chardin, who was banished to the hinterlands by the Christian Church because his scientific evidence and views contradicted the established doctrines of the Church.

The ancient authors tell us that all Greeks who sought ancient knowledge were drawn as a magnet to Egypt. Pythagoras was one of them. He was told that whereas Greece knew the wisdom of the gods, Egypt had the *science* of God, and this science, namely esoteric knowledge, was preserved in the temples, province of the high priests. Therefore, when we consider mythological Egyptian cosmology, we should not expect to find too much that matches the *science* of God known by the high priests. At the very least, we must recall that it took Pythagoras twenty-two years of arduous tests in order to finally be allowed the keys to the Egyptian mysteries, and, like every other student, he was sworn to silence to protect that esoteric knowledge from those that might use it in the service of selfish ambition. Thus, it is unlikely that we will learn anything of the Egyptian mysteries directly from anyone who swore an oath to uphold their secrecy.

And, what did this *science*, this knowledge of God confer upon the aspirant? First and foremost it conferred the initiation that presaged the merging of their soul with God, and the experience that their soul was indeed *a spa*rk of God. As such, it elevated the aspirant into a higher level of consciousness, such that ordinary people looked upon them as gods, or as immortals. They had *powers,* the powers of healing, of perceiving the thoughts of others, of predicting events in places far away, of piercing time and revealing their own and others's past lives. It also bestowed power over the forces of nature, the winds, the storms, the seas, and in the case of Jesus and others the power to raise the dead and to perform miracles. Some had direct instructions or visions sent by God to guide their understanding of the cosmic workings in their particular age, and their missions were to be spiritual leaders who could guide their respective peoples into new paths of religious, social and cultural evolution. As we have seen, the knowledge of the initiates was sacred and secret, too dangerous for ordinary men to be allowed access, with their passions unpurified, and, on occasion, tyrannical ambitions. The secret knowledge was thus conveyed by signs and symbols, in which the deeper truths were veiled, accessible only to true initiates.

We must not, then, expect to find very much information in the modern scientific investigation of Egyptian religion, and, as Schuré suggests elsewhere, whatever information we do find may be found in its esoteric history. We have provided a glimpse into that esoteric history by extrapolating the great powers known to be possessed by initiates such as Jesus and Pythagoras. But there is undoubtedly much more that was not divulged, and we must remember that, while for us it is mere rational knowledge to be accepted or dismissed as we see fit, for those great initiates the knowledge was *experiential*. Even today it is not easy to penetrate the wall of silence and secrecy surrounding the Egyptian mysteries, and in making it difficult for us, the ancient high priests attained their purpose! However, the ancient *religio*n of Egypt was mythological, and we must therefore expect that their cosmogony will also be mythological. We must not confuse the scientific understanding of the high priests of Egypt with the mythological understanding of the general population.

An Egyptian myth of origin holds that in the beginning the world was filled with the primeval waters of chaos (the god Nun) and that the god Re-Atum appeared out of the waters as the land of Egypt appears every year out of the flood waters of the Nile. Out of the spittle of the god Re-Atum were created the deities Shu (air) and Tefnet (moisture), and the world was created when Shu and Tefnet gave birth to two children—Nut (sky) and Geb (earth) (arguably the first duality if you discount the polarity between Nun and Re-Atum). Humans were created when Shu and Tefnet went wandering in the dark wastes and got lost. Re-Atum sent his "eye" to find them and upon reuniting with them, his tears of joy turned into more human beings.

Geb and Nut copulated, and when Shu learned of this, he inserted himself between them, so that now air existed between sky and earth.

He also decreed that Nut should not give birth on any day of the year. Nut implored Thoth to intervene on her behalf with the moon god Yah, who added five days to the calendar in order to accommodate her wishes. During those five days Nut gave birth to Osiris, Isis, Set, Nephthys and Horus-the-Elder, the Egyptian gods whose names we recognize.

The main Egyptian myth concerns Osiris, son of Re-Atum, or Geb, who was king of Egypt. His brother Seth was evil and coveted Osiris's crown. He devised an ingenious way to murder Osiris, tore his body into pieces (the One and the many) and made himself king. Isis rescued most of the pieces of Osiris for burial beneath the temple, but first she resurrected his body and copulated with him in order to create their son Horus, who, when he was grown, challenged and overcame Seth in order to take his place as the rightful king of Egypt. From him, the myth goes, are descended the pharaohs. As mythological history recounts, "Ra remained the supreme god in the solar religion, while Orisis, Isis and Horus were incorporated into his family" (Osiris, Isis and Horus parallel the Divine Triad of Pythagoras). Over time Osiris took over more of Ra's functions and became the judge of the dead. While the sun-god cult remained in existence until early in the fourth century BCE, the Osiris myth had transformed Egyptian religion greatly, by introducing a moral code and the promise of an afterlife, and in making the solar-cult knowledge more available to the everyday person.

In this myth of Osiris we see echoes of the philosophy of Pythagoras. We also see a reenactment of the Orpheus myth in which a god, or God, is originally One and ruling his kingdom, when he is murdered, dissolved into pieces, and becomes the many. Thus the myth metaphorically deals with the cosmology of the universe.

One of the most significant doctrines of the Egyptians, however, is what holds that the pharaoh is *a divine representation of God on earth*, and that it is the pharaoh's sacrifices to God (or the gods) that ensure the moral order as well as the fertility and prosperity of his nation. In this respect the pharaoh may fairly be called an initiate-king, one who ruled from higher, esoteric knowledge. The practice of revering the pharaoh as a deity was to endure through the Old Kingdom until the Fifth Dynasty, around two thousand four hundred BCE, after which time he was deified after his death.

Tracing the Source of those "Foreign" Doctrines

The Pyramid Texts, which date approximately to two thousand five hundred BCE, are considered by some to be the oldest known religious texts were specifically concerned with protecting the pharaoh's remains, reanimating his body after death, and helping him to ascend to the heavens.

This brings us to the Egyptian notion of the afterlife, in which there was a strong belief. Of prime importance was the doctrine that the *ka* (individual "I") needed to be reunited with the *ba* (the soul) to support the *ankh* (the spirit)—the part of each being that ascends to the heavens to take its place among the stars. (Note here the triadic nature of the higher principles.) It was believed that one took one's body into the afterlife, so elaborate rituals existed for preparing the soul for eternal life by embalming and mummifying the body. During the period of the Old Kingdom embalming was reserved for the select few, as it was in Zoroaster's religion, but in later periods it became available to wider sections of society. The Egyptian Book of the Dead contained important passages, often painted on the walls of the tombs, that would guide the journey into the underworld.

In the case of the pharaoh, his tomb would be filled with significant personal possessions that were judged to be needed in the afterlife. Some have suggested that later pharaohs were taken to the King's Chamber of the great pyramid of Gizeh, where the soul was said to leave by a shaft, carved in the stone, pointing toward the Belt of Orion, associated with the god Osiris, whereas the soul of his divine consort would depart by an equivalent shaft in the Queens's Chamber, which points directly to the constellation of Sirius, associated with the goddess Isis.[3] In this respect we may say that the Egyptians believed in the immortality of the soul (even if in the distant past this was reserved for the few).

As far as the laws of reincarnation are concerned, this does not appear to have been a point of exoteric doctrine with the Egyptians. However, one must assume that the high priests of Egypt were well aware of the doctrine of reincarnation because they, too, had been initiated and understood that their soul was immortal and a very spark of the Godhead. In addition, it was the Egyptian priests who possessed *the science of God* that Pythagoras sought as the fruit of his initiation, after which he was able to divulge several of his past lives to some of his students. Thus, although it

---

3 Bauval, *The Orion Mystery*, 5.

was not exoterically a tenet of belief, I think we can safely assume that the high priests were well aware of reincarnation. (Elizabeth's Haich's book *Initiation* contains valuable information on this topic.)

There are stories that as the Egyptian civilization eventually declined, the priesthood degenerated into those who practiced black magic and used their powers over nature for evil purposes. It has also been reported, even by as eminent a scholar as Paul Brunton,[4] that perhaps those modern-day archeologists associated with Howard Carter, who opened the tomb of the Egyptian boy-king Tutankhamun, were met with the awesome power of this ancient magic, and that too many of them died in unusual circumstances for it to be a coincidence. Considering the fact that they hacked the body of the pharaoh to pieces in order to remove the mummy from the sarcophagus, even in our own age their acts would be considered sacrilegious. For the ancient Egyptian high priests, whose magic enclosed the tombs, the offense of the twentieth century archaeologists was one that was punishable by death.

Exoterically, while there was no belief in the doctrine of reincarnation, there was a belief in judgment after death. In the Egyptian version, the soul of the dead person is taken into the hall of judgment in Duat by Anubis (god of mummification) and the deceased's heart is weighed against the feather of truth (Ma'at, who represents truth and order; she therefore also represents the laws of karma). If the person had led a good life, free of sin and guilt, he or she would be reunited with Osiris, god of the afterlife, but if the outcome was unfavorable, then the demon Ammi or Apopis (Eater of Hearts) destroyed the heart and the owner remained in Duat. If a person did not have a heart, they would essentially not exist. This was considered the most ghastly fate, as the Egyptians believed the heart to be the center of reason and emotion.

The Egyptian civilization is ancient, revered, and to this day somewhat inscrutable, and we have done it scant justice in our brief overview. However, the doctrine of immortality of the soul has been found to be present among the pharaohs, high priests, and those disciples in the mystery schools. Likewise that of judgment of the soul after death (the laws of karma in operation). And the high priests, with their esoteric knowledge, were well versed with all the ramifications of reincarnation. After all, it

---

4 Brunton, *A Search in Secret Egypt*, 236.

was after his twenty-two years in Egypt that Pythagoras had a revelation of several of his own past lifetimes.

Schuré can add to our knowledge in a number of ways. For example, he traces the earliest Egyptian civilization back to that of the Atlanteans, explaining that the one monument left on earth from that ancient time is the Sphinx, whose bull's body, with lion's paws, a man's head, and eagle wings represents the living unity of nature's kingdoms—evidence that they had solved the great mystery—that life is all One (Schuré 132).

Schuré also states that Hermes-Thoth was honored as the first initiator of Egypt at a time, before the Aryan period, when the white and black races were peaceful toward one another. The Greek disciples called him Hermes Tresmegistus, and he was called three-times great because he was considered king, legislator and priest. He was said to have written forty-two books on esoteric science, and the doctrine of the fire-principle and of the Word-Light contained in the *Vision of Hermes* was considered the highest expression of the Egyptian mysteries. One statement of interest by Hermes is: "None of our thoughts can conceive of God, nor can any language define Him. The incorporeal, invisible and formless cannot be comprehended by our senses. What is eternal cannot be measured with the short measure of time; God therefore is ineffable" (Schuré 135). Those who are initiates have...a "non-material vision" and...experience God as...a "living being" but the "First Cause remains hidden." Hermes thus confirms my view that in Plato's *Republic*, the *Good Itself*—as distinguished from the *Form* of the Good—is transcendental, One, and *formless*, and he also confirms Pythagoras in that the initiate experiences God as a *living* Being.

Schuré also tells us that the light kindled five thousand years prior by Rama in Iran and India shone down upon Egypt and became the law of Ammon-Ra, the solar god of Thebes. Rama's introduction of social organization, in which the priests, magistrates, and royalty each had their appointed tasks, amounted to government by initiates. The great pyramid was its symbol, as well as the mathematical *gnomon* (Pythagoras).

Around two thousand BCE, Egypt was invaded and partly conquered by the Phoenicians. While externally Egypt was forced to kneel to the invaders, the high priests withdrew to their secret sanctuaries in order to preserve the mystery tradition, and it was at that time and under those conditions that the oath of secrecy was then instituted under penalty of death. However, in order to perpetuate the eternal truths they propagated the ancient myth of Osiris and Isis, but covered its esoteric source with a threefold veil (Pythagoras, Plato, Orpheus). According to Schuré, the mysteries were preserved in these ways in Egypt for nine hundred years until Amos, the savior of Egypt, defeated the Hyksos and restored the religion of Osiris to its rightful place.

The Egyptian priests understood man was three-fold, comprising body, mind and spirit (Pythagoras, Orpheus, Plato) and that in order to attain mastery over one's lower nature, one's will, intuition and reason needed to be developed. And when a student, after many years of austerities and tests, was found to be worthy, they would finally have bestowed on them the sublime gift of initiation. Schuré gives a description—as far as allowed—of an actual initiation into the Egyptian mysteries that took place during the reign of Rameses II, around 1300 BCE. The account is best read in its entirety, but I will highlight one or two points of interest.

At one stage the initiate disciple is led into a hall where he has access to twenty-two paintings, which represented the twenty-two first Mysteries. "*The principles were fixed in the memory by their correspondence with the letters of the sacred language and with the numbers associated with these letters* (Pythagoras, Orpheus, Plato). Each letter and each number expressed in this language a ternary law, having its repercussion in the *divine world, the intellectual world, and the physical world* (Schuré 146). Thus the letter A, which corresponds to number 1, expresses in the divine world, Absolute Being from which all beings emanate; in the intellectual world, the unity, origin, and synthesis of numbers; in the physical world, Man, the head of related beings, who, through expansion of his faculties, rises into the concentric spheres of infinity."

This was merely the beginning of initiation. The disciple labored for many more years until he was ready for the final initiation—which consisted, in part, in the disciple experiencing his own death—and subsequent resurrection. If the aspirant was successful, he was given access to the Vision of Hermes, which shows him that the origin of the world has One God—Osiris—in three aspects: God the Father; union is Life (the Mother); and the Son (the Word).

Tracing the Source of those "Foreign" Doctrines

Another part of the vision consisted in the aspirant seeing himself enveloped in seven luminous spheres that emanated from infinite space and the star-studded heavens. He was shown that the seven circles were seven rays of the Word-Light and each of them governed a planet—Moon, Mercury, Venus, Sun, Mars, Jupiter, Saturn. The aspirant was shown how the soul originally left the realm of the Word-Light and descended from sphere to sphere, clothed in ever-denser coverings. In each incarnation he acquired a more corporeal body, and at the same time began to lose the memory of his divine origin (Plato). At a certain point in this process, when the individual was incarnated upon the earth and had suffered enough, the soul began to long for the experience of higher realms, and thus began the long journey of conscious evolution back toward its divine home.

The hierophant explained to the aspirant that the Vision of Hermes had been handed down as the archetype of initiation and that the words of the wise man, containing the secret knowledge, are like the seven notes of the musical lyre "which contain all music, together with the numbers and laws of the universe" (Orpheus, Pythagoras).

> And the prophet of the temple expounded the sacred text. He explained that the doctrine of Word-Light represents divinity *in the static state* in its perfect equilibrium. He pointed out its threefold nature, which at the same time is intelligence, strength, and matter; spirit, soul and body; light, word-life, essence, manifestation and substance...the laws of ternary unity which dominate creation from the highest to the lowest.... The second part of the vision represents divinity in *the dynamic state,* that is, in active evolution...which involves the visible and invisible universe...the seven spheres attached to the seven planets, which symbolize the seven principles, seven different conditions of matter and spirit, and seven varied worlds which each man and each generation must pass through in their evolution in the solar system.
>
> The Seven Genii of Hermes Vision (the seven cosmogonic gods), are identified with...the Seven Devas of India, the seven Amshapands of Persia, the seven mighty Angels of Chaldea, the seven Sephiroth of the Kabbala, and the seven Archangels of the Christian Apocalypse. And the great septenary law which unfolds the universe not only vibrates in the seven colors of the rainbow

and in the seven tones of the musical scale, but is also evident in the being of man, who is threefold in essence but sevenfold in his evolution. (Schuré 162)

As we review the Egyptian mysteries we cannot help but find echoes of Pythagorean doctrine. Chief among them is the notion of the incorporeal, invisible and *formless* God, which corresponds to the Pythagorean Monad, and I would suggest, to the notion of the *Good Itself* in Plato. Of particular interest are the clues that the great pyramid and the *mathematical gnomon* symbolized the expression of the form of government under the Egyptian initiates, and that the threefold nature of human beings has a *correspondence* to the divine world. Finally, the most tantalizing clue as to the source of Pythagorean number symbolism is found in the account of the student being shown the twenty-two paintings representing different aspects of the sacred esoteric language, but where the letter A = 1 and symbolizes a threefold expression; in the divine world as Absolute Being; in the intellectual world as unity, the origin of numbers; and in the physical world as humankind, which rises through the expansion of human faculties into infinity (Schuré 146). If we extrapolate this number-letter symbolism to the whole alphabet, we will indeed have a sacred language of the divine world! But, only the worthy initiate has access to that language and the divine world it symbolizes, whereas for the general populace it is reflected in signs and symbols. And, let us remember that for Pythagoras and Orpheus the science of numbers and letters was not an abstract theoretical exercise, for they both understood and experienced mathematics as a *living expression* of divine energies.

Pythagoras studied in Egypt for twenty-two years and thus absorbed the full power of the Egyptian Mysteries, but we also note from the historical record that Pythagoras spent twelve years in Babylon. According to Schuré (280), during that time he was able to increase his knowledge from the Persian Magi, but also to penetrate further into the mysteries of ancient magic. These mysteries included the manipulation of the hidden powers of nature, and it reminds us of the powers Jesus had: walking on the water, calming the storm, changing the water into wine at the wedding in Canaan, feeding the five thousand, and raising Lazarus from the dead. What is clear is that while the historical record shows Pythagoras spending many years in Egypt and Babylon, there is no doubt that Pythagoras was drawn, even by circumstances, solely to those places where the mysteries were still alive and being taught in secret.

THE PERSIAN INFLUENCE

Francis Cornford had mentioned a Persian influence on Ionians of the sixth century BCE, whereas Guthrie asserts, with Zeller, that in respect of a Persian influence on Pythagorean doctrines, the evidence was too weak and general to allow any definite conclusions, but he concedes that there was a remarkable persistence regarding the personal connection between Pythagoras and Zoroaster himself. In addition he recounts that the Greeks "in later days were strongly inclined to represent their early philosophers as the pupils of the Orient" (*HGP*, 252). However, history reveals there was an *indelible* Persian influence on Ionia in the sixth century BCE—none other than that of the Persian tyrant Polycrates who had usurped Ionia, deprived her of freedom, and stamped her with the corruption of "Persian voluptuousness" even before the birth of Pythagoras.

Schuré mentions Samos at the beginning of the sixth century BCE as "one of the most flourishing islands of Ionia. Its port faced the purple mountains of Asia Minor, from which came all wealth and culture" (Schuré 271). No mention is made of Orpheus in this connection or at this time period. Of course, Samos was the birthplace of Pythagoras. The tyrant Polycrates ruled Samos with an iron fist at the time of his birth, which is why his parents were guided to leave Samos for Sidon in Phoenicia in order that their child might be born far away from the turbulent influences of his homeland. We recall, too, that after Pythagoras had grown to manhood and had the cosmic vision of the Tetrad, he remembered the oracle given to his mother in Lebanon when he was only one year old, namely that the Egyptians possessed the *science* of *God*, and this powerful memory compelled him to go to Egypt. How this was brought about is fateful, because the tyrant Polycrates was a friend of the Pharoah, Amasis, and it was Polycrates who gave Pythagoras a letter of introduction to the Pharoah, who in turn, introduced him to the high priests of Memphis.

After twenty-two years in Egypt and having attained his final initiation, that country was invaded by yet another tyrant, Cambyses, son of the Persian conqueror, who with his vast armies sacked the temples of Memphis and Thebes and forced the last Pharoah, Psamettichus, to watch, humiliated and helpless, while all members of the ruling families were beheaded before his eyes. Pythagoras himself was taken prisoner and, along with some of the Egyptian priests, was taken to Babylon, where he remained in captivity for twelve years.

Here in Babylon, Pythagoras was able to "increase his knowledge of the Magi, heirs of Zoroaster...who had knowledge of the manipulation of hidden powers of nature" (Schuré 280). Schuré does not speak of direct contact between Pythagoras and Zoroaster, but of interaction with his descendants, the Persian Magi. After twelve years in Babylon, Pythagoras was finally free to return home to Samos. When he arrived, however, he was saddened to see that a tyrant was still in power and that under his brutal yoke, the country had been reduced to rubble. Pythagoras, reunited with his mother after an absence of thirty-four years, therefore left Samos for Greece.

Two points may be made about the account given here. The first is that the Persian Empire—the largest in the world until that of Alexander—had been the major influence upon Ionia for the entire life of Pythagoras until he finally departed for Greece at approximately age fifty-six. The wealth, culture, and religion of Persia had impressed Ionia with its indelible stamp, so when Cornford says that "any student of Orphic and Pythagorean thought cannot fail to see the similarities between it and Persian religion are so close as to warrant our regarding them as expressions of the same view of life, and using the one system to interpret the other," he is expressing in his own way what is a historical fact. Let us underscore that Cornford is telling us that the Persian and Orphic/Pythagorean *religions* were so similar as to be interchangeable.

However, as we have seen, it is *Pythagoras* and not Orpheus who had direct connections to Babylon and Persia in the sixth century BCE. The Orphic *writings* were traced back to the sixth century BCE, but Schuré has suggested that Orpheus lived in a much earlier time period, one that would have relied on an oral rather than written tradition. This would explain why the Orphic writings of the sixth century BCE are "adrift" from their charismatic creator—a passage of seven hundred years lay between them! Perhaps Cornford made the same surmise as Guthrie when he dates Orpheus to the Orphic *writings* of the sixth century BCE, but unless we find some evidence that there is a direct connection between Orpheus himself and Persia, we shall continue on with the assumption that Orpheus lived four centuries before Homer, around 1300 BCE. This leaves us free to explore the known chronological link between Pythagoras and Persian religion.

A brief sketch of the Persian Empire reveals that it took untold centuries to build, and that under its most famous leaders—Cyrus the Great, Cambyses, Darius the Great and Xerxes—it became the largest and most powerful empire in the world, swallowing vast amounts of territory along the way. The primitive beginnings of that civilization took place on the Iranian plateau, in central Asia, and the oldest written document (between an Akkadian and an Elamite king) is dated back forty-three centuries!

In the seventeenth century BCE, the Aryans apparently passed through Iran on their way to India, taking with them Indo-Iranian languages. Despite battles of domination lasting around seven hundred years between the Babylonians, Assyrians, Elamites and Kassites, the Iranian-speaking peoples—largely Medes and Persians—gradually moved, in the first half of the first millennium BCE into the area of the Zagros mountains of central Asia. The name Iran has its derivation from the word "Aryan."

History of Persian Empire

The Persian Empire had its beginnings on the Iranian plateau, dating to around 728 BCE, when the Median Empire was in power. A series of Iraniate rulers created early empires whose influence stretched into south, central and western Asia, as well as the Caucasus. The entire time period was characterized by wars between neighboring peoples for expanded power and territory. Under such circumstances the first Persian Empire was formed—under the Medians (728–559 BCE), who overcame the Assyrians in 612 BCE with the help of the Babylonians.

A unified Persian Empire was formed by Cyrus the Great, in 549 BCE when he in turn defeated the Medians and established The Achaemenid Empire (550–330 BCE). He became the first king of the Achaemenid Empire, and he conquered much of the Middle East, including the territories of the Babylonians, Assyrians, Phoenicians and Lydians. His son, Cambyses, who later became known as a mad, tyrannical despot, continued on the same path of imperial conquest. His most important prize, however, was that of Egypt, which he invaded and, after deposing the last pharaoh, Psamettichus, and perpetrating many atrocities, subjected to Persian domination. Cambyses therefore brought a three-thousand year old civilization to a brutal and ignominious end. Incidentally, the Neoplatonist Iamblichus records that among the slaves taken by Cambyses was the Greek philosopher, Pythagoras.

Cambyses was survived by his son, Darius the Great, and under his leadership the Persian Empire reached its greatest fame and influence. Darius led his conquering armies as far afield as the Indus River Valley as well as into Thrace in Europe. Several historical battles took place between the Persians and the Greeks, including the Battle of Marathon (in which the Greeks repulsed the Persians); the Battle of Thermopylae (which the Greeks lost to Xerxes, son of Darius); and the battle of Plataea. Revolts were often fomented by peoples who had been oppressed by the Persian Empire, and on one of his marches Darius sent forces to re-take Samos, birthplace of Pythagoras.

Philip of Macedon ascended to his throne in 359 BCE. He embarked upon a series of battles, and through might and political intrigue overcame the lands surrounding Macedonia—including Thrace and Illyria. Philip then took several important Greek cities including Potidaea, conquered northern Greece, and due to the power he had already amassed for himself, was the first outsider to force his way onto the Greek Delphic Council. He perpetrated invasions of Thessaly and the Balkans, and in 338 BCE he reasserted his authority in the Aegean by defeating the Thebans and Athenians at the Battle of Chaeronea, which effectively put an end to Greek liberty and history.

Philip organized all Greek states into a Greek league, called himself "Commander of the Greeks," and had ambitious plans to invade and overthrow the Persian Empire. However, Philip had made many enemies, was publicly assassinated in 336 BCE, and was succeeded by his son Alexander the Great. Despite his youth Alexander challenged the great Persian conqueror, Darius III, to a great battle at Gaugamela, in which against overwhelming odds and appearing to his troops as the very embodiment of godlike inspiration, courage and ambition, Alexander's armies took the victory, thus ending the Persian Empire—for the time being. Alexander went on to conquer most of the known world, and he died in 323 BCE, having surpassed even the Persian Empire in its vast scope and influence.

ZOROASTER

According to the Greek historian Herodotus, the religion of Zoroaster was already old when it entered recorded history in the mid-fifth century BCE, most likely during the period of the Achaemenid Empire (549–330 BCE), although it was believed to exist as far back as the ninth or tenth centuries BCE. Herodotus includes a description of greater Iranian society with recognizable Zoroastrian features in his work *The Histories,* considered a primary source on the early period of the Persian Empire, including the Achaemenid era.

Zoroastrianism was enthusiastically accepted by the rulers of the Persian Empire, and it became a defining element of Persian culture, such that eventually the Zoroastrian religion reached to all corners of the empire. One of the acknowledged authorities on this material is Mary Boyce, and it is from her book, *Zoroastrians: Their Religious Beliefs and Practices* that we find valuable information about its tenets and its influence. I will focus first on the teachings of Zoroaster himself (Boyce, 17–29), because they echo similar doctrines found in Orpheus, Pythagoras, and Plato. She starts out by declaring that Zarathustra is known to us because he composed seventeen hymns, or Gathas, "inspired utterances," many of them addressed to God directly, and that their poetic form was very ancient and inaccessible—tracing back to Indo-European times. Zoroaster believed he had been entrusted by God with a message to all humankind, and these inspired utterances, collectively referred to as the *Avesta,* incorporate a poetic form that is linked with a tradition of mantra characterized by *personal apprehension* of the divine.

Such teachings were understood only by the priestly seers (Pythagoras, Orpheus, Plato's guardians) but were handed down orally from generation to generation until they were finally committed to writing under the rulers of the third Iranian empire—the Sassanians. There are other teachings, the post-Gathic texts, which originated at a later time period and are referred to as the *Younger Avesta,* but they also contained some material that was considered very old.

Boyce tells us that the language of the Gathas themselves is archaic, and close to that of the Indian *Rig Veda,* whose composition has been assigned to around fifteen hundred BCE. Boyce suggests, based on new evidence, that Zoroaster himself should be dated to circa fifteen hundred BCE. If this is true it would tend to confirm that Pythagoras did not learn from Zoroaster directly, but rather from some of his disciples, the Persian Magi, when he was a captive in Babylon. More important, if Zoroaster is dated to circa fifteen hundred BCE, there is a time lag of almost a thousand years before the Zoroastrian religion entered history during the time of the Achmaenid Empire (549–330 BCE). Parenthetically, this is a situation that obtained in the case of Orpheus, who may be dated to 1300 BCE, while the written teachings surfaced hundreds of years later, in the sixth century BCE.

Tradition suggests that Zoroaster sought higher knowledge from various teachers (Orpheus and Pythagoras both go to Egypt, and Plato's teacher was Socrates, of whom the Delphic Oracle prophesied that he was the wisest man in Greece). Accordingly, he spent years in a wandering quest for truth, and after finally attaining such knowledge, he described himself as "one who knows," *an initiate*, possessed of divinely inspired wisdom (Orpheus, Pythagoras, Socrates, Plato).

He was thirty years old when a revelation came to him. He was attending a spring festival, and went to draw water for a sacred ceremony when he saw in a vision a Shining Being who revealed himself as Vohu Manah, "Good Purpose," who led Zoroaster into the presence of God in the form Ahura Mazda, and five other radiant figures before whom "he did not see his own shadow upon the earth owing to their great light" (Boyce 19). It was from this heptad of great Beings that Zoroaster received his revelation. After that Zoroaster worshipped Ahura Mazda, the master of order, righteousness and justice. Zoroaster, however, engaged in a startling departure from his own tradition when he proclaimed Ahura Mazda to be the One *uncreated* God, existing eternally, and creator of all else that is good, including other beneficient divinities (Plato's Good, Pythagoras's Monad, Orpheus's divine Word Light). Thus, for Zoroaster, in the beginning only One being existed in the universe, Ahura Mazda, the all-wise, wholly just and good.

In his vision, however, Zoroaster saw an Adversary to Ahura Mazda, the "Hostile Spirit" Angra Mainyu, equally uncreated, but ignorant and wholly malign. These two—Ahura Mazda and Angra Mainyu—were in perpetual conflict with one another. Each made a deliberate choice, based on his own nature, to choose between good and evil, and for Zoroaster this prefigures the identical choice that every human being must make in their own life (Plato, Pythagoras, Orpheus).

Zoroaster transformed the old cosmogony with fundamental new teachings. The first act of Ahura Mazda was to evoke, through his Holy Spirit (Spent Mainyu), six lesser divinities, the radiant beings of Zoroaster's earlier vision. These divinities formed a heptad, and, along with Ahura Mazda, they proceeded to fashion the seven creations that made up the world. The six great beings in their turn evoked other beneficient divinities of the Iranian pantheon, and despite these divine beings, called "Holy Immortals," having different appointed tasks, they nevertheless suggest the essential *unity* of divinity (Plato, Pythagoras, Orpheus).

Zoroaster held that Ahura Mazda accomplished creation in two stages. First he bought all things into a disembodied, or intangible state called "menog," characterized as spiritual and immaterial. Then, in the second stage he gave it "material," or *getig,* existence. Thus Zoroaster distinguishes between the intelligible or invisible world and the tangible and sensible world (Plato, Pythagoras, Orpheus).

Creation occurred three times. First of these was Creation itself. Angra Mainyu's attack upon the Creation inaugurated the second, called The Mixture, and it comprises the whole period of history when creation is no longer wholly good, but a blend of good and evil. According to Zoroaster, Angra Mainyu and his minions afflict humankind with every kind of physical, moral, and spiritual ill, and to withstand their assaults people need to bring into their own hearts the great goodness of Ahura Mazda and his heptad of great beings, the Amesha Spentas, so that no room is left for weakness or vice. Human beings are thus in a perpetual struggle to ensure that good overcomes evil in their own nature, and therefore share with Ahura Mazda the work of gradually ensuring that good overcomes and transforms the evil in the world. The third Creation will be brought about when the restoration of the world to its glorious original perfection has been finally accomplished, at which time world history will cease. This radical, eschatological interpretation regarding the end of history was also a profound break with earlier tradition.

Within these cosmic cycles, human beings had their life and being, but during the time of the Mixture, it was understood that at death, men and women, rich and poor, would be judged according to their good or bad deeds while on earth (Plato, Pythagoras, Orpheus). The souls of all people had to cross a "bridge" of judgment after their death, and the soul of the good person would meet a maiden (the personification of its own good deeds) who would lead it up on high to Paradise. The soul of a person who had done bad deeds would meet a deformed, ugly maiden (again, a personification of their own deeds) and would be led down to hell. However, during the time of the Mixture, souls could not achieve perfect bliss, even in Paradise, because Zoroaster introduced a new teaching about the afterlife, namely that the blessed must wait until the end of the world, Frashegird, for their souls to be fully and finally reunited with Ahura Mazda.

As we can see, there are echoes of Plato, Pythagoras and Orpheus in these teachings of Zoroaster. Nevertheless, there are bound to be some differences. For example, Zoroaster taught that souls must wait for the end of time to be fully reunited with the Ahura Mazda, whereas the Orphics, Pythagoras, and Plato all hold that an individual soul may be released from the wheel of rebirth even though other souls and external, material evolution continue onward. The Zoroastrians shared with Plato, Pythagoras and Orpheus belief in the immortality of the soul, and the law of karma as it applied to good and bad deeds and the corresponding rewards and punishments.

It is not known that the Zoroastrians believed in reincarnation. However, it is important to note that despite the fact that a religion does not explicitly endorse reincarnation as one of its public doctrines, there are nevertheless references to reincarnation found within the scriptures. For example, Christianity does not hold reincarnation as a principle doctrine, and yet in the *Gospel of Matthew,* Jesus states publicly that John the Baptist is "Elias (Elijah) which was for to come" (11: 7–14), which I interpret, along with many others, to mean that John the Baptist is a reincarnation of the Prophet Elijah. The Egyptians did not have a public doctrine of reincarnation, and yet the pharaoh was considered a reincarnation of Horus, the son of the god Osiris. On the other hand there are modern authors who include references to apparently authentic examples of reincarnation in their works. Some are scientific studies, such as that found in Ian Stevenson's ground-breaking book, *Twenty Cases Suggestive of Reincarnation,* the early pioneer in the field. There are today many, many personal experiences of reincarnation that have been revealed by Christians, starting with the famous story *A Search for Bridey Murphy*, by Morey Bernstein. An actual account of *her own* reincarnation occurs in Elizabeth Haich's book, *Initiation,* where she—in her current life as a European woman—had experiences that repeatedly took her back to a life as the daughter of a pharaoh in ancient Egypt. Brian Weiss, M.D., and a psychiatrist, tells of his introduction to reincarnation in his book *Through Time into Healing* (19). He used hypnosis as an important tool in his work and had a patient who was not responding to treatment. By a stroke of serendipity, he gave an open-ended instruction to the patient to go back to the source of the problem. To his surprise, the patient found that she was having an experience of an Egyptian life that contained the cause of the symptoms she presented in her current life. Through re-experiencing the ancient life, the client was cured of her problem. These examples call into question whether reincarnation was not a reality within the actual lives of people in these different religions, even when they were not declared as part of public doctrine. We do not know the reason why some cultures accepted reincarnation and others do not mention it, but there are too many documented cases to allow us to ignore it. It is more than likely that if we were to find suitable clients, there would be found cases of reincarnation by people who professed to follow every religion, including that of Zoroaster.

However, in the case of Zoroaster himself, as we have seen he changed the ancient traditions in a radical way. More research should be focused on the doctrines of the *ancient* Iranians, difficult as that may be due to lack of hard evidence, because their counterparts the *Vedic Indians did have a doctrine of reincarnation,* and if, as is claimed, these two peoples were interchangeable with one another it would point to a possible acceptance of reincarnation also being found among the ancient Iranians. As a whole, then, it is no surprise that Cornford described the Orphic, Pythagorean and Persian religions as "so close as to warrant our regarding them as expressions of the same view of life, and using the one system to reinterpret the other." We add the caveat that it is not the Orphics of the sixth century BCE that Cornford is describing, so much as 1300

BCE. Of course, this opens up the tantalizing possibility that Orpheus and Zoroaster lived at approximately the same time, because Mary Boyce states that although she believes Zoroaster should be dated at fifteen hundred BCE, she also held open the possibility that he lived around twelve hundred BCE. If Zoroaster and Orpheus were contemporaries, or near contemporaries, then, of course, Cornford's statement would hold true, except that it would hold for 1300 BCE and not the sixth century BCE, which he intended. One last possibility is that when Cornford refers to Orphics in the sixth century BCE, he must be referring to those Orphics who compiled or gathered the poems of Orpheus into the set of writings assigned to that time period. That still doesn't prove that Orpheus himself lived in the sixth century, merely that there was a renaissance of his teachings at that time.

On the other hand, Schuré tells us that Orpheus went to Egypt for twenty years and studied with the high priests, at the end of which time Orpheus called himself an initiate, "one who knows." On this view, Orpheus had *his own revelation*—and yet many of the core doctrines and beliefs found parallels, not only in Zoroaster, but also in Pythagoras and Plato. This seems to support Schuré's notion that great initiates were each receiving similar revelations from the same divine source, allowing for the exigencies of time, place, and culture of their different peoples.

One other point needs to be mentioned here. We have learned that Zoroastrianism had existed from ancient times, but that it only entered history in the mid-fifth century BCE. This suggests that there was an ancient oral tradition that carried the teachings forward. The very same case can be made for Orpheus. The dramatists, poets, and historians of the fifth and fourth centuries BCE flatly stated that Orpheus was already known to be of "great antiquity" in their own time. I suggest that the reason for this is that, like Zoroastrianism, Orphism was born during the period of prehistory that relied on the oral tradition, and that this can account for the fact that his writings did not surface until the sixth century BCE—some seven hundred years after his birth. Incidentally, as Mary Boyce will show, the exact same case pertains to the Vedas in India. According to her, the earliest compilation of the *Rig Veda* hymns is assigned to around fifteen hundred BCE, but they had an oral history and tradition going back, perhaps, *untold* thousands of years. As we can see, a similar pattern seems to apply to all three religions, a fact worth remembering as we go forward.

THE ANCIENT IRANIAN RELIGIOUS TRADITION

We have explored the teachings of Zoroaster as they applied to the period in which they entered history—during the period of the first Achmaenid Empire (549–330 BCE). However, as Boyce points out, Zoroaster is believed to have lived in the period of *prehistory*, somewhere around 1500 BCE, and he is credited with making some radical changes to a religious tradition that had predated his own birth by perhaps thousands of years.

As we explore this earlier tradition, Mary Boyce is again our guide.[5] She tells us that the religion of Zoroastrianism originated over three thousand five hundred years ago in a Bronze Age culture on the Asian steppes and reiterates that it became the state religion of three mighty Iranian empires in succession. It exerted influence in the Middle East—where Judaism developed and Christianity and Islam were born—and Iranian rule extended into Northern India, where it made a contribution to the development of Mahayana Buddhism. She tells us that there are elements in living Zoroastrianism that seem to go back to Indo-European times.

What is most interesting from our point of view is that important elements in Zoroastrianism date back to Indo-European times. As she states, *in times even more remote, the ancestors of the Iranians and the Indians had formed one people*, identified as the proto-Indo-Iranians. They were a branch of the Indo-European family of nations, living as pastoralists on the Russian steppes. As Boyce states: "During the centuries of this slow, stable way of existence—perhaps from the fourth to the third millennium BCE—the proto-Indo-Iranians forged a religious tradition of immense strength, so that to this day elements from it are preserved by their descendants, the Brahmans of India and the Zoroastrians of Iran" (Boyce 2). Eventually, around the third millennium BCE, they drifted apart to become the Indians and the Iranians respectively.

Boyce correlates the most ancient elements of the Zoroastrian scriptures and cult with the oldest religious works of India (notably, the *Rig Veda*) and with the Brahmanic rituals, which she dates, along

---

5   Boyce, *Zoroastrians*, xvii–16.

with Zoroaster himself, to approximately fifteen hundred BCE. The Zoroastrian scriptures are known collectively as the "Avesta"—a title that means "Authoritative Utterance"—while the language of their composition was Avestan.

Boyce mentions that Zoroaster had proclaimed changes to a much older tradition, and the most radical of those changes was his declaration that Ahura Mazda was the one uncreated God. However, the ancient Iranian tradition had held that there were many gods. In addition to the cult gods, there were nature gods—sky and earth, Sun and Moon, and two gods of the wind, Vata and Vayu. And, although Ahura Mazda was the master of order, righteousness and justice, there was, in fact, a divine triumvirate of *asha* (right) that recognized a fraternal pair, Mithra and Apam Napat, whose actions were ruled and directed by Ahura Mazda. The "three lords" were highly ethical beings, guardians of right (*asha*) and *rta* (order) (Pythagoras's Triad, Orpheus, Plato).

Boyce had mentioned in her earlier research (xiv) a long-held academic theory that the Indo-Iranians had also venerated personified "abstractions," but she corrects this view to state "that what they in fact revered were *the invisible forces* (Avestan, *mainyu;* Sanscrit, *manyu*) that they apprehended in all things, animate, or inanimate, some of which were felt to be very powerful" (Boyce xiv). This calls to mind Pythagoras and his apprehension of mathematical forces as alive, and as manifestations of the Monad. In the case of Plato and Orpheus the apprehension of divine forces appears to be mentioned only in relation to the Good and the Word-Light respectively—namely, in the experience of divine initiation.

Boyce tells us Zoroaster transformed the cosmogony with fundamental new teachings. He proclaimed that there would be an end of world history when the state of original perfection had finally been attained, whereas for the earlier tradition it was held that once the process of life (nature) had started, it was expected to continue forever. "No end was foreseen either for the generations of men, which were thought to follow one another ceaselessly" (Boyce 12).

Another radical change relates to death and the hereafter. As we have seen, after death the soul was judged, and according to its good or bad deeds ascended to Paradise or descended to the underworld. But, as Boyce states: "The pagan Iranians had presumably held, like the Vedic Indians, that soon after each blessed soul reached Paradise it was reunited with its resurrected body to live again a happy life full of sensation."

Somewhere in this period of prehistory, beliefs about the afterlife undergo a change. There was still belief in life after death for the individual, but now souls in the underworld, the realm of Yima, were deemed to live a shadowy existence, dependent on their descendants still living on earth to satisfy their hunger and to clothe them."

According to Boyce around the third millennium BCE, just before the Indians and Iranians separated to go their different ways, a new hope was conceived of the hereafter—"that some at least among them—princes and warriors and the priests who served the gods—might escape the dreaded fate of an eternally joyless existence in the underworld and that their souls might mount upward at death to join the gods in sunlit Paradise" (Boyce 14). Only those who were worthy could cross the "bridge" of judgment and find themselves in paradise. All other lowly souls, including women and children, went to the subterranean kingdom of the dead. Absent from ancient beliefs, however, were the doctrines of hell, or of blessed souls in Paradise having to wait for the end of world history to be reunited with the Godhead, Ahura Mazda.

At this same time period, around the third millennium BCE, there was also conceived a new belief in the resurrection of the body in which, after the first year after death, "the bones" of the physical body would be raised up and clothed in immortal flesh, to be reunited with the soul in heaven" (Boyce 14). At this time, the Indians changed their rite of burial to be one of cremation whereby the flesh was swiftly destroyed, whereas some of the Iranians adopted the rite of exposure where a corpse would be taken to a barren place, usually a mountain top and left for the vultures and scavenging beasts to devour it.

To synopsize, the Iranian religious tradition existing before Zoroaster held that there were three principles or Ahuras governing existence, and many gods, and they revered the invisible forces that they apprehended in all things, animate and inanimate. Once the process of life had started, both the evolution of nature and the generations of humanity were expected to go on forever. There was belief in life after death for the individual, but their initial beliefs in a happy and sensation-filled resurrection gave way to a darker notion, one where souls went to a subterranean realm of the dead to live a shadowy, joyless existence. Eventually that conception was modified to allow that *some*—those who were worthy—might escape into paradise. These older traditions must be held in mind when contemplating the religion of the early Indo-European people.

The Old Religion: The Cult

As with other ancient peoples, the early manifestations of religion were found in the cult. Boyce tells us that the basic objects of the Zoroastrian cult were fire and water (which brings Plato's *Timaeus* to mind). The proto-Indo-Iranians worshipped the waters as the goddess Apas, and the sacrificial offering consisted of three ingredients—a milk, and the sap or leaves of two plants. The number three was thus sacred (Pythagoras, Plato), and the offering represented the vegetable and animal kingdoms. The other cult object was fire, which was considered to be ever-burning and thus was a symbol of divinity (Pythagoras, Plato, Orpheus). The Brahmans knew the god of fire as Agni, while the Zorastrians called him Atar.

The offerings to fire and water formed the basis of the daily priestly act of worship, called by the Iranians the *yasna* and by Indians the *yagna*, from the verbal root *yaz*—to sacrifice, worship. The offering (Avestan, *zaothra*) to fire was obtained from blood sacrifice, but the Iranians felt such awe and danger at taking life that they consecrated it by the act of prayer, by which they believed the creature's spirit was enabled to live on. There was a strong sense of kinship between the human being and beast (Pythagoras). In fact, among the Iranians the belief grew that the souls of consecrated animals would, after death, be absorbed into a divine being, Geush Urvan. The end of the yasna was observed by a ritual offering to the waters prepared from milk, the leaves of one plant and the juice from pounding the stems of another. The Avestan term was *haoma*, while the Sanskrit described it as *soma*.

The Gods

In addition to the cult gods of Fire, Water, Haoma and Geush Urvan, there were "nature" gods such as Sky and Earth—Asman and Zam; Sun and Moon—Hvar and Mah; and two gods of the wind—Vata and Vayu. Vata was the wind that blows, but Vayu was a more mysterious being called in the *Rig Veda* the "soul of the gods" and regarded by the Iranians as the "breath of life itself" (Pythagoras, Plato). With Vata, the rain bringer, was associated Harahvati Aredvi Sura—the Sanskrit Sarasvati, whose name symbolizes a mythical river that pours down from a mountain at the center of the earth and flows outward carrying water to all lands.

The Indo-Iranians believed the world was divided into seven regions—the "seven karshvars"—and held that there was a natural law that ensured that the sun would maintain regular movements, thus providing order to the seasons and to existence itself. This law of order was known to the Indians as "rta" and to the Avestan people as "asha," and it was thought that order in the external world should likewise govern human conduct (Pythagoras, Plato). Truth, honesty, loyalty, and courage were felt to be appropriate virtues for mankind to cultivate. Virtue belonged to the natural order (Pythagoras, Plato, Orpheus). A person's word was sacred and considered to hold great power, a divine power that supported the upright one and brought down vengeance on those who betrayed it.

Eventually judicial procedures became lodged in Varuna—Lord of Waters—and Mithra, the Lord of Fire. Beyond these two there was the wise ruler, the single all-encompassing God, Ahura Mazda, the Lord of Wisdom, who controlled and directed their actions, while at the same time *not being connected with any physical phenomena* (Pythagoras, Plato, Orpheus). He symbolized the power of wisdom that should control all actions of gods and men alike. In the *Rig Veda* he is known as the Asura, the Lord. Boyce tells us that these lofty concepts are still deeply interwoven in the religions of both descendant peoples.

The proto-Indo-Iranians also venerated a number of other "abstract" gods—such as love, justice, courage, obedience, and victory (Plato). However, most of the Iranian gods were conceived anthropomorphically. Varuna speaks of the Immortals (Vedic, *Amrta;* Avestan, *Amesha*), or Shining Ones (Vedic, *Deva;* Avestan, *Daeva*—both words are Indo-European in origin).

There evolved a lucid picture of early cosmogony, which is reconstructed from Zoroastrian writings to show that the gods created the world in seven stages, first making Sky, solid like a huge round shell, with Water in the bottom half. Next they created Earth, resting on water like a huge flat dish, and at the center of the earth they fashioned three animate creations in the form of a single Plant, a single Animal and a single Man. Seventh, they created Fire—visible and invisible (Pythagoras, Plato, Orpheus). The world was brought into being motionless and unchanging, and the sun therefore stood still overhead, as if it were always noon. But then the gods offered triple sacrifice that set the cycle of being into motion: they crushed the plant, slew the bull and the man, and from this beneficent sacrifice more plants, animals and men came into existence. The cycle of being was set in motion, with death followed by new life, and the sun moving across the sky regulating the seasons in accordance with *asha,* order.

In reviewing the foregoing, we note that there are various places where the religious doctrines of Zoroaster remind us of doctrines similar to those we have encountered with Pythagoras, Orpheus, and Plato. One place in which it differs is where Ahura Mazda, the Lord of Wisdom, creates the world and controls all the lesser divinities below him. The Adversary, Angra Mainyu, he who is ignorant and has malign intentions toward the Good, comes into existence as well. Here is the schism for which Zoroastrianism is well known—the extreme dualism that divides the world into a place of perpetual conflict between good and evil, where each human being must make the choice as to which path he or she will follow. This has vague echoes in Plato's dualism, where the intangible and intelligible realm seems to oppose the material and sensible world, and where, too, each individual must make the choice about which path he or she will follow. The only difference is that Plato's dualism in fact constitutes a continuum, because the intelligible world has *unfolded* the material world and thus, in the final analysis, they have the same source. Zoroaster does not seem to highlight the continuum despite the fact that Ahura Mazda created the spiritual, immaterial world first, and then from it, the sensible world. There is, perhaps, a faint echo in Zoroastrianism's references to Vayu, the mysterious aspect of wind described as the "breath of life," and the relationship between the Monad and the Creative Dyad in Pythagoras and the Third, invisible principle in Plato's *Timaeus* that he calls the "nurse of all generation."

We also note that in Plato's *Timaeus,* after the One unfolds into three divine principles that are the creators of the cosmos, the elements of fire and water are introduced. The first elements in Zoroastrianism are also water and fire. The number three was sacred to Zoroastrians, as it was to Pythagoras and Plato, also to Orpheus, the founder of the mysteries. However, the number three could also be honoring the divine triumvirate of guardians of right and order. The Zoroastrian notion that the Sun maintains its movements, thereby producing order in the seasons and existence, and that we as human beings *reflect* this external order within us, *if* we are attuned to the higher side of life, is surely a mirror image of Pythagorean doctrine and the Platonic version of it in the *Republic*.

Likewise, the belief in the kinship of all life is paralleled in Pythagoras and Zoroaster. The abstention from flesh taught by Orpheus and Pythagoras reflects appreciation of the sacred nature of life, and that animals should not be made into an offering for expiation of *human* sins. Pythagoras, Orpheus, and Plato exhorted people to live according to their higher, soul-oriented nature, and to offer their *own lower self* in sacrifice to the gods for the expiation of bad deeds and the desire for higher knowledge. Thus, purity of mind and action was a pre-requisite to future development in each of these religious systems. This idea is reflected in the notion that one's good deeds can take one to a sunlit Paradise, whereas one's evil deeds will take one down to the realm of the underworld. Every religion in the world shares this notion that it is people's duty to make that *choice*, whether to act for good or for evil ends. And, naturally, it is the centerpiece in the teachings of Pythagoas, Orpheus, and Plato. The Zoroastrian virtues—love, justice, courage, and obedience—are clearly mirrored in the early Platonic dialogues. In Zoroastrianism they are unified within the notion of Virtue, while in Plato virtues are unified within the concept of the Good.

Cosmologically, the idea of Vayu—the Zoroastrian god of the Wind, the soul of the gods, the god of the "breath of life itself"—also evokes the concepts of Pythagorean and Platonic cosmogony, which holds that the creative Dyad, or the World Soul, surrounds the Earth, and that Earth must draw *breath from the World Soul* in order to have continued and expanded life. One takes note, too, that God, Ahura Mazda, the Lord of Wisdom, the wise ruler in ultimate control of the law, is not connected with any physical phenomena. This echoes the Pythagorean and Platonic notion that the Monad is originally unmanifest, formless, unified and transcendental, but the Monad creates the Indefinite Dyad—as its female counterpart—and she creates the temporal world. But, as we have seen, in creating the temporal and material universe, the Monad, or the Good, preserves part of itself in the eternal realm, where it is forever uncreated, unified and transcendental.

In addition, the Zoroastrian belief in the survival of the soul after death, its journey to the underworld, and for some its eventual release into the realm of sunlit Paradise has its echoes in Orpheus, Pythagoras, and Plato. Zoroastrianism does not seem to have a concept of personal reincarnation but rather the collective resurrection of all souls at the end of time. However, as we have seen, there was immortality of soul for the worthy and a universal law, karma, to determine how one's actions are judged as good or evil, which certainly has its echo in the Greek theogonies that parallel it.

India: The Vedic Era: Lord Rama

Now let us trace Zoroastrianism into its distant past and its connection to India, where Hinduism, the world's third largest religion, has been a major influence for millennia. Hinduism is often claimed to be the world's oldest religious tradition, with its roots going back to the time of the Vedas. Therefore, if we wish to compare Hinduism to Zoroastrianism we must focus on that period in the remote past when the Iranians and Indians formed one people with common religious beliefs. It will be reasonable to use the date fifteen hundred BCE, where Boyce eventually dates Zoroaster because it correlates to the same date for the earliest compilation of the *Rig Veda*, but it must be emphasized that, in my view, the oral traditions point to a *much* earlier date, perhaps *thousands* of years earlier.

Mary Boyce has shown that the proto-Indo-Iranians of the remote past shared the same ancient cult, worshipped the same pantheon of gods with Avestan or Sanskrit names, and shared common beliefs in the hereafter. And where Zoroaster received a revelation of Ahura Mazda and the heptad, it is claimed that the *Vedas* were not created, but "received" by the ancient sages of India in the same revelatory fashion, which is the reason why they are described as sacred texts that are "heard" rather than included with a different group that is "remembered." Where Ahura Mazda is conceived as the ultimate ruler, or creator of the universe, that same role is assigned to Brahman for the Indians.

There is a vast body of literature on Hinduism, and an equally vast literature on the *Vedas* and other significant Indian religious texts. A detailed comparison between them and Zorastrianism is beyond the scope of this book, but Mary Boyce has shown unequivocally that whether Ahura Mazda or the *Vedas* are cited, the religious beliefs of the time were held in common. The one great difference probably lies in the later development of Hinduism, namely in the Upanishadic period when it developed into a monotheistic religion, sometime in the period after eight hundred BCE and before the classical period where Hinduism acquired its typical form (500 BCE–500 CE). Again, these dates are questionably recent.

Zoroaster is known to have radically altered preexisting doctrine when he held that human history itself would come to an end, and that humankind shared with the gods the task of gradually overcoming evil and restoring the world to its original perfect state. Zoroaster also taught that the blessed would need to wait until the end of human history in order to be resurrected and then reunited with Ahura Mazda.

These Zoroastrian eschatological beliefs not only differed from the original Iranian teachings, but also from what we today know as Hindu doctrine. In fact, as we have seen, the remote Iranian teachings are more in consonance with *ancient* Indian religious beliefs. Although the Hindu religion is peopled with a great many divinities, nevertheless they are all under the umbrella of the One eternal, uncreated, Absolute principle, designated as Brahman. And the Hindu worshipper believed in the supremacy of the One eternal principle (Brahman) and understood that his soul was a spark (Atman) of that divine principle. Thus the Indians accepted the doctrine of the immortality of the soul, along with that of reincarnation, since it provided the means for the gradual purification of the soul until it was released from the wheel of birth and death in the divine moment of liberation, *moksha*. The framework of spiritual striving was imbedded in the law of karma, that divine universal law of justice by which one's actions were judged as good or evil, and that dispensed rewards and punishments accordingly.

These are the doctrines for which Hinduism has become renowned throughout the world, and that continue to provide the framework of religious belief for over eight hundred and fifty million people who follow those teachings today. What the ancient Indian understood was that they did not (like the later Zoroastrians) have to wait until the end of history in order to receive the collective reward of simultaneously being reunited with Ahura Mazda. Rather, they understood that their individual efforts, made through many lifetimes, would bring about their own liberation at a particular moment for them *individually,* while the other souls would continue on with their evolution in this temporal world. In this respect, the doctrine of Hinduism is more in keeping with Pythagoras, Orpheus and Plato than Zoroastrianism.

Such differences, however, should not alter our understanding that the Indians and Iranians, in the remote past, formed one people and shared common religious doctrines and beliefs, the origins of which the Gathas and the Vedas were "received" during the same time period and through direct revelation. When Mary Boyce makes the unmistakable connection between the Iranians and the Indians, she provides the last link we need in tracing the beliefs of immortality of the soul, transmigration/reincarnation, and the law of karma, backward in a direct line from Plato, to Pythagoras, to Orpheus, to the Persian Empire, to the ancient Iranians, and finally to India.

Before moving on, let us see what Schuré has to say about the Indo-Iranian period. Schuré concurs with Boyce that a migration of Aryan people entered Iran and India, but he gives a much earlier date of approximately 5000 to 4000 BCE. At that remote time, in Scythia, there were conflicts between the black races, the Semites—who worshipped a universal sky god—and the white races, the Scythians and the Celts, who worshipped the earth divinities of the forest. The female divinities were in high ascendance, but their cult had degenerated into one promoting human sacrifice amidst wild passions and orgies of blood.

Schuré states that a young Druid priest by the name of Rama led a fierce opposition to this barbaric practice of human sacrifice, which threatened to spill over into outright war between the black and white races. Rama had a visionary dream of a man and a woman as a divine couple in a temple, in which *the Greek god Dionysus* showed him a torch

Tracing the Source of those "Foreign" Doctrines

of a sacred fire, of the divine Spirit, and a cup of life and love. Dionysus told Rama to give the torch to the man, the cup of life and love to the woman, an act that not only transfigured the couple, but caused a light to shine upon a sacred altar such that the temple grew larger, its columns reached up to heaven and its vault became the firmament. Rama himself was transfigured and had revelations in which he saw the destinies of humanity in the constellations. Dionysus then gave Rama his blessing, told him he would spread His light on earth, and pointed him in the direction of the east. Rama asked to be told the source of this revelation. The being replied: "I am called Deva Nahusha, divine Intelligence" (Dionysus). The terrible war thus averted, Rama took the best of his (unmixed white) race, and led them safely into central Asia using the supernormal powers that had been bestowed on him.

Schuré says that when Zoroaster founded his new religion, the holy book of the Persians, the *Zend-Avesta* (or *Avesta*), refers to an ancient lawmaker by the name of Yima (Rama), who was the first man to whom Ormuzd, the living God, spoke. Zoroaster himself refers to Rama as "the leader of peoples, the most blessed monarch." In the the *Ramayana*, the Hindu epic, he is known as Rama, and in Greece he was connected with Dionysus, whose name is derived from the Sanskrit term *Deva Nahusha,* the divine restorer.

Rama led the white race in the conquest of Iran and founded the city of Ver. Owing to divine guidance, Rama was the first who conceived of social law as an expression of divine law, with the unmixed white race providing a center of light for all others. He divided people according to occupations (priests, warriors, laborers, artisans); taught them how to till the soil and sow seed; forbade slavery; and gave a new and honored position to women. He initiated the four annual great festivals, the holiest of which was Noel, the great sowing time. Here, too, the connection between the visible and invisible worlds was celebrated, since, at this particular winter festival, they bade farewell to souls leaving their bodies and extended a mystical greeting to those who were reincarnating into new bodies.

But most important, it was *Rama* who instituted the cult of the sacred fire. "The conception of *Agni,* the divine fire symbolized the cosmic agent, the principle of the universe... but its true domain is the unseen, mystical heaven.... The sacred fire [is] symbol of the divine unity of things" (Schuré 67, 63). Thus, with the ever-present *sacred* fire they celebrated, with fires and chants, the renewal of the earthly and solar year, the germination of nature in the heart of winter, and the promise of new life in the spring. Thus Rama linked human life with the cycle of the seasons and the movements of the stars, emphasizing their divine significance (Pythagoras, Plato).

The white race eventually settled in Iran, near the Himalayas. But Rama's mission was not yet accomplished. It was necessary to move onward into India and vanquish the remaining black race. This march on India is also mentioned in the *Zend-Avesta,* and the battle that ensued was viewed as one between white and black magic, which Rama was able to win by using the superhuman powers bestowed on him by Dionysus. Rama's battle reached its end in the conquest of Ceylon, now Sri Lanka, which was the last refuge of the black magician Ravana, a principle character in the Indian epic, the *Ramayana.*

According to Schuré, Rama, the chosen one of Dionysus, became master of India and spiritual king of the earth, ruled wisely and with compassion for many years until, when his end was near, he retired with his fellow initiates to the sacred mountain of Airyana-Vaeia, taught his disciples his secret knowledge, and sent them out to carry the divine message into Egypt and Occitania. Their message was that the sacred fire was the symbol of the divine unity of all things, and the horns of Ram were the emblem and symbol of the Aryan religion. In Vedic times, the Great Ancestor became Yama, the judge of the dead.

Mary Boyce has dated the earliest compilation of Vedic hymns at around fifteen hundred BCE, though there was undoubtedly an oral tradition that stretched back into the mists of time. The hymns of the *Vedas* established the rituals of sacrifice, and through "inspired utterances" brought forth the names of the gods we know as Hindu-Avestan, including Varuna (Greek Ouranos) and Indra. The sacred fire, the divine fire, was now the god Agni, the eldest of the gods and symbol of the *unseen, transcendent world*. The means to attain that world was embedded in the sacrificial offering of Soma, a drink that would confer immortality and turn men into gods. Agni, says Schuré, is the Eternal Masculine, creative intellect, pure spirit, while Soma, the Eternal Feminine, is the ethereal substance of the soul of the world, womb of all the worlds, visible and invisible, as well as Nature in her infinite transformations.

The *Vedas* make of the cosmogenic act a perpetual sacrifice. "In order to produce all that exists the supreme being sacrifices himself; he divides himself in order to emerge from his unity. This sacrifice is therefore considered the vital point of all the functions of nature... containing as it does, in embryo, the evolution of God in the world" (Schuré 68–69). The fire sacrifice, with its ceremonies and prayers, is a re-enactment of this great cosmogonic mystery, and the goddess Brahmanaspati symbolizes the crucible of prayer that accompanies such divine sacrifice.

The *Vedas* speak of the immortality of the soul, its transcendent origin and destination and the doctrine of reincarnation. In fact, Schuré refers to the doctrine of reincarnation as playing a major role in Brahmanism, in Buddhism, among the Egyptians and Orphics, in the philosophy of Pythagoras, and in that of Plato. (Parenthetically, Schuré makes the remarkable assertion that the philosophy of Pythagoras contains "a rational reproduction of the esoteric doctrine of India and Egypt." *That* is something to contemplate.) I think we can fairly include here the religious teachings of Orpheus and the philosophy of Plato, for as we have shown, their doctrines emanated from the same source. The *Vedas* are ultimately seen as an "organic religious system, a philosophic concept of the universe," whose light reflects, like a mirror, the eternal truths that are forever bestowed upon humankind from the divine source of life.

Schuré reveals that in those ancient times there was no distinction between the mysteries and popular worship; but much later, when the Brahmans had established their opulent form of authority, a rift began to develop between the king, the maharaja in his magnificent palace, and the ascetic recluse who lived near holy places and sought the direct revelation of God. A conflict between them would eventually ensue.

The Upanishadic Era: Lord Krishna

Around the year three thousand BCE (which *perhaps* coincides with the separation of the Indian and Iranian peoples) a great new initiate was born who would encapsulate the essence of the *Vedas* and crystallize their teachings in the world-renowned *Upanishads*. Indian legend has it that when the balance between good and evil dips too far to the side of evil, God sends a savior, an avatar, to restore the balance, and Krishna is considered to be such a savior, namely an "incarnation" of God on earth. (Christians may have difficulty in accepting that God has sent saviors other than Jesus to humankind, but Schuré shows that saviors and great teachers have been sent to different peoples with different religions during the history of the world, and that Jesus, the Christ, may perhaps be the only one of whom we in the West are aware).

According to Indian scriptural tradition, Krishna was born in 3228 BCE, a son of the royal family of Mathura. There is much anecdotal material about his early life, but he is famously known as the charming and mischievous boy-god who stole the butter offering at a sacred festival, or later as the enchanted flute player who divinely inspired the Gopi milkmaids to forget about their household duties and to follow the magic melodies of his flute into the forest. There, each gopi, believing that she alone danced with Lord Krishna, achieved moments of divine ecstasy and cosmic consciousness.

The events that shaped Krishna's mission, however, were those that concerned the balance between good and evil and are reflected in the other great Indian epic, *The Mahabharata*. In this time-honored tale, the good ruling family, the Pandavas, had been enticed into a chess game with the evil and ambitious family, the Kauravas, and during the game the Pandavas lost everything they possessed, including the kingdom. They were forced to retire to the forest for fourteen years, which they spent in religious austerities and purification. At the end of that time the kingdom was in even greater danger from the forces of evil, such that Krishna himself called a meeting between the Pandavas and Kauravas to determine its future. He offered a choice: take him as a guide, a champion in the inevitable war, or take all the armies and weapons to use in the battle. The Pandavas chose to have Lord Krishna as their champion, while the ambitious Kauravas chose the armies and the weapons. The die was cast. War would ensue.

One of the Pandavas, Arjuna, was a warrior and a special friend of Krishna. He was assigned the task of leading Krishna's army into the war—the war of good against evil. On the chosen day the two armies faced each other across the battlefield. Krishna, who would not himself take part in the battle, was nearby in his chariot. The war was about to

Tracing the Source of those "Foreign" Doctrines

begin—but when Arjuna looked across at the battle lines of his enemies, he saw with horror that the people he would have to kill included many of his friends and people that he knew! He grew fainthearted. Lord Krishna had to make a decision. There, with the battle lines drawn, and everyone waiting...waiting...waiting for the war to begin...Lord Krishna engaged in perhaps one of the most famous set of spiritual teachings ever undertaken. In order for Arjuna to understand and accept his mission, he would need to be instructed in the esoteric truth that lies behind the appearances of reality.

This teaching, found in the *Bhavagad-Gita*, comprises the central place of the scriptural teachings found in the *Upanishads* (the word means the teachings of those who sit near to the Master). Krishna instructs Arjuna about the nature of his soul, the Atman, revealing that it is part of Brahman, God, and that as a result his soul can never die. It is immortal, and only the body dies. Having finally understood his own immortality, as well as those of his enemies, Arjuna also has bestowed upon him a vision of Krishna in his cosmic form, and with his newfound wisdom, Arjuna is now prepared to do battle. The Pandavas eventually conquer the Kauravas, and the ruling family is restored to the throne. Good has been restored as the divine principle guiding human actions in the world.

Tradition has it that Krishna's teachings in the *Upanishads* encapsulate those of the *Vedas*, but make them more accessible to the ordinary people. They could more clearly understand the divine source and immortality of their soul, the doctrine of reincarnation, and the laws of karma, and apply them in their own lives. By making the choice to align oneself with good, one would ensure good circumstances in one's next life and hasten the time of their own liberation, *moksha*, or release from the wheel of life and death. The other great teaching—which perhaps had been forgotten or misunderstood from the prehistoric time of the *Vedas*—is that God is One. There may be many lesser divinities, but in the end, they all emanate from the One eternal God, Brahman. Such is the perennial teaching of the initiates.

Krishna lived a long life, and when he finally passed from this earthly plane, another important scripture, the *Puranas*, assigned a date to it of 3102 BCE, which marked the end of one long age, or yuga, and the start of the next age, which the Indians call Kali Yuga.

We cannot help noticing the discrepancy in the dates for both Rama and Krishna and ponder that it most likely goes back to the question of how ancient oral traditions eventually find their way into written scriptures in more "recent" times. The Indian tradition, which may be more trusted than western sources on their own history, date Rama around 5000 BCE and Krishna around 3000 BCE, whereas Boyce's more recent interpretations state that the Vedic hymns were composed and collected roughly from the latter part of the second millennium BCE to about 800 BCE. To fit into that time frame, it would mean that Krishna lived sometime around 800 BCE. Boyce states that the *Rig Veda*, the most ancient Vedic hymn, is dated to 1500 BCE, because that was when it found its way into a written form. But as she herself attests, the oral tradition goes back into distant prehistory.

The discrepancy of dating, if so it is, merely shows how very difficult it is to date ancient civilizations that are scarce on evidence of their existence. It also reinforces the idea, as shown in the section on Orpheus, that historians, striving for evidence, tend to the idea that *written documents* must be used to date a particular religion (Orphism, Hinduism) when in fact the oral history goes back so much further into prehistory that the original, charismatic leaders are no longer seen as historical figures but as legendary characters who may or may not have lived at all.

It is a tantalizing thought that perhaps Krishna lived around 3000 BCE, possibly coinciding with the period when the ancient Indians and Iranians drifted apart and forged their own distinctive languages and cultures. In fact, as we have surveyed the mystery school teachings backward from Greece, through Plato and Pythagoras, Orpheus, the Persian Empire, and the ancient Iranians, it may well be that Indian seekers came upon the knowledge of Krishna's teachings before they understood these doctrines could also be connected back to the original teachings of Lord Rama. Be that as it may, these two great avatars are immortalized in the epic poems the *Ramayana* and the *Mahabharata*, which tell their inspiring stories and continue to be recounted, performed, and revered by many millions of modern-day Indians. The main point, however, is that Lord Rama and Lord Krishna both taught the immortality of the soul, the concept of transmigration (reincarnation) and the law of karma, whose objective judgments reveal whether human souls are on the side of good or bad and how those actions affect individual future lives.

In concluding this section, let us review our findings. We have traced a path backward from Plato to Pythagoras (possibly as a result of the manuscript that Archytas acquired for Plato from the Pythagoreans); from Pythagoras to Zoroaster and the Persian empire (which shared religious practices and beliefs with the Pythagoreans and Orphics); and from the Persian Empire to ancient Iran and then to India, due to the fact that the Indians and Iranians had, in the distant past, shared a religion, a culture, and languages that were so similar that one was almost interchangeable from the other.

What we have tried to show, therefore, is that the idea of an *Eastern source* for the doctrines of immortality of the soul, transmigration/reincarnation and the law of karma is not a mere fancy but is entirely plausible. In fact, the crucial connection is the enormous influence wielded over a period of many centuries by the Persian empire, the largest empire the world had ever known until that of Alexander the Great. The Persian Empire dominated the Greek city-states of Ionia, Greece herself, much of the Middle East, and even the most ancient civilization of Egypt, which saw its end due to Persian invasion and subjugation. One thing is certain: the doctrines of immortality of the soul, transmigration/reincarnation, and laws of karma, or cause and effect, were utterly foreign to Greek state-sponsored religious beliefs at the time of Plato (as well as of Pythagorean and Orphic times) and that for similar and "peculiar" beliefs Plato's beloved teacher and mentor, Socrates, had been put to death by the state. As we have seen, such beliefs are ultimately traced back to India, and here we should remember that the direction of historical movement is not from Plato backward to India, but forward from India and the ancient proto-Iranian peoples into the Persian Empire, Egypt, Occitania, through Orpheus, and Pythagoras in Greece, and then to Socrates and Plato.

Conclusions

The main conclusions about Plato's dialogues are three in number, a fact Plato would no doubt appreciate. First, I have argued that there is a *grand design* in the dialogues; that they are not meant to be read in isolation, but rather as chapters of a book, which taken together, constitute Plato's philosophical as well as spiritual/religious teachings. I have put forth the thesis that the dialogues up to and including the *Republic encapsulate* the higher esoteric knowledge that leads up to the experience of the unhypothesized first principle, the Good, and that the dialogues following the *Republic* may serve as an *application* of those transcendental truths to human institutions. Such institutions include not only the *Laws* and the cosmology found in the *Timaeus*, but also extend to evaluation of other philosophical topics such as those embodied in the *Sophist* and *Parmenides*.

The *Timaeus*, in my view, may round out the group of dialogues that conclude with the *Republic,* since in bringing the notion of God into creation of the cosmos, it too deals with ultimate questions. I believe Plato placed it toward the end of his great work because dealing with the issue of cosmology would inevitably draw him into debate with the Pre-Socratics, the scientists and materialists. It is not an insignificant fact, and should not be overlooked, that Socrates's influence on Greek (and western) philosophy is of such paramount importance that he demarcates the historical line between its past and future, such that, in general, those who preceded him are referred to as *Pre-Socratic*s. Socrates is thus the historical marker for that evolutionary movement forward that has influenced western civilization for the last two thousand years.

The second point is that the *grand design* found in Plato's dialogues extends beyond the boundaries of philosophy and enters the realms not only of spiritual and religious teachings, but also encompasses mystical experience. Plato's protagonist for the dialogues up to and including the

Republic is Socrates, a man who was not only proclaimed the wisest man in Greece by the Oracle at Delphi, but who designated himself, not as a public teacher of philosophy, but rather as one who was "sent" by God, to persuade individuals, one by one, to focus on "care of the soul."

I maintain that, despite its low-key presence, this "care for the soul" is in fact the central, underlying theme of the dialogues, while on the surface another of Plato's goals is to move beyond Greek mythological thinking toward understanding the world in a new way by exercising the faculty of reason. Guthrie himself confirms that "care of the soul" was Plato's paramount concern. The implication of this focus is a religious and spiritual matter, not simply one of rational thinking. Thus, I have tried to show that Plato can be seen as a *religious teacher* inasmuch as his dialogues are not mere food for intellectual debate, but are meant to convey and inspire *a way of life*. This is accomplished through a framework of religious/spiritual teachings that start from the humblest beginnings with the acquisition of the virtues, and provide higher, esoteric knowledge, such that by the time of the *Symposium* and *Republic*, a dedicated disciple could reach the pinnacle of human evolution—the mystical experience that overcomes external dualism—and the corresponding subject-object split—and reunites one's soul with the Godhead in divine unity consciousness.

By providing a spiritual/religious framework for human beings to follow *as a way of life* Plato is revealing that he is providing no less a set of *religious* teachings than the Buddha before him and Jesus after him, the only difference between them being that Plato, or more accurately, Socrates, did not have a large public following because at that time, in Greece, it was considered the ultimate hubris for a human being to set himself up on a par with the gods or to regard his soul as part of God. As a result Socrates was guided, by God, to teach people individually. It was also not Greek political doctrine that people think for themselves; they were to be guided by the polytheistic gods of Homer and Hesiod, and to be governed by the political authorities and follow the religious traditions, ceremonies and festivals of the city-state. To go against these powerful forces meant persecution and death, as Socrates's own fate demonstrates.

In fact, in examining the multitude of references to Socrates in the dialogues, many of the hallmarks of a mystic are found, and it is my belief that the teachings espoused by Plato, at least up to the *Republic*, originated with Socrates, and that he is not accurately depicted, historically, as some do, as one who merely started out seeking *definitions*. As Socrates remarked to his accusers, he had been *"sent" by "God"* to remind all those he met to *take care for their soul*. As with Jesus after him who left no writings, but whose teachings were encapsulated by the Gospels of Matthew, Mark, Luke and John, Socrates left no writings, and, it was for his disciple, Plato, to commit the teachings to written form, and perhaps, after the *Republic*, to add those dialogues that embody the application of the transcendental truths to human institutions as they compare to God's *divine* law and justice.

The spiritual/religious/philosophical development offered to a student who was committed to the way of life that emphasized "care for the soul" is clearly delineated in the dialogues. It began with the acquisition of the virtues—courage (*Laches*), piety (*Euthyphro*), and the like—which were a pre-requisite in any tradition for religious development. It continued with the acquisition of higher esoteric knowledge not publicly current in Greece at the time, namely knowledge of recollection, immortality of the soul, transmigration, and the law of karma (*Meno, Phaedo,* and *Phaedrus*).

A word should be said here about the doctrine of the immortality of the soul. As has been mentioned on several occasions, this was a "foreign" concept in Greece when Socrates and Plato were alive in fifth- and fourth-century-BCE Athens. Immortality of the soul had been a central doctrine of Orpheus and Pythagoras, but in Plato's own time, as noted earlier, it was considered hubris for people to dare to claim they had an immortal soul, because this stepped over the invisible line between human beings and gods. The public mysteries provided, in some measure, experiences intended to hint at or actually provide a state of "initiation," but those participating in these public mysteries were forbidden to speak of them.

Socrates and Plato had the courage to publicly challenge the Homeric notion of the soul as a ghostly wraith that dissolved after death. In *The Collected Dialogues of Plato*, he placed the doctrine of immortality as *the very centerpiece* of his philosophical and religious teachings. As Walter Burkert puts it: "That the epithet which, since Homer, had characterized the gods in distinction from men now becomes the essential mark of the human person, is indeed a revolution.... It was Socratic care for the soul and Platonic metaphysics that gave it the classical form that was to predominate for thousands of years."[1]

It was this very knowledge of the human immortal soul that would eventually guide the worthy disciple who had shown dedication for many years to this *way of life*, into the experience of divine initiation or mystic union with the Godhead, as demonstrated in the *Symposium*. That ineffable experience had the power to finally overthrow the illusion of duality and the corresponding subject-object split, and to sweep the aspirant into divine Unity consciousness and the experience that his or her soul was not only a spark of, but *was* God. This experience is confirmed and reinforced in the *Republic*, which reminds us that the ideal city is in fact the *city of each person's soul*, the microcosm, as the external city is the macrocosm. In fact, Plato demonstrates the same metaphysical truth in the *Republic* by using rational argument. And, eventually, by going beyond rational argument into the unifying metaphysical science of dialectic, the disciple is shown that all the virtues—and all sensible things—are subsumed in the Forms; and all the Forms are eventually subsumed in the Good.

As has been pointed out, Socrates makes the most important distinction in the *Republic* between the *Form of the Good*—namely, what can be an object of thought and discussion, and the *Good Itself* that transcends the Form of the Good to such a degree that it is described as the unhypothesized first principle, eternal, unchangeable, and form-less.

This leads to the third conclusion, namely that when Plato speaks of the Good as the cause of all things and the truth of all things, there is no inference possible but that he means to equate the Good with God. Material from the *Timaeus* alone would support this view, where Plato clearly states that *God is the creator of our universe*. When we say that *God* created the universe we do not mean to limit God to that role of Creator. The ultimate designation of God is the One, the Absolute, the Monad, that which contains everything within its own incomprehensible transcendence.

But, as to the question that the Good is equated with God, I suggest that there are two main reasons why this view is not already a generally accepted truth. The first is that Socrates and Plato adopted a pedagogical style that did not pour "answers" into waiting and receptive student

---

1 Burkert, *Greek Religion*, 300–01.

vessels. Instead, they provided teachings that would allow disciples to come to the *realization of their own truth*, a principle of pedagogy that applies even to the earlier dialogues, where some scholars fault Socrates for not having arrived at the sought-after definition. I have argued that for *pedagogical* reasons, Socrates *could not* give a student the answer to the question posed by *any* of the dialogues, and thus wherever the student's knowledge terminates is where the dialogue also ends.

This principle also applies in the *Republic*, where, when asked by Glaucon to explain the *Good Itself*, Socrates replies that Glaucon would not be able to follow him there, but he *would* speak to him about the *Form of the Good,* something that Glaucon *could* understand and discuss, because the Form of the Good is a concept, whereas the Good Itself is beyond concepts and can only be experienced. Socrates's and Plato's form of pedagogy was wise enough and patient enough to allow each student to arrive, in their own time, at the truth of each dialogue. They were not only teaching their students to think rationally, but also *to think for themselves*, a new ideal in the Greek city-state, and thus bound to engender opposition, even persecution.

The second reason for refusing to deal with Plato's ultimate inference that the Good is God is that many modern philosophers would turn and run before even attempting to *think* of dealing with the issue of God as a matter of philosophy! This is due, in my view, partly to the fact that beginning with the seventeenth century Enlightenment, philosophy in general has adopted a more scientific way of describing the world, a method that has left most metaphysics beyond the interest of authoritative analysis, or even as a topic for discussion. Much of this thinking is modern, attributed to philosophy of science (or more accurately, the science of philosophy) but some of it may be attributed to an insistence in elevating Aristotle to the place of pre-eminent authority, not only in scientific but also in *metaphysical* matters. However, as has been shown, Aristotle himself was prey to the same kind of material explanations that modern philosophers espouse. He rejected metaphysical assumptions as vigorously as he rejected Plato's Forms or Pythagoras's mathematical interpretation of the cosmos.

Plato would have chided Aristotle—and theoretically minded modern philosophers—by pointing out that they had not examined their own basic assumptions and that they had not carried their investigations back to the unhypothesized first principle. This is one of my arguments with Aristotle, namely that he argues that Two Principles, the Unlimited and the Limited, govern this world and that they are material. *But he never explains how those two principles came into being.*

I return to this most important point, that when Plato speaks of the Good—and when one takes into consideration the transcendental descriptions of the Good in the *Symposium, Republic,* and *Timaeus*—it is well-nigh impossible to avoid the inference that Plato wishes to make—namely that the Good is God. But, consistent with his pedagogical style, Plato leaves it for each disciple, and each reader, to come to that discovery for him or herself, because every student must attain truth *by themselves.*

Taken together—the notion of a *grand design* in the dialogues; that "care for the soul" as a way of life constitutes both religious as well as philosophical teachings; and that the Good is to be equated with God—amount to a radical re-assessment of Plato's place in the philosophical tradition, and one that I maintain more nearly approximates what Plato had in mind when he originally wrote the *Collected Dialogues.* It is quite a dazzling fact that in the process he moves the doctrine of immortality of the soul to the center of philosophical debate and brings that doctrine out of the shadows of the mysteries and into the light of rational discussion. (As the myths, and the baffling teachings in the *Timaeus* demonstrate, however, there were still parts of the mysteries that were not to be revealed.) At the same time he is a force that helps move Greek thinking beyond mythological and symbolic modes to the development and use of reason as a new way of interpreting the world—a tool that would not only encourage each person to think for themselves, but also helped usher in new developments of philosophy and democracy that are the ultimate gifts Greece bequeathed to the world.

One last lesson we have learned from Plato is that although he separates the world into the intelligible world (objects that can be thought but not seen) and the sensible world (objects that can be seen but not thought) these two worlds are not in a duality of utter conflict such as might be found with the religion of Zoroaster or the Gnostics, but are instead part *of a continuum of existence.* One can posit with Plato that it starts with God creating the world, and then provides for intelligible objects to unfold into sensible processes and objects. Or from the opposite point of view, one can experience it—via the Divided Line—as four basic stages of development of the mind, each of which has corresponding objects. Thus at the lowest stage, that of conjecture, shadows and reflections are the corresponding objects. The second stage is belief, which has as its corresponding objects—all sensible things. The third stage is understanding, whose objects are scientific, mathematical, logical theories. And the fourth level is that of reason, which has as its corresponding objects the Forms, dialectic, the unity of things, and the eventual experience of the Good.

To reiterate, the sensible world and intelligible world are not in dire conflict, but through development of the mind the soul can be brought into a harmony where the transcendent and the immanent both have their place. What Plato appears to demonstrate in the Divided Line is that the world is *as you see it*. The higher your consciousness, the more likely you are to be able to grasp the transcendental truths, which, without developing such higher levels of consciousness, remain a closed book. What Plato demonstrates, however, is that there is a way to take "care for the soul" such that it adheres to a way of life that will propel itself upward toward knowledge of the transcendental realms and the truth of the soul's experience as a part of God. This is no more or less of an achievement than that of an innovating religious teacher, and demonstrates into the bargain that the tool of reason can be used in service of the divine just as much as it may be used in the service of science. *That*, perhaps, more than anything else, reveals the great genius of Socrates and Plato!

In Part II of the book I have asked the question: What made Plato's philosophy possible in fifth-century-BCE Athens? I have focused on precisely those aspects of Plato's doctrines that were almost certainly "foreign" to Greek thought at the time—the belief in immortality of the soul, the process of "recollection," transmigration of the soul, and the law of karma.

We have seen that Plato had a precedent for his beliefs in the early Greek philosopher, Pythagoras, who is well documented as sharing the doctrines of immortality of the soul, transmigration, and the laws of or karma, not only with Plato but with Orpheus before him. Another major debt Plato owes to Pythagoras is the quadrivium of subjects—namely, mathematics, geometry, astronomy and music—which Plato uses as the curriculum of higher knowledge studied by the guardians, those disciples who could potentially reach divine consciousness and then return to rule their cities with justice, peace, and with a social structure that reflected the divine nature of reality on earth. Again, I wonder if Plato actually used Pythagoras's school in Southern Italy as a model for the *Republic.*

On a purely philosophical level, however, I have undertaken an examination of Pythagorean doctrines to evaluate whether they compare with Plato's positions on two key issues, and I therefore asked the questions: Does Pythagoras accept the two-principle *material* theory of cosmic origin? And, are numbers immanent for Pythagoras? I have undertaken an analysis placing emphasis on the fact that Pythagoras is known to have spent twenty-two years in the Egyptian mystery school at Memphis studying *the science God* while seeking at the same time to attain the divine initiation that not only brought about union of the soul with the Godhead in unity consciousness, but was, no doubt, the source of his legendary achievements and powers.

As Aristotle summarized, the common view in Plato's time about Pythagoras was that he held that there were two principles governing existence, the Unlimited and the Limit. However, I have challenged that position on the grounds that it has a restricted view and understanding of Pythagoras's philosophy. I affirm, along with Schuré, that Pythagoras ascribed to the two-principle position *only as it pertained to the sensible world*, but as Schuré and my own conclusions make clear, Pythagoras subscribed to the notion that *beyond those two principles* was the unitary Monad, unmanifest, indivisible, unchanging, and totally transcendent. This Monad is described as the One, a divine principle that equates with the Absolute. Thus I have designated Pythagoras as a Monist of the first order, even though, as with Christianity, Hinduism, Buddhism and Zoroastrianism, there are three divine aspects in One.

I have argued that Pythagoras's philosophy clearly extends into the transcendent world, and that due to his initiation in Egypt, whose very purpose was divine unity-consciousness, it would be absolutely inconceivable for him not to have knowledge of—not to have actually *experienced*—that unity consciousness himself. I understand the difficulties posed by this position: the fact that there are no writings extant, and that Pythagoras's higher esoteric teachings, themselves a symbolic language, were sealed by an oath of silence to protect members of the mystery school from persecution, are obstacles to evaluating his place in philosophy. However, I have argued that those who persist in describing him as advocating the two-principle theory are only recognizing the sensible, mundane aspect of his philosophy, and have omitted or ignored that much larger, if secret part pertaining to the intelligible world, namely the unitary Monad.

I have similarly argued that those, like Aristotle, or the Pre-Socratics who hold to a scientific and material origin of the universe, have failed to examine their assumptions all the way back to the unhypothesized first principle. In their case, they observe physical manifestations including the elements, and are content to start from that point, not heeding, nor asking the final question as to *the source* of those manifestations. Pythagoras's position, however, is that the universe has a divine source, the Monad, the One, God, and that the celestial movements of the heavens are a reflection, in time, of the Monad's eternal nature, which human beings can emulate to mirror that same order, beauty, and divine law within themselves. I therefore reiterate that ultimately Pythagoras was a Monist and an Idealist.

The second common belief is that Pythagoras maintained numbers were immanent. I have shown a number of Aristotle's comments that clearly reveal his bafflement and irritation that the exact opposite was the case—namely that Pythagoreans held that *eternal principles* preceded and were the cause of sensible things—a view that Aristotle himself summarily rejected. In addition, despite the fact that in Greece number was considered both ideal and mundane, Aristotle did not wish to accept that mathematics could be transcendental because his four causes trap him in the sensible world and to material explanations for things. However, I believe I have shown that Pythagoras's mathematical interpretation of the cosmos is not only Idealist in nature (due in part to the ultimately Idealist nature of mathematics) and to the fact that number is a divine attribute of the Monad, but also, again, to the divine initiation that allowed Pythagoras the great gift of being given the *knowledge* of the mathematical interpretation of the universe, or what Schuré calls the science of God. We must take into consideration, as well, the fact that for Pythagoras mathematics was not a cold or abstract science, but was a direct manifestation of God's law in the cosmos, and that he assigned to mathematics a power that was not only divine, but was also *alive* in its manifestation.

Conclusions

Last, as Guthrie finally concedes, it became apparent that Aristotle had led his followers in the wrong direction in his understanding of mathematics, and Pythagoras was proved correct, because in the twentieth century mathematics became the standard language by which to couch all scientific interpretations of our cosmos. Pythagoras merely showed that he was aware of this truth over two thousand five hundred years ago! A Monist such as Pythagoras could not possibly ascribe to a purely immanent view of mathematics, because for him mathematics derived its source in the Monad—even though there was an immanent application of mathematics to the material world. Pythagoras's secret esoteric teachings are the cause of the opacity of ascertaining his views, but that should not prevent us from understanding that for a Monist such as Pythagoras, number was in its ultimate nature Ideal and, in fact, divine.

In challenging commonly held beliefs of Pythagoras some changes have obviously occurred. First Pythagoras has moved from a two-principle theorist to a Monist. And second, Pythagorean mathematics have been found to have their source in the Monad, and are therefore Ideal, albeit with an immanent application. These advances have now brought the philosophy of Pythagoras into more or less direct alignment with that of Plato, for as Plato reveals in the *Timaeus*, it is *God* who created the world, and Plato is clearly a Monist. And, although Plato's philosophy did not *publicly* emphasize mathematics in the way that Pythagoras did, Plato nevertheless clearly uses the Pythagorean quadrivium of arithmetic, geometry, astronomy, and music to educate the future guardians. Also, Plato clearly assigns Number as a Form and, therefore, as a transcendental truth, one that is only truly understood when one detaches consciousness from the senses. When not fully detached, as in interpreting geometrical diagrams, Plato argues that an individual is operating at the theoretical level of the Divided Line but has not approached the highest level, that of reason that includes as its objects both dialectic and the Good—the cause of all knowledge and truth in the universe.

With a revised view of Pythagoras we can finally appreciate that Plato and Pythagoras shared an almost identical philosophy. They share the doctrine of the One, the Monad, God, as well as the creative Dyad, and the Divine Triad (*Timaeus*). They share the continuum between sensible and the intelligible worlds. They share doctrines of the immortality of the soul, transmigration, and the laws of karma as providing a cosmic framework for the journey of the human soul from the divine realms into matter, its experiences in its lives on Earth, and its eventual journey back to the divine realms. And most significant, they share the ultimate goal of human evolution as the divine initiation that transcends the duality of the external world and the corresponding subject-object split, where the soul is merged into the unity-consciousness of God.

I would like to add a note on the Neoplatonists, Plotinus, Porphyry and Iamblichus, who, although they lived approximately seven hundred years after Pythagoras (in the second and third centuries CE), are precisely those philosophers who wrote biographies on Pythagoras that are a valuable source used by modern researchers, despite, in some cases their obvious reservations.

Guthrie summarily dismissed them as overly naïve, and as willing to ascribe any and all teachings directly to Pythagoras. What Guthrie omits to mention is that their own writings document that both Plotinus and Porphyry had experiences of divine initiation themselves, and thus were in a unique position to evaluate the true achievements of Pythagoras. If they ascribed all of the teachings to Pythagoras, it was because they understood that such high teachings could only have been created by someone who was permanently immersed in a divine state of consciousness. Therefore, they did not hesitate in revering him. And Kahn, after wondering if Philolaus was the creator of Pythagorean doctrine, at the end came to believe that great ideas came from great minds and that, therefore, the teachings should be ascribed to Pythagoras himself. It is my position that a new open-mindedness should be accorded to these Neoplatonists, who contributed a large part of what we know about Pythagoras from a spiritual perspective.

In Part III of the book, I seek the origin of those "foreign" teachings—immortality of the soul, transmigration, and the law of karma—that found their way into Plato's dialogues. We have seen that such beliefs were also attributed to Pythagoras, the Egyptian mystery school in the temple of Memphis, and also to Orpheus, founder of the mysteries in Greece. We also recall that Guthrie described the Pythagorean Orphics as holding the same religious doctrines.

As far as Zoroaster is concerned, we have noted Cornford's statement, confirmed by Guthrie, that the Orphics shared with the Zoroastrians such similar doctrines and beliefs as to be interchangeable with one another. And yet, such religious views are not connected to the Persian Empire by Guthrie or others, despite the fact that it was the largest empire in the world until the time of Alexander. Nor was it emphasized that Zoroaster's religion had been adopted by the state and had permeated to every far-flung corner of the empire, including to Samos, where Pythagoras was born and lived until he departed for Egypt as a young man.

The Persian Empire had an *indelible influence* upon those peoples it had subjugated. Pythagoras saw that first hand. When he was still in Egypt the Persian conqueror Cambyses invaded Egypt, subjugated the last Egyptian pharaoh, Psamettichus, and ended that ancient and illustrious civilization. Pythagoras himself was arrested and sent to Babylon, where, as a prisoner for twelve years, he was exposed to the teachings of Zoroaster, most likely from his descendants, the Persian Magi, as well as to the mysteries of Chaldean magic.

Mary Boyce's book, *Zoroastrianism: Its Beliefs and Practice,* provides most invaluable clues about ties between Zoroastrianism and the doctrines of ancient India. She reveals that in the ancient past the Aryan people migrated through Iran and into India, and at that time the ancient Iranians and Indians had shared common beliefs and gods, their languages so close as to be seen as interchangeable. Our journey thus ends in India, passing backward through the Upanishadic Era with Krishna, around 3000 BCE, and ending up in Vedic times with Rama, the great savior, who, according to Schuré, founded the first major civilization some 7,000 ago.

Although the *Vedas* are dated to 1500 BCE, this does not take into account an immense period in which the oral tradition was the sole way in which sacred knowledge was passed from generation to generation. Thus, the date of 1500 BCE refers to the date the *Vedas* were written down, but as we have seen from the examples of Orpheus and Zoroaster, there is often a great time-lag between the lifetime of the Teacher and when their teachings appear in written form, a lag sometimes stretching into hundreds or even thousands of years. In tracing the threads of these teachings back from Plato to Pythagoras, Orpheus, Zoroaster, Krishna and Rama, and despite the challenges of correlating mythological representations of the cosmos and rational representations of divine truths, some general themes are shown to be common to all.

First, the notion of God as the creator of the universe, a God who is transcendental, unified, immutable, and formless. Second, they share the belief in a unitary God with Three Divine Aspects, or Persons. In India they were Brahma, Vishnu, and Shiva; in Egypt, Osiris, Isis, and Horus; for Pythagoras, the Monad, creative Dyad, and Harmonia; for Orpheus, Zeus as the Father the firmament as the divine wife, and Dionysus as the Son; for Plato it is God, the World Soul, and the nurse of generation, who forms the Divine Triad; in Christianity, it is God the Father, God the Son, and God the Holy Spirit (the Mother). What these cultures also share—despite vastly different social, religious, political and cultural structures, and time periods—are the central doctrines of immortality of the soul, transmigration, and the laws of karma—the very doctrines that place the individual human soul within a cosmic framework and, at the same time, verify and confirm that the human soul is a spark and, indeed, *is* God. Considering the diversity of these different civilizations, these facts carry great weight.

Second is that in the case of each of these Teachers—Plato, Pythagoras, Orpheus, Krishna and Rama—they appeared as leaders of their peoples at a time when those peoples were beset by political or religious turmoil, if not actual wars. In the case of Rama, a great struggle was taking place between the black and white races. Where the black races dominated, the Semitic form of mythology was propagated, a belief in the One God, the universal Spirit; and where the white races dominated, the Scythians and Celts found their gods in the form of many feminine spirits in the heart of the forests. The feminine cult, Druidic in origin, which was originally a visionary cult, had turned ambitious and cruel and instituted human sacrifice on a widespread and gruesome scale. Thus a war was about to break out between this degenerate feminine cult and the masculine gods who had been consigned to the mountains. As a young Druid priest, Rama publicly protested the barbaric practices of human sacrifice, and it was on the eve of war that he had his famous visitation from Dionysus, Deva Nahusha, who instructed him to take the unmixed white race eastward and into India. As a result of this revelation, war was averted.

Conclusions

As Schuré tells us, during the two thousand year period between the birth of Lord Rama (circa 5000 BCE) and that of Lord Krishna (circa 3000 BCE), there gradually emerged a split between the opulent kings who ruled India and the mendicant hermits and anchorites—seekers of the truth who lived solitary lives of poverty and spiritual austerity. The kings persecuted and hunted the anchorites so that they were forced to take refuge in the most remote and wild parts of the forest. Eventually, the leader of the anchorites, a blind sage of great renown, Vasistha, went to the king of Madura and warned him of impending doom due to his past actions.

It was the destiny of Lord Krishna not only to meet the great Vasistha, but to receive divine initiation from him, such that when the blind, hundred-year-old sage passed away, Krishna took his place as the leader of the anchorites, and he challenged the evil deeds of India's corrupt kings. Perhaps that is the origin of the famous battle between good and evil that takes place in the Indian epic, the *Mahabharata*.

Moments before the battle between the good Pandavas and the evil Kauravas begins, Arjuna, the military leader of the Pandavas, becomes fainthearted, seeing family and friends on the side of the enemy army. In order that the battle might proceed and the balance of good be restored in the kingdom, Krishna has to instruct Arjuna about the immortality of his soul. Only when Arjuna understands that the souls of his enemies are also immortal can he accept the terrible bloodshed and loss of life that will ensue in the battle to restore good to the kingdom.

Similar conditions are to be found with Orpheus. Before his birth Schuré tells us (224) that Greece was deeply divided by religion and politics. In Greece as in Thrace, the feminine cults were in supremacy, but they had appropriated the old cult of Bacchus and had given him a bloody and dreadful character. Their practices gave rise to dangerous passions indulging even in human sacrifice. Thrace had been divided into two enemy camps, the female earth cults and the male gods, consigned to the mountains. Thus, after his return from twenty years in Egypt, where he had become an initiate, and at a moment of great turmoil, Orpheus assumed the leadership of the peoples of Thrace. He created the mysteries in Greece, instilling them in a veiled form into poetry so that ordinary people might be exposed to their beneficial influences, and he used the magic of his music to subdue the passions of the people. By the end of his life the mysteries had spread, like a secret lifeblood, not only into all the temples of Jupiter and Apollo, but into the very veins of Greece. Nevertheless, the myth tells that the Bacchantes, feeling offended by Orpheus, killed him and tore his body to pieces.

Schuré tells us:

> Once he had disappeared, darkness covered (Greece) once again. After a series of revolutions the tyrants of Thrace burned his books, overturned his temples, drove out his disciples. The Greek kings and many cities...imitated them. They wished to erase his memory, to destroy his last remains, and this was so well done that a few centuries after his death, a part of Greece doubted that he had ever existed. In vain the initiates preserved his tradition for more than a thousand years; in vain Pythagoras and Plato spoke of him as a divine man.

And so it was with Pythagoras. In the seventh century BCE, according to Schuré:

> Greece began to be threatened, in that the commands of Delphi were no longer respected; sacred lands were trespassed upon; the spiritual and moral level had lowered; the priests sold themselves to political power; even the Mysteries began to be corrupted. The ancient priestly and agricultural royalty was followed here by tyranny pure and simple, there by military aristocracy, elsewhere by anarchical democracy. The temples had become powerless to warn men of impending dissolution.
>
> A popularization of esoteric teaching had become necessary. In order that the thought of Orpheus could live and expand in all its brilliance, it was necessary that the wisdom of the temples should pass into the ranks of the laity.... The evolution of which we speak...gave birth to physicists like Thales, legislators like Solon, poets like Pindar, heroes like Epaminondas; but its official leader was an initiate of the first order...Pythagoras...for he coordinated the Orphic inspirations into a complete system....

We have discussed the philosophical, mathematical, and religious teachings of Pythagoras and we recall that his esoteric teachings were mathematical and symbolic, not committed to written form. According to Schuré the *"essence of system* can be found in the *Golden Verses of Lysis,* in the commentary of Hierocles, in fragments by Philolaus and Archytas, as well as in Plato's *Timaeus,* which contains Pythagoras's cosmogony.... The Neoplatonists of Alexandria, the Gnostics and even the early Church Fathers quote him as an authority." (Schuré 265–268, 269)

We cannot refrain here from noting that immortality of the soul is one of the central tenets of Christianity. Jesus, like the other great Teachers, taught that man has a choice between acting for good or evil, but he did not provide the sophisticated cosmic justification for that Eastern doctrine found explicitly in Plato, and in India. In the *Gospel of Matthew,* Jesus mentions that John the Baptist is Elias, or Elijah (one of the great Israelite prophets), come again, thus hinting at his knowledge of the doctrine of transmigration (11:7–14). We would not be amiss, then, in describing Jesus as the consummate initiate who carried forth the perennial teachings into Christianity, where they have since become known and practiced by millions of people all over the world.

Schuré mentions that at the time of Pythagoras there were great teachers in other parts of the globe—in China, Lao-Tse; in India, the last Buddha, Sakya-Moni; in Italy, King Numa, who, armed with the Sibylline Books, sought to restrain the threatening ambition of the Roman senate. "And it is not by chance that these reformers appear at the same time among such different peoples" (Schuré 270). According to Schuré the higher esotericism found among these different reformers was part of a single spiritual current passing through all of humankind, so much so that Schuré could state that in Pythagoras's system "we find a rational reproduction of the esoteric doctrine of India and Egypt, to which he gave clarity and Hellenistic simplicity, adding a more forceful feeling and a more exact idea of human freedom" (Schuré 269). A central part of that doctrine, of course, are the tenets of immortality of the soul, transmigration, and the law of karma, those very doctrines that prompted this book because they were "foreign" in Greece at the time of Plato.

As Schuré points out, "Although he appears in the broad daylight of history, Pythagoras has remained an almost legendary figure. The main reason for this is the dreadful persecution he experienced in Sicily, and that cost the lives of so many Pythagoreans. Some perished, crushed under the debris of their school that had been set afire, others died of starvation in a temple. The memory and teaching of the Master was perpetuated only by those survivors who were able to flee into Greece" (Schuré 267–269). (Alas, we note that Krishna, Orpheus, Socrates and Jesus were all to suffer the same fate.)

We have now come full circle, back to Plato. In Greece, an agrarian society had developed into the city-states, but as Schuré relates "somber and troubled was the political horizon during Plato's childhood and youth. He passed his childhood during the dreadful Peloponnesian War, that fratricidal battle between Sparta and Athens that paved the way for the dissolution of Greece. The great days of the Medic wars had passed; the time of Marathon and Salamis had gone. The year of Plato's birth, 429 BCE is that of the death of Pericles, the greatest statesman of Greece.... Inside Athens were the discords of a demagoguery held at bay; outside the Lacedaemonian invasion was ever at the gates, war on land and sea, and the king of Persia's gold circulating like a corrupting poison in the hands of tribunes and magistrates. Alcibiades had replaced Pericles in the public favor.... [He] led his country to ruin while he laughed.... Plato took part in the capture of Athens by the Spartans.... He saw the entrance of Lysander into his native city, which meant the end of Athenian independence; saw the enemy literally dance upon the ruins of the country...then came the Thirty Tyrants and their proscriptions" (Schuré 374–376).

It is not surprising therefore that after the sobering experience of Socrates's execution, Plato withdrew from politics and, in his greatest work the *Republic*, revealed a system of governance inherited from Pythagoras, which posited that only *philosophers* were worthy to be rulers, due to their pursuit of spiritual illumination and their complete lack of political ambition.

And other challenges were on the horizon, namely those of the Pre-Socratics who were attempting, in their various ways, to reduce the creation of the universe to material origins, often to one of the four elements fire, water, earth or air. Heraclitus's philosophy also offered an unsettling view of the human place in the universe, because he had argued that all is change and that, because of this, people could never know the truth of things. Plato vigorously opposed such views by counteracting them with his dialogues where he extols the immortality of the soul (*Phaedo, Phaedrus*) and the divine origin and destination of humankind

(*Symposium, Republic*). The formidable Parmenides offered a philosophy that negated any kind of movement or change in the sensible world, and described God in a way that depended upon logical formulations and arguments, which Plato analyzed and in my judgment successfully countered (*Parmenides*).

And the last of the great challenges lay with the Sophists, those who claimed "man is the measure of all things," by which they meant that each person's experience was so subjective that no objective standards could ever apply, thus implying anarchy. Plato found that the Sophists twisted and distorted the truth into a mere "appearance" and sold their teachings for money. Socrates mocked them because they bamboozled ordinary citizens with their false reasoning, and Plato unmasked the sophist in the dialogue of the same name.

Amid these challenges on all sides, scientific, political, and philosophical, Plato taught his students to think for themselves; by stressing the human need to live a virtuous life—by encouraging people to "care for the soul" and seek higher knowledge of their origins in dialogues that revealed the immortality of the soul, recollection, transmigration, and the laws of karma. He revealed that humankind has the capacity, if worthy, to reach the pinnacle of human evolution—namely, divine initiation, the experience of which would confirm that the human soul is a spark—indeed, a part of God.

Thus, couched in the philosophy of reason, Plato taught "care for the soul" *as a way of life*. These were *religious/spiritual* teachings, kept secret by an oath of silence in Pythagoras's day, but made (mostly) public by Socrates and Plato despite the possible charges of hubris and blasphemy that could be leveled against them. *These* were the very doctrines that could counter the materialism of the Pre-Socratics, the flux of Heraclitus, the logic of Parmenides, and the distorted truth of the Sophists. They proclaim the truth that God created the universe and that human beings, because of their immortal soul, have a faculty by which they can not only come to understand their place in the universe, but also by which they can rest assured that the universe has a loving and beneficent source rather than intimidating, implacable, abstract principles.

Like the initiates before him, Plato (and let us not forget Socrates) sought to restore the teachings of humankind's divine heritage and destination in a world that was shaken by political uncertainty and scientific interpretation. This is why Plato is a religious/spiritual teacher, namely because in an uncertain world he restored the existence and reality of God to front and center in his teachings. And, in proclaiming his debt to Pythagoras in the *Republic*, Plato appropriated those doctrines that started this quest—namely, the beliefs in the immortality of the soul, of transmigration, and the law of karma—the doctrines that we described as "foreign" in fifth-century-BCE Greece. Our search has shown that such doctrines spanned all continents and time periods, but that they had their ultimate source in the East, and specifically in India. That is something with which modern philosophers will need to grapple and eventually integrate. Let us hope we do not have to wait until another initiate appears on earth to verify this truth!

BIBLIOGRAPHY

Bauval, Robert. *The Orion Mystery*. New York: Crown, 1994.

Bernstein, Morey. *A Search for Bridey Murphy*. Garden City, NY: Doubleday, 1956.

Boyce, Mary. *Zoroastrians: Their Religious Beliefs and Practices*. London: Routledge & Kegan Paul, 1979.

Brunton, Paul A. *A Search in Secret Egypt*. New York: Samuel Weiser, 1970.

Burnet, John. *Early Greek Philosophy*. London: Adam and Black, 1948.

Burkert, Walter. *Lore and Science in Ancient Pythagoreanism*. Cambridge, MA: Harvard University, 1972.

Clark, Gillian. *Iamblichus: On the Pythagorean Life*. Liverpool: Liverpool University, 1989.

Cooper, John M. (ed). *Plato: Complete Works*. Indianapolis: Hackett, 1997.

Cornford, F. M. *Before and After Socrates*. Cambridge, UK: Cambridge University, 1932.

———. *Plato's Theory of Knowledge*. London: Kegan Paul, Trench, Trubner, 1935.

———. *From Religion to Philosophy*. London: Harper, 1957.

Curd, Patricia. *A PreSocratics Reader: Selected Fragments and Testimonia*. Indianapolis: Hackett. 1996.

DeVogel, C. J. E. *Pythagoras and Early Pythagoreanism*. Assen, The Netherlands: Van Gorcum, 1965.

Dillon, John. *Iamblichi Chalcidensis*. Leiden, The Netherlands: Brill, 1973.

Gaye, R. K. *The Platonic Conception of Immortality and its Connection with the Theory of Ideas*. Cambridge, UK: Cambridge, 1904.

Gill, Mary Louise, and Paul Ryan. *Plato–Parmenides*. Indianapolis: Hackett, 1996.

Gould, John. *The Development of Plato's Ethics*. Cambridge, UK: Cambridge, 1955.

Guthrie, Kenneth Sylvan. *The Pythagoras Sourcebook and Library*. Grand Rapids, MI: Phanes Press, 1988.

Guthrie, W. K. C. *History of Greek Philosophy*. Cambridge, UK: Cambridge, 1975.

———. *Orpheus and Greek Religion*. Princeton, NJ: Princeton, 1933.

———. *The Greek Philosophers: From Thales to Aristotle*. New York: Harper, 1950.

Hadas, M. and Smith, M. *Heroes and Gods: Spiritual Biographies in Antiquity, Porphry's Life of Pythagoras*. New York: Harper, 1965.

Haich, Elizabeth. *Initiation*. Palo Alto, CA: The Seed Center, 1974.

Hamilton, Edith and Huntington Cairns. *Plato: The Collected Dialogues*. Princeton, NJ: Princeton, 1965.

Hemenway, Priya, *Divine Proportion: Phi in Art, Nature and Science*. New York: Sterling, 2005.

Herodotus, *The Histories of Herodotus*. New York: Dutton, 1964.

Humphreys, Christmas. *Buddhism: An Introduction and Guide*. New York: Penguin, 1990.

Huffman, Carl A. *Philolaus of Croton: Pythagorean and Pre-Socratic*. Cambridge, UK: Cambridge, 1993.

Isherwood, Christopher. *Ramakrishna and His Disciples*. Hollywood: Vedanta, 1965.

Kahn, Charles. *Pythagoras and the Pythagoreans, A Brief History*, Indianapolis: Hackett, 2001.

Kraut, Richard. (ed). *The Cambridge Companion to Plato*. Cambridge, UK: Cambridge University, 1992.

Laertius, Diogenes. *Lives of Eminent Philosophers*, trans. R.D. Hicks. London: William Heinemann, 1925.

Magee, Glenn Alexander, ed. *The Cambridge Handbook of Mysticism and Western Esotericism*. Cambridge, UK: Cambridge, 2012.

McKeon, Richard. *The Basic Works of Aristotle*. New York: Random House, 1941.

Menn, Stephen. *Plato on God as Nous*. Carbondale: Southern Illinois University, 1995.

Philip, J. A. *Pythagoras and Early Pythagoreanism*. Toronto: University of Toronto, 1996.

Robinson, Richard. *Plato's Earlier Dialectic*. Ithaca, NY: Cornell University Press, 1941.

Schuré, Édouard. *The Great Initiates*. Great Barrington, MA: Steinerbooks, 1992.

Stevenson, Ian. *European Cases of the Reincarnation Type*. Charlottesville, VA: University Press of Virginia, 1975, 1980.

Taylor, A. E. *Plato*. London: Archibald Constable, 1908.

Bibliography

———. *Plato: The Man and his Work*. New York: Meridian, 1952.

———. *Plato's Mind*. Ann Arbor, MI: Ann Arbor Paperbacks, 1960.

———. *Platonism*. Norwood, MA: Plimpton, 1924.

———. *Socrates*. Edinburgh: Peter Davies, 1932.

Teresa of Avila. *The Interior Castle*. New York: Viking Penguin, 1957.

Turnbull, Grace H. *The Essence of Plotinus*, Stephen MacKenna, trans. Oxford, UK: Oxford, 1934.

Weiss, Brian L. *Through Time into Healing*. New York: Fireside, 1993.

www.ingramcontent.com/pod-product-compliance
Lightning Source LLC
Chambersburg PA
CBHW021914180426
43198CB00035B/466